PLAYHOUSE TO POWERHOUSE

PLAYHOUSE TO POWERHOUSE

LOCATING BLACK POWER WOMEN AND THEIR MOVEMENT IN THE BLACK THEATRE

KERRY L. GOLDMANN

The University of Arkansas Press
FAYETTEVILLE ▲ 2025

Copyright © 2025 by the University of Arkansas Press. All rights reserved. No part of this book should be used or reproduced in any manner without prior permission in writing from the University of Arkansas Press or as expressly permitted by law.

978-1-68226-277-1 (cloth)
978-1-68226-278-8 (paper)
978-1-61075-841-3 (electronic)

29 28 27 26 25 5 4 3 2 1

Designed by William Clift

Library of Congress Cataloging-in-Publication Data

Names: Goldmann, Kerry L. author
Title: Playhouse to powerhouse : locating Black power women and their movement in the Black theatre / Kerry L. Goldmann.
Description: Fayetteville : The University of Arkansas Press, 2025. | Includes bibliographical references and index.
Identifiers: LCCN 2024059301 (print) | LCCN 2024059302 (ebook) | ISBN 9781682262771 cloth | ISBN 9781682262788 paperback | ISBN 9781610758413 ebook
Subjects: LCSH: African American theater—20th century—History | American drama—African American authors—History and criticism | American drama—Women authors—History and criticism | African Americans—Intellectual life—20th century | African Americans in literature | Black power—United States—History—20th century | LCGFT: Theater reviews
Classification: LCC PN2270.A35 G65 2025 (print) | LCC PN2270.A35 (ebook) | DDC 792.08996073—dc23/eng/20250331
LC record available at https://lccn.loc.gov/2024059301
LC ebook record available at https://lccn.loc.gov/2024059302

CONTENTS

Acknowledgments — vii

Introduction — ix

ONE
Where Shall We Play? Staging Struggle
Before a Black Theatre Movement — 3

TWO
The Keepers of the Culture at 3201 Adeline Street:
The Black Repertory Group of Berkeley, California — 27

THREE
The Temple of Liberation at 125th Street and Fifth Avenue:
The National Black Theatre of Harlem, New York — 53

FOUR
The Entertainers, Enrichers, and Enlighteners at 3535 Main Street:
The Ensemble Theatre of Houston, Texas — 79

FIVE
Beyond the Movement: Inheriting the House of Revolution — 103

CONCLUSION
Co-Opted, Compromised, and Commercialized: Historical
Legacies and Living Revolution in Today's Black Theatre — 131

Notes — 145

Bibliography — 175

Index — 191

ACKNOWLEDGMENTS

FIRST AND FOREMOST, THIS BOOK is dedicated to the women of these theatres for remaining indelibly open in their art, their stories, and their houses of theatre and social change. Thank you, Dr. Mona Vaughn Scott, Sade Lythcott, Abisola Faison, and Eileen Morris, for speaking with me and allowing me to be audience to your work.

I'm indebted to the mentors and colleagues over the years who have fostered my intellectualism, my critical eye, and, most importantly, my empathy. Andy Harris, Jennifer Wallach, Natalie Ring, Charles Hatfield, Annelise Heinz, Kimberly Hill, and Ashley Farmer were especially central in shaping my work and me as a scholar of history and culture. I also want to acknowledge *California History* for publishing my article on Black Repertory Group that has become a central chapter in this book. No one has impacted my work more than my husband and life partner, Blake. For his unyielding support, patience, and draft reading, I am eternally grateful. Our first love was theatre, and that's where we met. Over the years, as I have poured further into my scholarship and academic work, he has become even more devoted to theatre and has in turn kept me tethered to what matters above all else: the art. As much as I write about its utility now, nothing compares to the feeling of watching live theatre or performing onstage. Whenever I become too technical in my writing or discussions of theatre, Blake is always there to remind me of the humanity and emotionality theatre carries in its most pure form.

Finally and formatively, I thank my parents for raising me to never accept the status quo, to remain ferociously curious, and to know that my role in this world should never be a passive one.

INTRODUCTION

The time is over for asking or even demanding human rights, in and out of the theater. We no longer ask for manhood or womanhood or dignity; all we can do is express what we have to the degree that we have it. Soon we may have to read our works on the sidewalks of inner-city and 'mainstream' Broadway. Time is up. I've a play to write that may never be seen by any audience anywhere, but I do my thing. Who has ears to hear, hear . . . all others, later.

—ALICE CHILDRESS, "BUT I DO MY THING,"
THE NEW YORK TIMES, FEBRUARY 2, 1969

AS THE 1960S CAME TO a close, Black playwright, arts theorist, and social activist Alice Childress lamented the persistent lack of control felt by Black artists: a symptom of the long, complex struggle to stake a claim in the American theatre. She underscored the fact that establishing a Black theatre institution was an arduous undertaking but that outright ownership of a stage would ultimately serve to uplift Black artists and the community as a whole. Childress's words captured the surging sentiments in Black America between the 1960s and 1980s that supported militant Black self-determinism in building a Black nation and the physical structures to house it. The long Black freedom struggle is marked by Black Americans' efforts to emancipate themselves from oppression, and it has often been designed, organized, and led by Black women. This fight is unruptured in United States history, though it has often regenerated itself and changed in character both to meet the evolving needs of the Black community and to outmaneuver state campaigns to undermine the movement's defining ideologies, organizers, and institutions. Beginning in the 1950s, arts activists such as Childress yearned for more innovative, militant strategies to effect more immediate racial uplift, and Childress stressed the powerful role of theatre in this mission.

Black nationalistic ideals emphasizing both personal and communal empowerment rose to the forefront of the movement in the 1960s and 1970s. Though Black Power ideologies and rhetoric preceded the classically defined Black Power movement of the 1960s and 1970s, this new era was distinct in its mass mobilization, prioritization of culture, and establishment of various institutions to build a thriving Black nation through economic and cultural autonomy. Black art similarly took on a more militant and functional approach during this time and ushered in the formal Black Arts movement. Within Black Arts, the Black Theatre movement was further distinguished by its extensive and unprecedented amount of theatre institution building, craft, production, and autonomy. Women played a key role in each movement: a role that ensured longevity. Black Power and Black Arts converged in their calls for Black ownership of historically exclusive realms. Nowhere was that mission more fully realized than in the Black theatre.

The creation of Black-centric art was intrinsically meaningful for the theatre movement, but its effecting potential remained limited unless Black artists could produce autonomously in their own institutions without white oversight or funding. Childress believed a Black-owned theatre could foster self-determinism in political, artistic, educational, and economic spaces by encompassing the tenets of Black nationalism in a single institution. She also believed the need for these theatre houses would be permanent.[1] When the call for the nationwide establishment of Black theatres resounded from famously recognized Black Arts leader Amiri Baraka in 1965, Black women were already building theatres in the spirit of constructive separatism, and they had their own ideas about how to run Black theatres and for what purpose.[2]

Childress's movement ideology stemmed from her extensive experience in the theatre. She held a central role in the American Negro Theatre in New York from its inception in 1940 until 1949, but she grew frustrated with the company after nearly ten years of being unpaid and cast as a subordinate theatre member because of her gender. The theatre also refused to commit to producing Black plays for Black audiences.[3] Childress left the theatre and became a published theorist and playwright to gain autonomy and exercise an unapologetically Black female voice in the American theatre. She used her arguably most famous play, *Trouble in the Mind* (1956), to call out white male theatre leaders for their colonization of Black artists, with one of her female characters stating, "It's the man's theater, the man's money, so what you gonna do?"⁴ Even Childress, who remains one of the most published and produced Black playwrights, recognized the limitations of her art with no permanent stage, steady funding, or rooted audience. She was not alone. Black female theatre practitioners around the country were professionalizing through education and experience. They held similar torches that pushed them toward institutionalizing and physically manifesting their theatres in this era.

This book foregrounds female leadership in the Black Power and Black Arts movements by investigating three significant local Black theatres that were founded, led, and built by Black women between 1960 and 1980 and that are still in operation today. The most noteworthy theatre houses constructed in this period were Nora Vaughn's Black Repertory Group in Berkeley (1964), Barbara Ann Teer's National Black Theatre in Harlem (1968), and George Hawkins and Eileen Morris's Ensemble Theatre in Houston (1976). Though many Black theatres were founded in this period, these three most reflected the tenets of Black nationalism and ensured movement persistence in their exceptional survival. These nationalistic theatres thrived on Black female organizing, presenting Black-centric art, exerting unprecedented amounts of financial control over their theatre facility, and funneling revenue back into the Black community. Each theatre began with local grassroots organizing, as many Black Power initiatives did, but they eventually achieved national presence and connectivity.

Scholarship and popular perceptions of the Black freedom struggle have evolved since the 1970s, and the story of these theatres expands them further. Even today, scholars continue to disrupt the conceptualization, periodization, and geographical focus of the declension narratives of the civil rights and Black Power movements. The classic narrative asserts that the modern civil rights movement sprang up in the 1950s after the *Brown v. Board of Education of Topeka* ruling led to nonviolent mass mobilization in pursuit of court-granted freedoms. For years, scholars argued that the movement devolved in the late 1960s with the rise of a mostly younger generation who were radicalized with impatience over slow-moving nonviolent strategies. They asserted that Black Power arose as a supposedly new, separate movement concerned with militarizing Black neighborhoods and instituting self-imposed segregation out of racial animosity towards white people. Earlier scholars of Black Power, such as Allen Matusow and Charles M. Payne, defined the Black

Power movement as violent and disorganized, leading to its lack of popular momentum and subsequent demise by the end of the 1970s.[5]

In the early 2000s, scholars began reassessing this narrative by challenging early notions of fractured, short-lived movements at odds with each other. Jacquelyn Dowd Hall, Jeanne Theoharis, and Komozi Woodard were instrumental in this historical turn by identifying what they called the "Long Civil Rights Movement."[6] In arguing for continuity over rupture, these scholars expanded the geographical and temporal landscape of a complex movement that could not be collapsed into one region or the decades of the 1950s, 1960s, and 1970s. Hall argues that the purpose of the classic narrative (which asserts the movement was temporary, geographically limited, and ineffective) is typically to serve the political agendas of the movement's opponents and cast the movement ultimately as a failure. The long movement doesn't collapse history but rather demonstrates the historical tradition of Black adaptability for sustaining an ongoing movement in new historical contexts. Because innovation was necessary for the movement to persist within new atmospheres and against new obstacles, historians must take a similar approach in assessing unconventional methods and presentations of Black Power.[7]

Pragmatism and innovation were at the heart of the long Black Power movement and, therefore, provided a foundation for the era of mass mobilization beginning in the 1960s. According to Mumia Abu-Jamal, a political activist of the era, the movement centered on "self-determination through self-reliance and Black control of significant businesses, organization, agencies, and institutions."[8] Black nationalists of the 1960s saw the conventional methods of the 1950s as too conservative; they were slow-moving, inaccessible to many Black communities, and not easily adapted to the changing circumstances of new decades. Methods of direct political engagement and appeals to the white public fell short of achieving social, political, and economic equity by the mid-1960s, and Black nationalists were forced to be more creative as they paved ancillary avenues to liberation. These activists valued a more radical approach and advocated for innovative methods, a sense of urgency, and ultimately the building of a thriving Black nation within a nation to reach sovereignty through separatism. However, not all civil rights movement methods were discarded in this new era. Pragmatism, for instance, was a traditional tool used within the various eras of the Black liberation movement, and Black nationalists used it to ensure both movement effectiveness and longevity.

This book not only highlights the ingenuity of Black Power but also its subsequent endurance. Even within recent works on Black Power, the longevity of the movement is denied. Black Power scholarship of the last two decades marks the beginning of the movement in the 1960s and the end between the mid-1970s and early 1980s. Scholars such as Peniel E. Joseph attribute the passing of the movement to divisions between Marxists and anti-Marxists and to Black activists becoming more moderate, while Robyn C. Spencer equates the death of the larger Black Power movement with the death of the Black Panther Party.[9] Some scholars, such as Sundiata Keita Cha-Jua and Clarence Lang, warn that the designation of "long" causes the movement of the 1960s and 1970s to lose its distinctiveness as a significant phenomenon by considering other time periods, regions, and presentations as noteworthy in the fight.[10] However, the meaning of this movement is not lost, only re-signified with new characteristics of the freedom struggle, most notably found in the creative strategizing of Black women in their cultural institutions. In looking beyond the declension narrative, another narrative is recovered that underscores the historical roots of Black radical politics marked by a reverence for how cultural expression could lead to widespread liberation and enduring agency.

In laying the foundation for this long movement, the tenets of Black nationalism date back to early utterances from abolitionist Martin Delany in the nineteenth century and organizing by Jamaican-born activist Marcus Garvey in the early twentieth century. The movement of the 1960s, however, was defined by more widespread organization and the formation of Black nationalist models of American institutions. Black Power figures and groups suffered from media misrepresentation and public attacks—namely, in Black Power's most iconic manifestation, the Black Panther Party, founded in 1966.[11] Though the party began in Oakland, California, the movement was nationwide and resided in various organizations. The sentiments of Black Power, now recognized as a highly organized movement, posed a threat to the country's status quo on racial equity. Therefore, the movement immediately garnered negative attention from the white American public and the FBI, who deemed it "dangerous."

Robert L. Allen argues in his book, *Black Awakening in Capitalist America*, that to suggest the movement didn't end in the 1970s overlooks the vast efforts of the FBI witch hunt to destroy radical Black Power organizations and offer state support for moderates through organizations such as the Ford and Rockefeller Foundations.[12] The FBI campaigns were, indeed, effective in many ways. They contributed to the end of many Black Power groups, such as the Black Panther Party and Baraka's Harlem theatre, the Black Arts Repertory Theatre/School (BARTS). However, BARTS was incidentally surveilled due to his individual image as a radical, and it closed mostly due to internal issues.[13] For the most part, the FBI did not focus on dismantling Black theatres because the theatres projected Black Power in a different image. Those who wished to participate in and perpetuate Black Power had to perform Black Power inventively in an effort to evade government surveillance and interference. These alternative iterations of nationalism, such as cultural centers and theatres, were harder to attack due to their registered status as artistic, not political, organizations. Arguably, their production of Black plays and construction of communal infrastructure were inherently political, as they stood in opposition to white America's cultural and economic hegemony. However, these theatres most often avoided becoming targets of federal surveillance and hostility because, as artistic institutions, they weren't seen as overtly radical.

The limitations that are still placed on defining what constituted movement activity negate the important work of Black theatres founded in the 1960s and '70s. Black Power theatre spanned these supposed chasms between the civil rights and nationalist movements and ultimately revealed the utility of theatre as a permanent house for cultural healing as well as collective community uplift. With Black women at the helm, Black Power theatre spaces managed to inclusively house the wide range of institutions that had been historically underdeveloped in the Black community, including cultural, educational, political, economic, and health structures. The stakes of investing in the long movement lie in ultimately liberating the radical cultural work from confined definitions that undermine the effecting labor of these movements and activists then and now.

The atmosphere of the revolutionary 1960s fostered a celebratory attitude in the Black artistic community toward unapologetically Black art that did not submit to white aesthetics or whitewashed Black aesthetics. While groups such as the Black Panthers referred to themselves as *revolutionary nationalists* in seeking radical separatism from white society, Maulana Karenga, who in 1965 founded the cultural nationalist group Us, defined *cultural nationalists* as those who sought complete liberation from white cultural institutions.[14] For Karenga and his contemporaries, cultural nationalism was an ideology that asserted the cultural front was as significant as the political and economic fronts of Black nationalism. In fact, they believed that fully realized cultural nationalism would lead to both political and economic gains. It was an era that encouraged a raised racial consciousness through Black-centric cultural production, which Karenga termed *Kawaida*.[15] Despite the common genesis and rhetoric in cultural nationalism and Black nationalism, their tactics were at odds with each other at times, creating dissention between the movements.[16] However, their ultimate objective was a shared one: instituting a sovereign nation within a nation that would cleanse white historical and cultural stains and work to preserve and celebrate Blackness.

Historically, Black artists struggled to combat white public performance of Black life and character in the form of blackface worn in minstrel variety shows since the mid-nineteenth century.[17] Minstrel stages were common throughout the South and the North and functioned as sites where white audiences could simultaneously delight in and disparage African and African American cultural expression.[18] White audiences received these performances as validation of the current racial ordering of society and justification of their perceived cultural, and therefore, social inferiority of Black Americans. Black performance theorists Thomas DeFrantz and Anita Gonzalez assert that only autonomous Black performance can cleanse Black artists and audiences of damaging double consciousness and white audiences of racial misconceptions. To stage such productions for cultural and social recovery, Black artists needed their own physical stages.[19]

For some movement activists, cultural ownership was the key to all-encompassing liberation. This fact was further demonstrated by the widespread participation and leadership roles taken on by Black women, who battled subjugation on multiple fronts and were central to theatre institutionalization and continuation. As Childress expressed, Black women were forced to contend with a dual misrepresentation in white popular culture and theatrical performances under the direction of both white and Black men. Though Karenga verbally defined cultural nationalism for this era, Black women defined it through practice. They demanded a reorientation and resignification of gender roles within the cultural nationalist movement because they saw themselves as necessary figures in the fight for cultural autonomy and overall Black liberation. Therefore, they would accept nothing less than equal treatment and opportunity.

These women based their gender ideals on their reading of societal roles in ancient African societies, which were more equitable than European gender expectations. They defined cultural nationalism moving forward as a movement of gender consciousness.[20]

Cultural nationalism set the foundation for the Black Arts movement as the artistic branch of the Black Power movement. Black Arts was another long-form movement with roots in the Harlem Renaissance in terms of producing Black art for Black audiences.[21] Still, the arts movement mobilized in the 1960s was distinct due to a militant tone, the mass production and consumption of Black art, and an emphasis on how art could offer economic and other practical benefits for Black communities. This movement also marked a major break from Eurocentric cultural hegemony, mimicking the broader mission of Black Power separatism. Breaking away from Eurocentric definitions of theatre meant that these "theatres" could define themselves more broadly as cultural institutions with vast artistic investments, and they could indulge more in Afrocentric performance styles. They used their stages for so much more than plays. I discuss the traditional play productions of the Black Repertory Group, National Black Theatre, and Ensemble Theatre minimally, as each founder demanded that their institution be seen as more than a theatre. Though the plays of any theatre movement are important, the focus of this book remains on the broader artistic programs and definitions of performance that serve each theatre's historically rooted mission of cultural nationalism.

The Black Arts movement has been the subject of monographic study and is also treated in histories of Black theatre.[22] Black Arts scholarship generally aligns with the limited timeline of the traditional Black Power and civil rights scholarship, insisting that the movement ended in the late 1970s.[23] James Smethurst partially blames the Reagan administration for major cuts to public funding of the arts, whereas Kelli Jones argues that it ended due to the rise of multiculturalism and the commercialization of the Black Aesthetic in the blaxploitation films of the 1970s.[24] Lois P. McGuire, executive director of Karamu House, a Black theatre founded in 1941, gave an interview in 1979 and stated that the Black theatre movement was currently in decline. She partially blamed musicals and waning white interest in Black theatre: "Black isn't in anymore."[25]

Despite the perception that it was in decline, the movement was transitioning in character to keep pace with a shifting atmosphere.[26] Current narratives that assert that the movement was dead by the 1980s have yet to give due attention to how the spirit persists in the theatres founded during the movement, necessitating further analysis of how they survive, function, and thrive today. Similarly, the works of Smethurst and Jones, foundational as they are, ignore the significant turn of Black artistic autonomy staged by theatre companies and their venues, the continued existence of which negates the supposed demise of the movement. Theatre historians who specialize in Black Power arts have studied plays and playwrights in relation to Black nationalist ideology, but there has been no study of the social and economic implications of the process by which Black theatre companies constructed institutions. Black theatre scholar La Donna Forsgren has expanded the field in recent years and drawn attention to Black women's theatre. She argues that the Black Theatre movement timeline is muddled because a distinction has to be made between theoretical and institutional sustainability. Forsgren, similar to other movement scholar Mike Sell, asserts that movement theories and aesthetics persisted as metaphysical legacies outliving the theatre institutions that began to fall in the 1980s.[27] Though these scholars are correct about the period of institutional waning, they often overlook the stories of sites that survived and house a continued movement. By merely focusing on the plays and theory of this movement, the field has neglected the lasting impact of theatre institutions and property ownership, which, under Black female leadership, became movement vessels that materialized the art and theories and carried them forward into new moments. These leading women believed that structural ownership could determine communal accessibility and outreach, aesthetic standards, funding, and, ultimately, survival. An understanding of this shift in Black theatre reshapes the purview of how long-form social movements have been waged in American history and broadens public imagery of Black decolonizing efforts.

    The radical imagination of those in the Black Theatre movement foresaw unprecedented cultural and economic prosperity, which would manifest through the physical ownership of Black theatres. Historian Robin D. G. Kelley was instrumental in unveiling the utility and politics surrounding Black cultural expression in his 1994 book, *Race Rebels: Culture, Politics, and the Black Working Class,* and his 2002 book, *Freedom Dreams: The Black Radical Imagination.* Kelley defined the *Black radical imagination* as the power to manifest dreams into social reality.[28] Though it is not the most discussed artistic medium of Black Arts, Black Theatre movement leaders prioritized theatre for its social protest roots, collaborative and communal nature, and potential to speak to wide audiences. Additionally, they hoped it would function as drama therapy for diasporic trauma, which had a lasting impact on Black American ideas of selfhood and the security of proprietorship.[29] Transgenerational displacement created both a physical and psychological diaspora for Black Americans who strove to reclaim roots through home ownership, self-representation, and a central position in American history and culture. The arts, and theatre especially, were long-standing practices in the Black community that helped Black Americans repossess physical and intellectual property. Theatre seemed the most fitting artistic medium to heal diasporic trauma, mobilize the community, and facilitate tangible change. The continued struggle to feel rooted inspired metaphysical ideas of ownership in the form of cultural practice and artistic expression, and physical ideas of ownership in the form of venues in which dreams could be reverently manifested and securely housed.

For all Black theatre companies, the physical venue proved the most difficult necessity to secure, yet also the most significant aspect of theatrical autonomy. Throughout America's history, property ownership has been a privilege afforded to whites and wealthy individuals. As Dylan Penningroth, Cheryl Harris, Laura Warren Hill, and Julia Rabig have explored, these exclusionary efforts were meant to reinforce social hierarchies by limiting property ownership and therefore citizenships rights such as participation in politics, economics, and culture.[30] Despite white Americans endeavors to keep American proprietorship inaccessible and individually based, Penningroth explored how Black property ownership, dating back to Reconstruction, has been historically communal in a collective effort to gain access.[31] This pattern of collective ownership and redefinition of American property is found through the investigation of these theatres. The movement of the 1960s was even more radical, with female leadership bucking against historical traditions of male proprietorship; Black women were historically central to property acquisition.[32]

Black Power theatre companies strove for full autonomy, meaning outright ownership of each aspect of theatre: playwriting, direction, production, revenue, company, audience, and stage. The battle for Black autonomy and equity was as much an artistic battle as it was an economic and geographical one.[33] Theatre set the stage for a multifaceted revolution intent on economic and cultural emancipation in Black communities across the country. If run effectively, control over these institutions held potential for economic self-sufficiency, job creation, Black-centric performances, opportunities for Black women to lead and express themselves, educational programs, and community outreach. Moreover, the theatre spaces were utilized for free health screenings and hosted town hall meetings for community concerns, such as human trafficking and police brutality.

Despite its critical functions and legacies, the theatre movement has not been given the same extensive scholarly exploration as other movement art forms, such as literature and visual arts, and the founding of Black-owned theatres of the era has not received a full-length study. Bernard L. Peterson's 1997 book, *The African American Theatre Directory, 1816–1960*, is the most comprehensive study of Black-owned theatres, though its encyclopedic structure lacks critical analyses.[34] Peterson highlights issues faced by early Black theatres and companies, but he stops short of this critical period in which a major proprietary shift occurred. Prior to the 1960s, most Black theatre was barred from mainstream white venues, instead relegated to Black schoolhouses and churches, which limited public accessibility and cultural ownership. Tracking the rise of Black theatre institutions during the height of this era reframes understandings of Black culture and Black Power by unveiling the ultimate goal of the era: that a sovereign Black nation would be found within cultural institutions. Furthermore, while many of the movement's organizations were short-lived, theatrical institutions persisted beyond the era as lasting houses of Black Power. This book aims to expand the field, not just by rescuing the narrative of Black theatre, but also by rightfully centering it as the most active and long-lived site of connection between Black Power and Arts.

By locating theatre as a significant stage for the Black Power movement, Black women are unveiled as active agents and leaders of the movement who bring about the most concrete and lasting changes in the Black theatre. Gender consciousness, which Patricia Hill Collins tracks in her 1990 book, *Black Feminist Thought*, was a revolution within the revolution, though it volleyed between harmony and contention with the broader movement.[35] In recent decades, attention has been drawn to women within Black Power (by scholars, such as Ashley Farmer, Jeanne Theoharis, and Kimberly Springer) and women within Black theatre (by scholars, such as Kathy A. Perkins and La Donna Forsgren). Forsgren's work has been especially pivotal in centering Black women's roles in the Black Arts movement and Black feminist theory (as it relates to arts activism). Her first book, *In Search of Our Warrior Mothers: Women Dramatists of the Black Arts Movement* (2018), focuses on Black women theorists and dramatists, and effectively demonstrates their leadership in shaping the movement. Forsgren's next book, *Sistuhs in the Struggle: An Oral History of Black Arts Movement Theater and Performance* (2020), grows out of her earlier work and provides a platform for Black women intellectuals of the Black Arts movement to share their stories of performance, institution building, and historical legacy.

Playhouse to Powerhouse is enriched by these scholarly works, such as Farmer and Springer's frameworks of Black women's organizing traditions, Theoharis's breakdown of movement building, and Forsgren's intermingling of Black feminist theory with artistic action and centering Black women's theatre in the age of Black Power. As foundational as these texts remain, there has yet to be a focused, monograph-length study of how Black women leveraged unprecedented autonomy and movement longevity through the building of Black theatre institutions.[36] Black women found meaningful ways to reorient Black theatre from patriarchal direction. These women reimagined what true liberation would look like for the whole of Black America and were convinced that they held a substantive role in this revolution. Along with the struggle to gain access to professional white-owned institutions, Black women were still subjugated to low-level roles within arts institutions owned by Black men.[37] In recognizing their own unique position of agency within the community, their historic role as cultural creators and keepers, and their historical traditions of forming united collectives and proprietary campaigns, Black women sought to establish cultural institutions to foreground the fight for true intracommunal equity.

By focusing on the constructive women of this period, this project additionally deviates from the most discussed theatre of the era: Amiri Baraka's Harlem theatre, BARTS. According to leading Black Arts movement scholars, including James Smethurst and Kelli Jones, the movement was ignited by the founding of BARTS, which Baraka founded in 1965 in response to the assassination of Malcolm X.[38] Baraka was determined to build an artistic institution inspired by the activist's vision for Black cultural production. Though Baraka's *Revolutionary Theatre* dogma outlived BARTS and remained influential, the Black women who ran theatres (such as those in Berkeley, Harlem, and Houston) were not ultimately striving to follow guidelines set by one leader or cultural icon.[39]

In order to be lasting and effective, they had to follow the internal pulse of their individual communities, as well as more broadly consider the effect they could have on the Black world. Despite the centrality of his ideology in shaping the movement, Baraka's model for the Revolutionary Theatre should not be posited in the center of Black Theatre movement scholarship since BARTS was fraught with dysfunction, and ultimately failed to serve the movement or the community. The theatre was also, as Forsgren notes, preceded and outlived by other significant theatres, such as Doris Derby's Free Southern Theater.[40] In general, historians have placed weighted attention on short-lived Black theatres, as opposed to those that succeeded and remain operational. Destabilizing the central position of BARTS in the Black theatre and broader arts movements expands the periodization, democratizes the movement's narrative, and re-characterizes the movement's nature as a constructive, women-driven revolution that continues unruptured.

This was a national movement with localized distinctions and individualistic turns that were epitomized in the theatre houses of Berkeley, Harlem, and Houston. The local nature of both Black Power and theatre ensured efficacy. Sociologist Doug McAdam argued in his book, *Political Process and the Development of Black Insurgency, 1930–1970*, that Black Power caused the demise of the civil rights movement by fracturing a national movement into local operations.[41] However, local organizing ensured the movement would persist in many ways, as a central notion of Black Power emphasized individual actions for the revolution and the collective power those individual actions could build.[42] These three theatres present as impactful, local brands of Black Power. They represented a national call for Black theatre autonomy, yet also reflected local distinctiveness and a complex movement. Today, they stand not only as honorific monuments to the Black women who founded and led them but also as pivotal cases in Black Arts scholarship. They herald the significant, active role Black women played in the past and present currents of the movement and the continued stakes of owning a Black separatist theatre today.

For the length of their tenures, these companies have operated as community theatres, meaning they hold legally recognized nonprofit status and must maintain a primary purpose of existing in service to their community. To adhere to the mission of cultural nationalism, theatrical institutions had to be planted within the Black community they wished to uplift. Community proved historically foundational and transcendent in fostering dignity, support, racial optimism, and tangible proprietary gains. Black nationalists espoused the need for collective community organizations to prepare for a fully mobilized revolution. Therefore, groups like the Black Panther Party for Self-Defense focused on establishing community survival programs, offering free bus service, shoes, clothing, food, health clinics, and even education through the People's Liberation School.[43] The Black Power creed and actions that were deemed extremism by critics were seen by movement activists as simply fundamental. Once institutionalized, the Black Repertory Group, the National Black Theatre, and the Ensemble Theatre implemented similar communal programs with the addition of creative initiatives, and they were able to adapt over the decades to address evolving issues in their neighborhoods, ensuring long-term viability.

Foregrounding Black theatre houses in terms of their history, impact, and continued presence provides the public with physical addresses to step into today and see Black nation building at work. Current production seasons continue to celebrate the Black Aesthetic, and the companies themselves continue offering community programs, including production and training opportunities for local artists, public service workshops for community members, and a space of cultural healing. Despite past and present obstructions to operations, and the deaths of the founders, the women who inherited each of these theatres continue running the institutions to ensure their survival for a new generation.

Other major cities, such as Detroit, Chicago, Los Angeles, Atlanta, New Orleans, and Dallas hosted noteworthy Black theatres. Like Berkeley, Harlem, and Houston, these large urban centers were sites of substantial Black populations, especially in the postwar years, and therefore experienced a simultaneous denigration of racial coexistence alongside a flourishing of concentrated Black culture. Additionally, other Black theatres of note were created within this era alongside the aforementioned three theatres. However, the Black theatres established in other major cities and in the same timeframe are not included in this book because they either did not survive beyond the movement,[44] or their mission was not as tied to cultural nationalism.[45] Vantile Whitfield, founder of Performance Arts Society of Los Angeles, said that it is not truly "Black Theatre" simply because they produce Black plays for a Black audience; the theatre must be actively working for Black liberation.[46] The Black Repertory Group, the National Black Theatre, and the Ensemble Theatre are unique because they exemplified the significance of the Black female liberation front in creating sustainable Black Power institutions, remaining tethered to Afrocentric aesthetics, employing Black artists, and uplifting the Black community. Still, a number of other theatres remain significant emblems of artistic institution building by Black women. Doris Derby's background as an artist and a teacher helped her foster educational programming for rural communities in Mississippi through the Free Southern Theater (1963–1985), and though Jackie Taylor championed racial cooperation over separation in her Black Ensemble Theatre (1976) in Chicago, her mission has been historically centered on eradicating racism through theatre.

The chapters of this book frame the start and continuation of the Black theatre movement through the lens of three significant theatres and the women who founded and lead them. Chapter 1 sets the stage for the subsequent discussions of specific theatres by examining the theoretical and historical turns in Black theatre history arriving at the 1960s with the centrality of Black women in roles of art and activism. The next three chapters cover the three highlighted theatres and contain original interviews I conducted with the current CEOs of each theatre, all inherited from the founders. These interviews offered intimate insights into the theatres' histories, operations, and art, as well as access to previously unanalyzed archives held at each of the theatre houses.

Chapter 2 covers the West Coast movement, epitomized by Nora Vaughn's Black Repertory Group of Berkeley, California. Their operations are in some ways unique to their region, but the theatre also represents national trends and the melding of varied regional experiences due to the founders migrating from the South. Vaughn's theatrical institution provided a space in which to operate significant welfare programs that both preceded and outlasted the Black Panther Party in institutional support for the impoverished communities of Oakland. The third chapter examines Barbara Ann Teer's National Black Theatre of Harlem. New York is widely regarded as a central locale for Black cultural capital. However, female-driven arts institutions, such as the National Black Theatre, have been largely ignored despite their survival and unruptured communal and cultural uplift. Though several works have been written on Teer, none have focused on how she utilized her physical spaces for her artists and the Black community of Harlem. Teer navigated the male-dominated theatre scene of New York and sought to bring prosperity to Harlem through her brand of cultural nationalism in which all artists were revolutionaries in training.

The fourth and final local chapter presents what seems to be an outlier in this narrative with George Hawkins's Ensemble Theatre in Houston, Texas, founded in the late 1970s. Texas is rarely explored as a central hub of Black Power activity, as most attention is placed on the East and West coasts. However, this third coast was blazing with similar sentiments, revolutionaries, and cultural institution building in the spirit of nationalism. Although Ensemble has a male founder, from the beginning, Hawkins hired Black women to lead, and he left the theatre in the hands of several women, namely Eileen Morris, to continue theatre operations after his passing. Ensemble Theatre has continually stood out in the Black theatre landscape of Texas by rooting Black nationalist ideals in Texas and ensuring they persist as the national movement waned.

The fifth chapter brings the three theatres into conversation with each other. It focuses on the continuation of nationalistic theatre in the "post-movement" era. Though regional distinctions set the stage for long-standing local movements, they converge in methods, efforts, and persistence through struggle to form a broader movement. The Black Power and Arts movements supposedly died by the 1980s, followed by the passing of the theatre founders in the subsequent decades. This chapter checks in on each of the theatres in the so-called post-movement era of the 90s and 2000s to see how they survive when the cause is inherited by the next generation of Black women, two of which are direct heirs as daughters of the founders. The central aim of this chapter is to determine whether these theatres survived the "death" of the Black Power and Black Arts movements, or if the movement indeed survives because the theatres do.

I conclude with a discussion of the current moment. The theatres are well established and have been inherited to carry the mission through generations. However, the theatres face other obstacles now, such as gentrification, prestigious white theatres co-opting Black theatre, the question of position within the Black Lives Matter movement, and, most recently, the impact of COVID-19. Despite these obstacles, the aim of this chapter is not to present a bleak picture of the future of Black theatre. Instead, I reiterate the stakes of these theatres surviving as emblems of the long-form revolution and, once again, foreground theatres as central to housing the Black liberation front.

Signifying Black Power as a cultural movement recuperates the true aims and nature of a woman-driven movement centered around humanism, innovation, survival, and ultimately Black joy. The Black Aesthetic was the artist's answer to the grueling images and dark realities facing their community, and theatre ownership was the activist's answer to economic, cultural, and social oppression. Understanding these theatre structures advances the studies of the Black Power movement, the Black Arts movement, Black women's history, Black American theatre, Black culture, and American culture. This book garners a more cohesive understanding of theatre as a revolutionary art form and sheds light on the broader legacy of Black Power and cultural nationalism. Subsequently, it yields new conclusions by showing how Black women fulfilled the mission for Black sovereignty through artistic and cultural institutions and revealing the larger tradition of Black-owned theatres as a form of nation building for ultimate autonomy. Examining theatrical institutions run by Black women in the era of the movement and beyond makes it clear that artistic institutionalization not only mirrored Black nationalism, but indeed these structures were the physical manifestations of the heart of the movement and persist today as the lasting houses of Black Power.

PLAYHOUSE TO POWERHOUSE

ONE

WHERE SHALL WE PLAY?

Staging Struggle Before a Black Theatre Movement

No people come into possession of a culture without paying a heavy price for it.[1]

—JAMES BALDWIN

BLACK THEATRE EXISTED IN AMERICA long before the Black Power movement, with the first scatterings evident in the early nineteenth century. Due to the difficult search to house these early productions, iconic Black scholar and playwright W. E. B. Du Bois gave a resounding call for an independent and autonomous Black theatre in 1926. Though many in the Black artistic community agreed on the importance of Black-owned venues, Black theatre companies founded prior to the 1960s suffered short lifespans due to the struggle to establish a fully operational theatre space.[2] They were forced to produce their theatre in alternative structures, white spaces, or abandon their communities altogether and become transient in their search for opportunities to participate in mainstream theatre.

The lack of physical venues meant that Black artists most often played for white producers, directors, critics, and patrons. Still, there was a long history of Black artistic production, consistent and undisrupted. Because theatre speaks to the most marginalized groups, Black women were consistently participating in and leading in artistic theorizing, play crafting, and theatre ownership. The scope of Black theatre history ran on balances struck between establishing theatre companies versus structures, valuing public versus private performance, and prioritizing cultural responsibility versus individual artistic expression. Despite intercommunal debates, there was a cohesive acknowledgement of theatre's social potency. Even before the renewed renaissance and proprietary gains of the 1960s, many in the Black community continuously made attempts to house the performing arts.

In the spirit of the long civil rights movement, the push for Black theatre has been a consistent, long-running process. Neglect of the broader timeline "undermines the gravitas" of gains long fought for.[3] The turn of the twentieth century set the stage for the battle for full artistic autonomy, and Black women were fortifying these efforts by securing communal, cultural, and economic capital. Each decade of the twentieth century presented new social contexts, along with opportunities and limitations in establishing a Black theatrical institution. This burgeoning century invigorated Black theatrical endeavors that would ultimately gain ground approaching the widespread founding of institutions in the 1960s.

Black Women's Early Theatre History and Theory

As America entered the twentieth century, the country was transforming into an industrial, urban society. Americans were plagued with anxieties about modernity and struggled to define what it meant to be an American in the new century. For Black Americans, this struggle was further complicated by their efforts to be identified as Black and American citizens, reconciling with dual identity and double consciousness.[4] Black women contended with an additional marker of gendered marginalization, which Alice Childress referred to as a "double-blacklisting system."[5] For most Black Americans throughout the country, it was a time of uncertainty but also one of promising change in the air.

The influx of immigration and Black migration in the late nineteenth and early twentieth century sparked a national identity crisis as white America attempted to renegotiate its position in a diverse society. The idea of cultural pluralism promised an unmerged coexistence between US-born citizens and newcomers, and the rise of nativism brought renewed hostility towards the Other, drawn on ethnic and racial lines.[6] For the first time in history, the American theatre scene began to reflect the country's character, history, and aesthetics, as opposed to simply mimicking the

European stage. Modernist and racial anxieties played out on the young American stage with celebrations of white supremacy, nativism, and romanticized history with plays such as white dramatist Thomas Dixon's *The Clansman* (1905).[7] White-centric performances were granted access to mainstream stages, sponsored funding, and large-scale audiences.

Throughout early American theatre history, the vast majority of audiences were white, forcing Black actors to perform as criminal or comedic caricatures if they wanted to appear on professional stages.[8] Black women were presented as either defeminized mammy or oversexualized jezebel archetypes. Patricia Collins discusses this form of popular representation as controlled by the oppressor and its damaging effects on the self-efficacy of Black women. Because these images were so engrained in popular culture performance, such as theatre, negative perceptions of Black women were heavily normalized and naturalized.[9] Furthermore, white theatre critics routinely undermined Black theatres in order to maintain a cultural and, therefore, social hierarchy.[10] Few white people attended the staging of Black plays; when white drama critics did, they wrote reviews based on their own aesthetic standards for how Black characters and circumstances should be portrayed.[11] White playwrights were able to stage their works in major American theatre houses due to both private and public funding, but many Black playwrights of this time had to self-subsidize their productions, which were most often housed in non-theatre institutions.

Prior to the twentieth century, there were few Black-controlled theatrical venues in operation. Of the 160 existing theatre groups, only a handful managed to secure a temporary theatre space, and they were often afflicted with structural issues and external pressures to shut down.[12] Even after emancipation, it was difficult for Black Americans to acquire funding, property, or municipal support to establish new institutions.[13] As Black theatre artists navigated limited staging for what seemed like an unlimited stream of artistic expression, debates erupted, often regarding the racial makeup of creative teams, actors, audience, and theatre owners. Ultimately, many in the conversation were drawn to a nationalistic approach that echoed Du Bois's 1926 call for a holistically Black theatre:

> One: *About us*. That is, they [the plays] must have plots which reveal Negro life as it is. Two: *By us*. That is, they must be written by Negro authors who understand from birth and continual association just what it means to be

a Negro today. Three: *For us*. That is, the theatre must cater primarily to Negro audiences and be supported and sustained by their entertainment and approval. Fourth: *Near Us*. The theatre must be in a Negro neighborhood near the mass of ordinary Negro people.[14]

Rather than being concerned with authentic representation, Du Bois believed that the Black theatre would have to politicize performance to ultimately break down the double consciousness of Black performers and audiences.[15] Those who followed this nationalistic theatre approach argued that the theatre had to stay physically within the Black community in order to truly serve that community.

Though Du Bois ignited these conversations, other artistic theorists, many of whom were women, did not blindly accept Du Boisian theatre.[16] Georgia Douglas Johnson, Angelina Weld Grimké, Caroline Bond Day, Alice Childress, and Zora Neale Hurston, along with Alain Locke and Langston Hughes, responded with their own theories on theatrical representation and calls for a Black theatre. They agreed with embracing cultural nationalism in the theatre but bucked against rigid rules for representation Du Bois also tried to set forth, instead wanting to celebrate a vast spectrum of Black humanity and experiences.[17] Culture scholar Izabella Penier argues that "black folk culture became the only location from which an authentic and legitimate black female voice could be heard."[18] These women artists were not decidedly against politicized art but concerned with portraying a nuanced group onstage due to their personal experiences of exclusion from the Black male-centric political and artistic conversations. Artistic debates arose in all other eras of Black theatre, exemplifying that the Black community was not monolithic and that the image of revolution would vary among regions and individual theatres. One aspect that was not up for debate was Black women remaining insistent on their active roles in the theatrical revolution.

From the beginning, even when men were leading discussions and organizations, women fought for their seat at the table. At the start of the twentieth century, Du Bois and Jamaican-born Black nationalist Marcus Garvey pushed the ideal of cultural nationalism forward by emphasizing that Black people had something intrinsically valuable to offer the world that was unique from other groups.[19] Garvey's Universal Negro Improvement Association (UNIA), founded in the name of Black nationalism in 1914, established a drama program with Black playwrights, actors, directors, and designers. Garvey recognized and championed the significance of cultural nationalism, referring to it as "self-culture," in the fight for institutional autonomy and Black nation building.[20] By devoting a sector of his campaign to theatrical performance, Garvey made a convincing case that popular theatre, or theatre of the people, was a decolonizing force.[21] Women such as Anne Cooke, Henrietta Vinton Davis, and Amy Jacques Garvey performed and directed within the UNIA drama program, staking a historical legacy for Black women's central roles within the Black theatre.[22]

The search for a Black stage grew more fervent in the 1920s and 1930s as the mass cultural production of the Harlem Renaissance converged with pressing issues of racial injustice. As artistic philosophies and modes of creation began to take shape in these decades, the rise of nativism, the second iteration of the Ku Klux Klan, and acts of domestic terrorism perpetrated against Black communities across the nation raised the stakes for artists to respond. Many respondents were women. Black women were primed to lead theatrical movements for social change with their long history of culture bearing and the persistent need to protect themselves, their families, and their communities.[23] Artists were producing in this time but with a pressing question: Without access to existing stages, or the funding to build new ones, where would they play?[24] If Black theatre groups were determined to produce plays that reflected more authentic representation and artistic expression, they needed to find spaces that were unconventional for theatrical staging but familiar to Black communal organizing.

Black Women Find Alternative Stages

Performing within existing communal institutions fostered the vision of Black art being fully appreciated by a Black audience and Black artists creating in service of their own community. These ideals become cornerstones of the cultural nationalist movement in the 1960s. Women used their resourcefulness and community leadership roles to transform existing structures, such as churches, schools, and even private homes, into theatrical stages. Established institutions, such as churches, schools, and homes, historically operated as multifaceted spaces, serving varied social purposes and adapting to changing communal needs. Each of these structures is tethered to deep roots of communal service, expression, and uplift dating back to enslavement.[25] They offered privacy and protection from the white gaze; they were spaces where Black Americans could shelf social performance that veiled their true selves. Similarly, these venues served as more private stages where theatrical performance was neither monitored nor standardized by Eurocentric culture. These stages were exclusively for Black theatre, providing opportunities for artists to showcase their work as well as offering Black audiences an atmosphere that was free of racial tensions and filled with an Afro and Afro American aesthetic. The spiritual remnants of these first structures are visible in the Black theatre houses established in later decades.

CHURCHES

One public space that was already autonomous from white institutions by 1900 was the Black church. The power of religious resistance was not merely in the ritual of practice but in the retention of African cultural traditions and the refusal to fully adopt America's dominant religion.[26] The retention of African culture, especially in artistic expression, planted the roots of nationalism early on. Enslavers recognized culture as a significant force and tried to strip enslaved people of distinctive cultural markers to dehumanize them, as well as establish a hierarchy which positioned African culture below American culture. This constructed perception continued long after the demise of enslavement and maintained white cultural hegemony.[27] Black women are historically revered as "keepers of the culture" for continuing traditions even when faced with hegemonic hostility and erasure.[28]

Before and after emancipation, Black Americans institutionalized religion in their churches, which functioned as centers for the Black community's cultural expression, social gatherings, women's clubs, spiritual affirmation, and political rallies. Over time, religion and the Black church even became intermingled with the market economy. Black Americans, especially women, traveled to raise money for their churches, which would then offer communal assistance.[29] This practice set a precedent of collective support that was a model for later efforts to fund Black nationalist theatre institutions. Because of their centrality to the community, churches quickly became an alternative structure in which Black plays could be produced.[30] Church structures operated off communal funding, and audiences were already established for these venues.

The Black church, however, had limitations as a house for art. In 1926, in *Crisis Magazine*, Du Bois noted that "now and then a church is liberal enough to house a play."³¹ However, at times, churches attempted to regulate performances to uphold politics of respectability. Respectability politics dictated social behaviors and what was deemed "acceptable" performance for Black Americans both in public and on the mediated stage.³² Black women were especially subject to the politics of respectability and, therefore, were often enforcers of it in the community as well.³³ However, women would also come to shape the tenets of 1960s cultural nationalism as they grew more preoccupied with presenting the authentic Black self, unencumbered by the pressure of white gaze and judgement. There were theatre companies, however, who abandoned their church stages but kept an essence of religion in their new theatrical homes. Though Christianity, and general spirituality, continued to play an important role for some revolutionaries of the 1960s, the activists moved away from heavy reliance on organized religion to focus more on active communal assistance and self-reliance.³⁴

SCHOOLS

Similar to churches, schools were significant historical institutions in the Black community and theatre. In the nineteenth century, Southern states passed laws making it illegal to teach enslaved people how to read and write, as education was linked to resistance.³⁵ This educational disparity persisted in the era of Jim Crow segregation and was included as a major platform during the Black Power and Arts movements.³⁶ Black women activists of the late nineteenth and early twentieth centuries, such as Ida B. Wells, often led the charge for Black education. They fought not only for the education of Black people but for an Afrocentric curriculum that fostered racial pride and knowledge of the self.³⁷

Many Black Americans viewed schools as valuable commodities due to the social potency of education and its restriction by those in power.³⁸ Similar to churches, schools disseminated cultural education and operated as centers for cultural production. A few missionary schools established in the South after emancipation stressed a classical, liberal arts education of literature, oration, and theatre. Black students extensively studied the Bible, ancient Greek and Roman drama, and Shakespeare.³⁹ In his preface to his play *Dessalines*, nineteenth-century Black dramatist, William Easton, referred to Black intellectuals educated through these programs as a "new emancipation literati."⁴⁰ He saw theatre as a powerful tool for reform, arguing, "On the mimic stage were portrayed the direful results of the abuse of power . . . the stage in those days, as it is today, was a mirror for despots to view their own iniquity."[41] Easton stresses in his preface that it is the obligation of Black Americans to honor the posterity of their "distinguished dead" by not allowing white artistic representations to falsify Black historical experiences.[42] This stance would be echoed by cultural nationalists in the next century.

Prior to the national movement, schools became spaces for Black nationalistic thought and theatrical production. The first Black female playwright to have her work semiprofessionally produced onstage was Angelina Weld Grimké in 1916.[43] Grimké was a Harlem Renaissance playwright who was active in the NAACP branch in Washington, DC, and had connections with Du Bois. Grimké's anti-lynching play, *Rachel*, was performed at a schoolhouse in DC. However, the play only had a two-day run and could not attract a wide audience.[44] Grimké felt the weight of cultural responsibility and wanted a large playhouse and an audience to bear witness. Though individual expression was important, her ultimate objective was to utilize art as an educational tool to curb white racism and violence. Du Bois funded Grimké's venture through the NAACP Drama Committee for a one-weekend run at the Neighborhood Playhouse in 1917, though it was a white-owned theatre.[45]

Even with her ties to powerful members of the Black community, Grimké was still unable to secure wide viewership, or a stage, for more than three performances. Due to the lack of a centralized Black arts institution, and as a continuation of the tradition of school-based Black theatres, historically Black colleges from around the country became involved in this artistic surge of the 1920s and 30s, highlighting the centrality of Black institutions within artistic movements.[46] Overall, schools were pivotal starting points for Black theatre, but they had exceptional limitations in that they were still small venues, often white-owned and funded, and lacked proper accommodations for full-scale theatrical productions. Even with these limitations, cultural nationalists valued schools as both physical structures being used to stage productions and as metaphysical structures, imbuing theatre companies with curriculums to educate their artists, audience, and local community.

PRIVATE HOMES

In the same way that schools offered a space of empowerment and collectivity, the Black community also made use of the home as a private space for expressions of individuality and resistance that were not welcome in public spaces.[47] Furthermore, the action in many Black plays is set in the home, which underscores the significance and centrality of the Black family within the community, as well as the extensive nature of the "Black family," which included community members.[48] Home, often structured by Black women, historically held a communal value, as opposed to being defined by individual proprietorship. Those emancipated from enslavement could not afford to purchase single-family properties; instead, they relied on funding within the community, creating collective ownership, and, therefore, the uplift of whole groups of people. As historian Dylan Penningroth noted, this system changed the perception of property: "Ex-slaves thought that what made an object into property was not that it disappeared into the private sphere of a single person but that it was associated publicly with people."[49] This meant that even a community member's "private" home could be utilized for public engagement and organizing. Therefore, the Black home became not only a thematic device within plays, but also a stage for production. The theatre houses of the 1960s would follow this pattern of collective ownership, often funded and physically built by the Black community.

With no professional stage to call home, several Black women artists, notably Harlem Renaissance playwright Georgia Douglas Johnson, used their parlors to present their latest works and network with other Black artists.[50] Johnson facilitated a Black theatrical stage and communal collective as an earlier version of the later theatrical properties secured by the women of the Black Theatre movement. The home was advantageous in that it was a comfortable space that allowed for private performance and avoided a racially charged white audience. The audience, instead, was usually small and made up of members of the community who became artistically engaged. They bore theatrical witness and collaborated to hone the aesthetics and aims of present and future Black theatre. Just as the Black mother character is frequently featured as the impelling agent of Black plays that drives the action of the plot forward, Black women remained constant impelling agents driving the theatre movement forward in their homes.

Several Black theatres of the 1960s were inspired by the tradition of producing plays in Black homes, and this informed how they designed their theatre house. These stages were designed to be literally closer to Black audiences through extended apron stages, actors playing in the orchestra and aisles, and maintaining small theatre houses.[51] This structural design fostered a more personal connection and mutual interaction between performers and audience. However, there were arguments over public versus private performance and which method would best actualize the artist's intention.[52] As with propaganda or protest, dramatic theatre loses intended meaning if it is not witnessed and critiqued by an intended audience. The audience plays a participatory role in actualizing the artist's intention of a play.[53] As the community became more collectively minded in terms of theatrical and social revolution in later decades, Black theatres shifted their goal to broader public accessibility.

TRAVELING STAGES

Despite some success with alternative stages, many Black Americans were still in diasporic transition in the late nineteenth and early twentieth centuries, continuing to migrate in search of a place that embodied the values and comforts of home. They also established artistic migratory patterns in a transient search for a stage. In addition to performing in existing communal structures, Black theatrical performance became communally uprooted at times in the form of traveling troupes. Just as the institutions of churches, schools, and homes, are deeply and historically engrained in the Black community, migration was another familiar aspect. Mobility and migration are recurring motifs in both Black American history and theatre. Voluntary migrations that followed emancipation were a means of resistance that created a shared experience among Black Americans, further binding them as a collective community in constant transition.[54] The same was true for theatric opportunities, and these migratory patterns began to change the theatrical landscape of the nation.

Around 114 out of the five hundred African American theatre organizations between 1820 and 1960 were touring variety, vaudeville, comedy, musical, and dramatic companies that were not tied to one theatre building.[55] The trend of these "suitcase theatres" highlighted the continued physical and psychological fallout of the African diaspora. These companies were unable to establish structural roots or a loyal audience base, and they were forced to close following short tenures.[56] Black traveling troupes could not find affordable property, welcoming neighborhoods, or financial means necessary to establish a theatrical home. These troupes, such as famed Harlem Renaissance poet and dramatist Langston Hughes's Harlem Suitcase Theatre (1937–1939), had short lifespans, which can be attributed to their lack of long-term, communal roots. Furthermore, company members were forced to devote time to their primary jobs to afford basic necessities.[57] This was indicative of the persistent question as to whether culture was a necessity in economically desperate situations and if the cost was outweighed by the gain.

During the Harlem Renaissance, Black Americans reached a new level of emancipation through more assertive art. However, the Black theatrical ambitions of the 1920s and 1930s lacked permanence, stability, and accessibility while operating outside of professional theatre venues. The question remained as to who would bear witness without physical sites of presentation. The theatrical models of church, school, home, and even traveling troupes did not completely dissipate in new spaces. Many of the Black theatres founded between 1960 and 1980 remained rooted in their heritage of traditional Black institutions and resourceful alternative stages by including educational programs, spiritual elements, and an atmosphere of home in their new theatre. Pragmatic artists struck balances between adapting to new cultural contexts and retaining ties to tradition, and that practice helped sustain continuous, evolving Black art operations, as opposed to existing as periodic renaissances that ebbed and flowed. This early period was also heavily defined by Black playwrights, especially women, who geared their efforts towards artistic creation but struggled with public production. Though their creations did not move past alternative stages in these decades, Black women in the decades to come would construct the houses needed to showcase the long history of Black play crafting and cultural retention.

Black Women, the Black Theatre Movement, and Cultural Nationalism

The gains in theatre ownership separate the Black Arts movement from pre-1960 Black theatre endeavors. Within the arts movement, artists formed the Black Theatre movement. This new era was distinct because, more than ever before, Black artists mobilized to build a nation of Black theatres that was first called for by Black women and men artists four decades prior.[58] In the age of Black Power, artists and activists prioritized permanence by establishing cultural centers within the Black community with the promise that internal, collective support would lead to communal gain. Women remained instrumental to cultural gains in this new era and helped lay groundwork for it to be called a movement.

There were several factors that set the stage for cultural nationalism and fostered the Black Theatre movement in the post–World War II era, but migration was pivotal. Between 1940 and 1970, the Second Great

Migration marked the mass exodus of five million Black Americans who moved from the South to the Northeast, Midwest, and West. Black women were at the forefront of this migration as community organizers, and they sought more employment opportunities for themselves and their husbands.[59] The migrations yielded little opportunity for better living standards or race relations than in the South due largely to white resentments against Black economic competition on the national scale.[60] However, Black women encouraged these moves as the keepers of their families, communities, and culture. This was an exercise in voluntary mobility, promising at least the possibility of improved living conditions. It was also an undeniable opportunity for raising cultural consciousness, connecting broader communities through cultural transplantation, and mobilizing for a theatre movement.

After World War II, Black migrants moved into urban centers, and they sometimes brought their theatres with them. Cities with larger Black populations of at least 20 percent presented atmospheres that were more conducive to sustainable Black institutions but not without obstacles.[61] The horrors of economic destitution and heightened racial tensions in the North and West led to a burst of cathartic artistic expression and the endeavor to improve the community from within. Women were drawn to the business of art because they had even less job opportunity than Black men in their new cities.[62] Emerging from the 1940s, artists saw new potential for the utility of theatre as a tool for social change. However, it could only be potent for change if in the hands of Black artists.

With migration, the world of Southern Black artists was expanded, which meant their worldview, experiences, and artistic expression would also expand. By the late 1950s, there was growing ideological enchantment with nationalism and the idea that Afrocentric cultural institutions could revitalize both the spirit and living standards of Black America. Playwright Lorraine Hansberry serves as an emblematic marker in the year of movement transition away from integration and towards nationalist ideologies. On the cusp of a new decade and movement, Hansberry became the first Black female playwright to have her play performed on Broadway, when *A Raisin in the Sun* premiered at the Ethel Barrymore Theatre in 1959. This play depicts the struggle of a Black family, the Youngers, living in a white neighborhood.[63] *Raisin* premiered on Broadway on March 11, 1959, and ran for 530 performances, becoming one of the most performed plays by a Black playwright. Hansberry was inspired by the rise of the nationalist movement in Egypt and saw theatre as a tool for dismantling cultural perceptions.[64] Because she was able to secure a mainstream stage with a wide audience base, Hansberry was affecting as a playwright. Her contemporaries credited Hansberry with shifting the perception of Black theatrical identity from "American Negro" to "African American" in popular culture.[65]

Hansberry garnered mostly positive reviews of her Broadway hit from several white critics as well as some Black critics, including James Baldwin.[66] However, some Black critics condemned *Raisin* for being an inconsequential integration piece. Harold Cruse, called it a "glorified soap opera," shallow in its depictions of Black struggles.[67] Baraka viewed it as too "middle-class" when he first saw it, though his opinion of the play became more favorable in the late 1980s.[68] Today, Hansberry is recognized for invoking nationalistic themes in her plays by Black culture scholars such as Peniel E. Joseph and Fanon Che Wilkins.[69] Perhaps the most telling nod to Hansberry operating as an artist revolutionary was FBI agents surveilling from the Broadway audience.[70] The varied reviews from Black intellectuals reflected increasing disunity in the late 1950s as civil rights organizations fractured over cause, strategy, and varying levels of radicalism. Despite criticism from Black male artists, her success on Broadway was undoubtedly a step forward in making Black theatre more accessible and making further strides in the theatre industry for Black women. It also posited that Black women would have something different to offer, in terms of their theatrical theories and practice, in the burgeoning age of cultural nationalism.

By 1960, the Black Power movement was already underway. As Black art prepared to enter a new decade, the question remained as to what theatre could really offer the Black community when it played on white stages for white audiences. This new era was concerned with achieving a nation within a nation. Activists embraced separatist ideals to counter the state of Black neighborhoods as "internal colonies" or "urban plantations."[71] They wanted the colonized population to build up its own infrastructure and thrive independently. The rhetoric of the Black nationalist era cautioned that advancing into white society meant compromising a distinct Black identity, pride, and culture.[72] The emergence of cultural nationalism and call for unapologetically Black art inspired the new movement of Black artistic production. Assimilation and integration were now regarded by cultural nationalists as the genocide of Black culture, as opposed to an equal merging.[73]

While movement leaders were working to distinguish themselves, their ideals, and their rhetoric, a shared value among many was culture. When Stokely Carmichael, later Kwame Ture, became the head of the Student Nonviolent Coordinating Committee (SNCC) in 1966, he pushed for cultural nationalism, stating, "Color and culture were and are the key in our oppression... Black Power not only addresses itself to exploitation but to the problem of cultural integrity."[74] Similarly, Black Power organizer and icon Malcolm X had an affinity for culture, founding the Organization of Afro-American Unity (OAAU) in 1964. The OAAU's "Statement of Basic Aims and Objectives" stated, "Culture is an indispensable weapon in the freedom struggle. We must take hold of it and forge the future with the past. We must recapture our heritage and our identity if we are ever to liberate ourselves from the bonds of white supremacy."[75] He agreed with cultural nationalists that Black identity, pride, and potential would only be fulfilled through Black-controlled institutions and cultural centers. He also believed that Black-centric performances promoted identity affirmation.[76] According to Black Power scholar Ashley Farmer, cultural nationalists also believed that "redefining gender roles was the basis of social and political transformation."[77] Black women saw an opportunity to renegotiate their positions socially by asserting themselves culturally. They, therefore, fought to participate in and lead these cultural nationalist efforts. Female advocates led fundraising campaigns, served on various educational and cultural committees, ran and taught in the Us School of Afro-American Culture, and organized a women's unit within Us, known as *Malaika*, to protect women's interests.[78]

The convergence of Black Power discourse with exhausted cultural submission mobilized Black artists and intellectuals to sever ties with white culture and construct an open stage for Black art that would also serve as a pillar for the Black community. Cultural liberalism, which celebrated the individual, gave way to cultural nationalism, prioritizing cultural responsibility in service of the whole community to run a more cohesive movement.[79] The ideals of Black and cultural nationalism flourished with rallied support from Black artists and activists in the same historical context of the 1960s and with similar grassroots foundations. This new renaissance merged the artistic spirit with the practicalities of theatre ownership and production.

To become embedded in the community and operate on an effective, widespread, and lasting level, the revolution needed to be institutionalized.

Black women held strong ideas about how institutionalization could be both achieved and maintained. When discussing Black Theatre movement theory, Amiri Baraka is often centralized as the ideological crux of the movement. In 1965, Baraka wrote "Revolutionary Theatre" as a call for Black artists to stage a racial revolution in the American theatre. In his essay, which is often cited as the theoretical underpinning of the movement, he issued a call for "a theatre about, with, for Black people—and only Black people," similar to Du Bois's call four decades prior.[80] He demanded an end to Black integration into white culture in the name of embracing Black-centric theatre.[81] Though his essay is often cited as the compelling call for theatrical nationalism, Black women crafted theory and full-fledged theatre companies that were already gaining momentum by the 1960s.

In the 1950s, playwright Alice Childress began writing theory. While her plays proved artistically significant to the movement, her theories provided an impelling foundation for the building of theatre institutions and set the stage for Black women to carry theory into theatrical practice. She called for a fully autonomous Black theatre in her 1951 essay, "For a Strong Negro People's Theatre." In her essay, she imagines a theatre that is fully funded, operated, and artistically managed by Black artists for a Black audience.[82] White theatres, funders, directors, and audiences touted control over Black playwrights, actors, and companies through funding and proprietary control. Each of these white entities were only interested in Black theatre if it was presented in the artificial style of minstrelsy, which parodied and trivialized Black personhood and experiences, thus funneling money back into white pockets.[83]

Childress framed the art of theatre as a weapon of revolution and accentuated the necessity of securing venues to operate as community centers and sites of radical artistic autonomy and social responsibility. She insisted on using theatre as a social tool because it aligned with the fact that culture serves a utilitarian purpose, especially when manifested through what is known as *Developmental Theatre*.[84] Developmental Theatre is an interactive style of theatre that is used by a group to tell their story in their own words on the stage, and it should adhere to cultural and expressive traditions of the community. The extrinsic purpose of this theatre style is served by artists deeply engaging with an underserved neighborhood and addressing present issues to develop and improve the community's standard of living.[85]

Despite Black women finding ways to participate, and at times lead in these nationalist movements, their fight for gender equality was ongoing, and it ultimately fostered a more radically inclusive movement towards liberation. Black female intellectualism, social work, and leadership were present and persistent, but the compounding struggles of gender and race were not highlighted in some of the male-run organizations and cultural institutions.[86] La Donna Forsgren even argued that some Black Power women found cultural nationalist groups to be more hostile to women than Black nationalist groups.[87] Women such as Nikki Giovanni, Sonia Sanchez, Ntozake Shange, Alice Walker, and many more challenged their male counterparts to examine gender discrimination while insistently positioning themselves in the movement's foreground.[88] Izabella Penier states that "By creating strong and charismatic female characters, commemorating formidable black foremothers, and celebrating unique feminine folk cultures, these authors created their own feminist version of black cultural nationalism."[89] The activism and inspired visions of Black women ensured the stability of nationalist institutions, like Us, and the communities they served, just as they would come to lead the most enduring Black-owned theatres. Though culture was a uniting force, the high stakes of these endeavors led to ideological ruptures over how the movement should be structured, and Black women would have to contend with the balancing act.

Tensions over Scope and Funding in the Black Theatre Movement

As the Black nationalist and cultural nationalist movements formalized, movement leaders, artists, and intellectuals found themselves divided on ideological and practical issues regarding the intended scope of the theatres and how they would be funded. In terms of scope, tensions arose over the question of Black theatres operating as local, national, or even global entities. World War II had a globalizing effect that both united and divided people along ideological lines. This metaphysical expansion fostered a new global consciousness, igniting both a search for widespread connection with the current world and a radical reimagining of the future Black world. Ideas of art, identity, and consciousness were in transition, and an atmosphere of cosmopolitanism dominated postwar intellectual debates regarding the Black Aesthetic. The art itself was marked by a level of urban deterioration that was emblematic of the 1920s. Instead of creating art to protest the circumstances peculiar to Black Americans, there was a new emphasis placed on connecting those of African descent around the world who had been victimized by colonization and enslavement. Individualism gave way to globalization, which heavily informed the coming Black Theatre movement.

For Black Americans, the global consciousness of the 1950s and 1960s was a boost to the already existent Pan-African movement, which emphasized uniting the diasporic Black world through a connected consciousness and celebration of Black culture. Pan-Africanism has deep ideological roots in the nineteenth century, but truly took hold as a formalized political movement in America by the late early twentieth century with Du Bois at the helm.[90] The cultural aspect of Pan-Africanism was similar in its global aims, but it also sought to capture the distinct voice of Black Americans.[91] This new consciousness condemned "art for art's sake" and stressed "art for the sake of the world spirit," emphasizing high stakes in the face of racial oppression in America as well as the Pan-Africanist ideal of a global Black liberation movement.[92] 1960s cultural nationalism, therefore, placed a dueling emphasis on both localization and globalization. Harold Cruse, one of the major ideological architects of the Black Arts and Black Theatre movements, and a cofounder of BARTS, agreed with Baraka that culture should act as a loud, radical voice to communicate and connect those of African descent around the world, while staging a domestic confrontation of white America's imperialistic ideology and action.[93] Black women such as Alberta Hill and Malcolm X's widow, Betty Shabazz, led educational organizations, conferences, and cultural campaigns to practically actualize the ideals of Pan-Africanism.[94] However, there was also resistance to Pan-Africanism being too broad to speak to the unique character of local Black communities across the nation or address their particular needs. To thrive in this new movement towards cultural nationalism, theatres, and the women who ran them, had to strike a balance in their scope being both localized and globalized.

Theatres needed to be local enough to have communal roots and support, while being broad enough to foster a national, and even international, movement for greater stability. Often when Black theatre companies procured white funding, such as the Negro Ensemble Company, investors moved the theatre to white stages within white communities.[95] This trend became a point of contention by severing local ties with the Black community. In striving for localism and separatism, many Black artists felt that the authentic spirit of Black culture and the needs of the Black community were sacrificed on the altar of white stages, communities, and audiences. If they controlled their own local space, the global aspect could be reflected in the themes and content of the art. Many Black community theatres sought to capture the "Black world spirit" through the art they produced, while the theatres themselves functioned as local communal entities. Childress, for instance, was preoccupied with the establishment of a Harlem theatre. However, she also asserted that with enough local theatres established on a national scale, there was "potential to open a window on the black world."[96] Rooting these theatres within the community was significant because it was an acknowledgement of the deeply unique character of local Black communities and culture.

This complexity of fostering both local and global cultural efforts was exemplified in the search for a theatre. Though some found balance, inconsistency persisted as movement leaders pushed for a globalized, metaphysical landscape for Black art, while also trying to settle into a community structure with localized goals. This also raised a question for theatres in terms of viewership and accessibility: Would these institutions produce theatre for a global, national, or local audience? Cosmopolitan rhetoric thrived in tandem with a localized emphasis on creating rooted communities through organized cultural projects. As Black theatres of the 1960s and '70s found security in their local positions, they began organizing and collaborating regionally, nationally, and internationally with other Black theatres. This was, therefore, a mass-mobilized theatre movement that still held reverence for the diverse landscape of the Black world.

Another tension arose within the Black Theatre movement regarding the practical necessity of funding. The Black Power ideal of self-determinism placed special emphasis on developing economic uplift within the Black community, and business ownership was viewed as the most effective avenue to gain autonomy.[97] The most iconic Black Power organizations and figures argued for the significance of the cultural front because it was seen as a form of social liberation, and it encouraged creativity in the search for communal revenue. The spectrum of institutions established by these groups, like the Black Panther Party, was broad, encompassing commercial businesses, schools, and cultural centers. Development Theatre was the artistic equivalent of the corporate development corporations of Black Power, which created jobs, were often run by women, and "put economic development in the hands of the community themselves."[98] The separation of Black theatre from white stages benefitted the Black community in various ways and consequently hurt white pockets by removing Black art and artists from exploitation and commodification for white economic gain.

The idea of a cultural nationalist theatre was fully fledged, but it still required funding to be securely institutionalized. Due to the difficulty of self-funding, some Black theatres had to rely to some degree on white funding. President Johnson's War on Poverty initiative. Congress passed the Economic Opportunity Act (EOA) of 1964 to carry out his vision of eradicating poverty in the United States.[99] EOA funds were to be allocated at the local level through branches of the Community Action Program (CAP) located throughout the nation. The CAP provided financial assistance to both public and private nonprofit entities that promised to engage all members of the impoverished community. Though they regarded it with cautious optimism, Black women had hope in what this funding would mean for their communities.[100]

Black theatre artists saw this as an opportunity to financially jumpstart their theatres, and many received federal funds through this program. CAP's willingness to fund these theatres demonstrated their awareness of the connection between property ownership and community welfare, though their funding was mainly in the interest of curbing urban rebellions.[101] However, external funding was riddled with problems. In accepting these funds, theatres were forced to adhere to nonprofit standards according to the funding entity.[102] This meant that local CAP officials could pull their support if they found a theatre to be too political, citing it for misappropriation of funds. Additionally, the federal government could surveil these theatres under the guise of tracking their funding. Therefore, although the theatre companies were given the necessary finances to operate in their venue, they did not have complete autonomy over their theatrical and social aims as they operated under a watchful eye.

CAP funding furthered intercommunal discord over the question of whether Black producers and directors should accept white assistance and the subsequent standardization and supervision.[103] White sponsorship presented another obstacle of racial control that obstructed the view of a fully actualized Black theatre. In 1966, Robert Macbeth, director of New York's New Lafayette Theatre, argued that cultural issues must be realized and solved within the community, stating a Black theatre "would be developed from within that body of people, using methods and concepts organic to the body."[104] In that same vein, Clayton Riley, a Black theatre theorist and newspaper critic, wrote an article in *The New York Times* accusing the Negro Ensemble Company of indulging white audiences. He stated that "NEC's most significant gesture would come in the presentation of one proud work offered on its feet, rather than a hundred plays produced in a kneeling position before its dubious benefactors and critics."[105] These critics feared that NEC was creating nothing more than cosmetic diversity with a theatre that led with the Black image onstage and white hands backstage.

Funding led to another issue of surveillance and company interjection by government officials. The political organizing and nationalistic rhetoric of some theatres eventually caught the attention of the FBI who began surveilling Black artists, such as Du Bois and Childress, and later Harold Cruse and Amiri Baraka. Former FBI agent Tyrone Powers retrospectively articulated the bureau's intentions to "weaken and unlink the unified chain" of Black artistic and civil rights movements.[106] The FBI's efforts highlighted government fears of an effective Black liberation movement if it proved un-ruptured. Therefore, they played up tensions between company members and even disbanded several companies, falsely—yet effectively—framing these movements as disjointed, dysfunctional, and defunct.

Childress drew attention to these issues and the necessity of self-funding, stating "any attempt to 'buy our own' puts us in the position where they can cut off our supply lines ... at a moment's notice."[107] She argued that everything about the new Black theatre should be self-determinist, but that would require leaders prepared for that fight. Though external funding presented a continuous balancing act for Black theatre, this crucial period between 1960 and 1980 marked a rise in Black professional individuals and organizations that were instrumental in sustaining these theatres. In the 1960s, Black female producers emerged with a combined force of artistic passion and business acumen.[108] Most of these producers started their careers on the artistic side of the theatre but learned the business side through a mixture of experience and higher education. Acknowledging successful theatre founders and leaders as highly trained and educated professionals dismantles the same myths that soften the activism of civil rights women like Rosa Parks. Their theatres of longevity were born from intention, experience, and as Childress noted, preparedness. Survival could not have hinged on luck or fated timing because the role of a theatre producer carries many responsibilities, including grant writing, financial management, play choice, marketing, and hiring theatre personnel. At Black theatres, producers faced greater external pressure. Therefore, it was significant for Black artists to take on that role to elevate theatrical ownership and agency. Black female producers recognized that their level of opportunity was often inaccessible to many in their community and established programs in their theatres to assist other Black artists in becoming producers, thereby creating a positive industry cycle.

Over time, through professional development and organization, Black theatres found their own independent funding and business strategies. This became especially important after the EOA was dismantled during the Nixon and Reagan administrations. One key to survival for these theatres was forming connections and networking opportunities to aid in sustainability. The Black Theatre Alliance (BTA) was founded in New York in 1971 and was heavily led by women. Seven theatre companies banded together, forming the alliance to help each other fund their theatres and social programs. They held festivals that operated as collective fundraisers and printed newsletters to spread awareness of financial opportunities for Black theatres. The BTA was funded by New York City's Parks, Recreation and Cultural Affairs Administration (PRCA).[109]

Eventually, white funders moved the BTA out of the Black community to an office farther downtown on Broadway, but the group remained connected to the core of the Black theatre community and began to see themselves as more of a national entity than a local one. With the help of the Theatre Communications Group (TCG), BTA published the Black Theatre Resources Directory as a resource to develop and connect other Black theatre communities, effectively nationalizing the movement and encouraging collaboration. They defined themselves as "a collective to solve common problems, to share information and resources and to create an instrument to validate Black Theatres as community institutions."[110] The Alliance proved effective in creating a supportive network offering connections to Black theatre members across the nation, including the three theatres in California, New York, and Texas. By 1980, they constituted three of 139 professional theatres on the alliance list.

According to Black Theatre movement scholar, Mance Williams, the "biggest factor controlling the destiny of a viable Black theatre movement, during whatever moment in time it has sought to express itself, is that of a permanent audience."[111] BTA was conscious of this issue and because they were defined by their collaborative nature, they sought assistance from

Vivian Robinson, who founded the Audience Development Company (AUDELCO) in 1973 "to stimulate interest in and support of performing arts in Black communities."[112] In general, it was nearly impossible for a theatre, white- or Black-owned, to support themselves. Black companies launched aggressive publicity campaigns on the phone and engaged in walking door-to-door because they were not covered in mainstream media.[113] AUDELCO bused people from their neighborhoods to attend performances at discounted prices. These theatres needed to conduct aggressive audience campaigns because the box office should be the majority funder of every theatre. Traditionally, outside funding intentionally does not fund a majority of theatre operations because then there would be no incentive for the theatre to produce popular theatre. Therefore, if a Black theatre company wanted to be independently funded, they needed audiences. In turn, they could give back to their community of patrons.

Black Women and Their Theatres in California, New York, and Texas

The 1960s came with a new ideological framework, constructed by Black Power and Arts figures, to gain more than they had in any previous decade. They now prioritized institutionalism built on a foundation of artistic and economic autonomy. This new age of Black theatre was a national phenomenon, yet it reflected regional and local contexts. California, New York, and Texas had distinct histories of racialized oppression, resistance, Black cultural signifiers, and values attached to property. The theatres led by women in these states were products of both these particular contexts and of the broader historical moment. Artists in these states sought to rectify troubled histories by self-producing more authentic performances of Black history and experience. They also cultivated new paths towards liberation that differed from prior Black theatres and renaissances by prioritizing communal aid, individual uplift, cultural assertion, and economic self-sufficiency, all of which operated independently of white America.

The stories of how the significant theatres of the era survive include the broader social, political, and economic trends of the time and the deeply personal sacrifices and work of exceptional individuals. The investigation of these theatres requires a biographical element because individualism was valued in the theatres. The individual had to be empowered before they could empower and mobilize the community for collective ownership in the name of cultural nationalism. This ideal was also heavily tied to early ideas of Black nationalism in the first half of the twentieth century. Garvey's nation-building rhetoric was entrancing but not seen as a reality to many who lacked even basic infrastructure in their communities. Prior to a mobilized movement to collectively create a nation within a nation, Black people had to seek individual paths in their physical or metaphysical "return to Africa," often going no further than one's own backyard. The practicalities and ideologies of that journey differed. This fact was reflected in Black nationalist theatres in that they remained connected to each other through a nationwide spirit but retained individualistic brands of cultural nationalism within their institutions.

Three theatres founded in the era of Black Power—Black Repertory Group, National Black Theatre, and Houston Ensemble Theatre—embodied a radical vision for the future of Black theatre that was determined to break from the long line of Black theatres under white control. The theatre histories in California, New York, and Texas all reflected racial marginalization, yet each presented unique landscapes for the formation of long-sustained Black theatrical institutions. Black theatre proved to be a constant stream of performative expression, and it continued to reflect and shape the national and regional contexts of each decade. The hope within the community was that this strong artistic spirit, if persistent and mass mobilized, could eventually lead to a fully realized autonomous Black theatre and a liberated Black America. The burst of revolutionary energy in these nationalistic decades promised a widespread movement and lasting change.

Du Bois threw down the original gauntlet for the establishment of a Black theatre four decades prior. However, the fight for Black-owned theatres goes back even further, and many women artists took up the gauntlet thereafter with eager, individualized authority for self-definition and communal leadership. In the Black Theatre movement, more than ever before, Black women arts intellectuals engaged with new artistic ideals for the Black Aesthetic and explored creative yet practical avenues for theatrical liberation to be followed by social, economic, and political liberation. This new age surged with radical energy that was unapologetically Black and irrevocably female. It rang out for a Revolutionary Theatre to be formed in its name. The atmosphere was now ripe for the construction of a mass theatre movement, and women took center stage. By the time Ture and Baraka entered the public scene, nationalistic Black theatres were already being established in local communities throughout the nation. The three coasts of the United States each had unique theatres to offer that operated on the same goals to create a nationwide Revolutionary Theatre as well as advance the lives of Black Americans and redefine the American stage.

TWO

THE KEEPERS OF THE CULTURE AT 3201 ADELINE STREET

The Black Repertory Group of Berkeley, California

When my mother died, the city tried to revoke our mortgage for the theatre building. They didn't think I would be confrontational enough to fight it. I fought it, and I won. The building is the starting point for keepers of a culture. You must have consistency and a stationary place to help with income and provide people a place to be somebody.[1]

—DR. MONA VAUGHN SCOTT

IN 1978, NORA VAUGHN BEGAN an ardent campaign for a new home to house her theatre company, the Black Repertory Group, or Black Rep, the oldest Black theatre company in California's Bay Area.[2] Fire marshals condemned their previous building for violating fire codes, and Vaughn was in search of more than a structure. She wanted a rooted institution and community center dedicated to Black nation building through cultural uplift and economic assistance that could impact current and future generations. This need was made ever more pertinent amid the declining Black Panther Party and Black Arts Movement. Black Rep had to ensure their survival as an enduring anchor for a community in dire economic conditions. When she found the perfect site on the border of Oakland and Berkeley, California, city officials refused to meet with her to negotiate the lot purchase. In response, Vaughn staged regular protests for nine years, sitting just outside of the lot with a sign that read, "Here I sit, till Black Rep stands!" Not garnering enough attention from officials, she took her demonstration to the steps of Berkeley City Hall and picketed right outside of the Mayor's office and received a meeting to negotiate the purchase of her lot the next day.[3] Though Vaughn and her husband established the group in the Bay Area in the early 1960s, they struggled to secure the funding and support necessary for a proper stage, therefore hindering their mission to utilize culture for communal uplift, a cornerstone of Black Power. But, on October 11, 1987, the Black Repertory Group Theatre finally stood with physical permanence to house both cultural performance and communal purpose. This institution thrives today as a lasting legacy of the Black Power movement and an emblem of West Coast Black theatres established in this period with the goal of Black empowerment.

As of 1964, when the Black Repertory group was formed, Black Power was still a burgeoning movement seeking definition and leadership. Black women in the West, such as Vaughn, saw their communities entering a new era of hardship in the 1960s with postwar deindustrialization. Though the end of World War II set the stage for strife, the Second Great Migration during the war caused a demographic shift in California, providing for a more substantial Black population that could mobilize against emerging oppressive social and cultural structures. Consequently, California became a central site of intermingling revolutionary and cultural nationalists by the 1960s. These two groups varied in strategy but held a shared mission of liberating a deeply impoverished Black Californian community. Black Power and nationalistic art converged in the neighboring cities of Berkeley and Oakland in Alameda County of California's East Bay Area in direct response to economic and cultural oppression following World War II. Similar to the location of famed Black Power sites, such as Merritt College, Black Rep's search for a stage continually straddled the boundary between Berkeley and Oakland, both of which were in need of economic assistance and innovative strategies to bolster property ownership, financial securities, and autonomous cultural expression.[4]

California followed the national trend of the Black Power and Black Arts movements, embracing autonomous Black art and sovereign Black institutions for nation building. Yet it also remained distinct. Robert O. Self's *American Babylon* asserts that the Western fight was distinct from the Southern civil rights model in that it was a mostly economic front, and he argues that Black women in California consistently participated in and led antipoverty programs, despite themselves being overrepresented among the area's impoverished.[5] Therefore, Black artists in the West merged their need for autonomous cultural performance with the goal of collective uplift. Though profit would be a far reach for most local theatres, a modest revenue cycle could fund antipoverty programs, as well as undercut external funding and, therefore, oversight. Holistic autonomy would be difficult, but the fight would begin with owning a stage. Vaughn's Black Rep came to embody these goals.

The West held distinct theatrical, gender, and racial histories that set the stage for Black Rep's entrance. Due often to financial constraints, there were few Black-owned theatres before 1960, and those that existed were often located in regions with a substantial Black population. Of the only 200 Black-owned theatres, there were 130 in the South, forty-eight in the North, thirty-seven in the Midwest, and only one in the West.[6] The first known Black theatre in the Bay Area of California is the Bay Cities Dramatic Club at the turn of the twentieth century. Setting an early standard for the operational goals of Western Black theatres, the theatre offered communal assistance in poor Black neighborhoods and fostered the early career of famed Black stage performer Bert Williams.[7] However, the only Black presence on the Western stage prior to the Black Arts movement, including Bay Cities, presented minstrel-style characters and held only temporary runs due to reliance on white funds. The lack of funding, along with the small Black population in the region, cast the theatrical stage of the West exclusively for white performance, or Black performance under white financial and aesthetic oversight.

Racial tensions rose for Oakland residents in the postwar years. During the war, industrial mobilization created a surplus of jobs in Oakland. Industrial expansion brought thousands of Black Americans, mainly from the South, into the Bay Area for economic opportunity beyond what was offered in the South.[8] This migration included the Vaughn family, who migrated with their young theatre company from Mississippi. However, de-escalation of war production around 1946 resulted in job shortages, and the influx of Black Americans created tight economic competition with white residents. Black residents, consequently, faced greater difficulty in procuring jobs and property.[9] Though they worked in construction and various types of property development, Black migrants did not benefit from what they built. Bay Area institutions, businesses, and residential property remained mostly white-owned due to discriminatory loan practices and low wages afforded to Black laborers. Postwar Berkeley reflected the nation's long history of exploiting Black labor for white gain. Though difficult to obtain, Black residents knew that property and business ownership were key to economic nationalism, facilitating jobs for Black workers and selling to Black consumers to keep money within the community.[10]

Reflecting national trends, Black female professionals had even less opportunity than their male counterparts in the Bay Area. The postwar period pushed millions of American women who had enjoyed a temporary holding in the workforce back into the domestic sphere. Though they did not leave the workforce entirely, Black women were forced to return to old positions of white household servitude by the 1950s. In the Bay Area, these women were desperate to find new avenues of employment that could instead serve their own communities.[11] Historically, Black women held dual roles serving and leading their households as well as their communities, holding more autonomy and decision-making power than their white counterparts.[12] This position primed Black women to navigate creative or unconventional job opportunities and to be instrumental constructers in institution and nation building.

The 1950s sparked white flight from urban to suburban areas further decaying urban Black neighborhoods nationwide and in California.[13] Western residential segregation was codified through state efforts of highway building through Black neighborhoods and redlining, which only allocated development funds and refinancing to white neighborhoods as property rates increased in the postwar period.[14] Segregation in the West was a reaction to a perceived threat to economic, social, political, and cultural capital posed by the expanding Black community. In the 1960s, home ownership was considered the key to upward economic mobility in California's Bay Area. The Berkeley housing shortage, coupled with housing discrimination practices, leveraged racial exclusivity on Western property.[15] White artists further solidified this monopoly by asserting metaphysical ownership over the distinct cultural capital and performance of the region. They employed the longstanding practice of espousing Black cultural inferiority.[16] This argument was used to justify discriminatory and segregationist practices, asserting that Black Americans are incapable of assimilation and therefore integration.

By the 1960s, the collapse of the Western promise radicalized California's Black population. In August of 1965, amidst the rising Black Power movement, riots erupted in Los Angeles which had a positive impact on Black theatre development. The Watts riots were predominantly a reaction to lack of capital and property claims. Rioters looted white businesses, constituting a forcible seizure and radical redistribution of property. Ironically, the damage caused by looters lowered property rates, and Black theatre companies were now able to take up residence and convert buildings, such as furniture stores, into performance spaces and community centers, including the Inner City Cultural Center, the Performing Arts Society of Los Angeles, and the Watts Writers Workshop.[17]

Due to the prioritized economic front of the civil rights fight in the West, developmental theatre proved an exceptional strategy because it historically merged art with the economic development of underserved communities, especially in decolonization efforts and popularizing after World War II.[18] Black nationalists were committed to building an economically fortified infrastructure for the Black community, and many Black artists, including Black Rep, merged with this ideal of economic betterment through art and were able to actualize it through developmental theatre. Margaret Wilkerson, a scholar of Black Arts on the West Coast, argued that the "singular distinction that distinguishes these black-run theatres" in this period was that they now sought Black audiences.[19] In reality, the reach for cultural autonomy in this era differentiated itself from previous Black theatre eras beyond audienceship. These artists believed that economic self-sufficiency began with ownership of a building in which to produce art and culturally driven community initiatives. Black Rep embodied each of these distinctions that defined a truly new social, economic, and theatrical movement.

Oakland, California, represented the spectrum of racial injustice visible in urban areas across the nation. The city boasted a powerful chapter of the Ku Klux Klan (KKK) during its resurgence in the 1920s and again during the civil rights movement.[20] However, it was not simply a place of hardship. This city was the birthplace of the Black Panther Party (BPP) in 1966. As racial tensions rose alongside the growing Black population, Oakland became the central site for the materializing Black Power movement. Black Power ideologies and figures of the West Coast were localized in some of their community aims, yet informed by their experiences from across the country, similar to Black Rep.[21] Kwame Ture's cry for "Black Power" rang out in 1966 in Greenwood, Mississippi, but the idea found true organizational roots in Oakland. The families of BPP founders Bobby Seale and Huey P. Newton migrated from the South to Oakland during WWII, just as the Vaughns migrated with their theatre from Mississippi.[22]

From the beginning, the efforts for Black liberation in Oakland were centered on founding Black-owned businesses, communal institutions, and fostering cultural expression.[23] Activists utilized performance as a tool for unifying, educating, and economically improving Black neighborhoods. Demonstrating the centrality of Oakland for both Black Power and Black Arts figures, Seale and Newton first met at Oakland's Merritt College, where they began organizing students with Black nationalist discourse, and Black Arts activist Marvin X attended Merritt in this same period.[24] The location of the college reflected the nationalistic formula for institution building by operating within the Black community. Merritt was in the heartland of the impoverished North Oakland neighborhoods, or "flatlands." Therefore, those who attended the school were politically and socially charged. The movement needed to be led by community people, but it also had to be organized within Black institutions, like Merritt and Black Rep, to ensure structural support and longevity.

With development in mind, Bobby Seale and Huey P. Newton formed the Black Panther Party for Self-Defense, a foregrounded organization and emblem of the Black Power movement, in 1966. Their platform focused on community protection from police brutality and providing communal assistance for the impoverished.[25] From the beginning, women were instrumental in building the party's infrastructure, organizing communities, and creating art and campaigns to garner support and ensure the party became a movement. Government officials cast the image of the Panthers as one of deep misogyny to undermine their community work and political organizing. Though Black women contended with gender disparities within the organization, male leadership made concerted efforts to create spaces that were somewhat gender neutral and fostering for women to earn powerful positions.[26] The women who joined early on, such as Judy Hart, Emory Douglas, Kathleen Neal, Elendar Barnes, and Tareka Lewis, offered skills, ranging from shooting to typing to artistry, and platform contributions, such as childcare networks, free food, and campaigns to end violence against women.[27] Like Nora Vaughn, several of these women were also Southern transplants who brought the tradition of Southern organizing to the Bay Area.

Despite their militancy, the Panthers recognized the power of art and culture. Within their ranks, they created a position of "minister of culture," a position first held by Ed Bullins in 1967.[28] The Black Panther Party wanted community development efforts to be widely participatory, such as marching through the neighborhoods, a type of street theatre, in Oakland.[29] Public demonstrations, constituted developmental work because they engaged audiences on issues and encouraged heightened political consciousness. Therefore, the street also became a venue for artistic theatre. In 1968, Bullins stated that street theatre allowed for "communication with diverse classes of people, the Black working class, or with special groups... who would not ordinarily come or be drawn into the theatre."[30] Because theatre was mostly inaccessible to those of lower socioeconomic status, and due to the continued struggle of attracting Black audiences to attend theatre in this period, street theatre was an effective alternative to a professional venue in order to foster theatre hype and collective experience. However, street theatre could not fulfill the organization's goals of economic development or self-sufficiency. This security would only come from established long-running institutions, and theatres proved to be the longest lasting of the cultural institutions.

Bullins moved to the Bay Area in 1964, the same year Black Rep began operating in Oakland. Seale became acquainted with him when he acted in Bullins's theatre troupe in San Francisco.[31] After the failure of BARTS in Harlem, Baraka traveled to San Francisco where he collaborated with Marvin X, Bullins, Newton, Seale, and Eldridge Cleaver to build a new artistic institution, resulting in the creation of Black House Political and Cultural Center of San Francisco (1967). However, it was not long before Black House fell victim to the disunity that plagued Baraka's BARTS.[32] Despite the Panthers holding similar tenets in cultural nation building, the Panthers' theatrical endeavor, and the group in general, were both preceded and outlived by a neighboring cultural institution that embodied the use of nationalistic culture for economic uplift: the Black Repertory Group, or Black Rep.

The story of Nora Vaughn and the founding of her Black Repertory Group theatre, or Black Rep, is emblematic of this period of Black theatre with individuals in search of a collective to actualize their ideal of a thriving Black theatre that would function as a mutual aid organization for those in poverty. Black Rep was one of the earliest Black theatres established during the Black Power era and is one of the few that still exists today, as it continues to carry on its programs. This narrative illustrates how Vaughn faced the complexities of theatrical ownership, especially as a Black woman in the 1960s, as well as the broader narrative of Black theatres struggling to self-sustain through this era and what it meant to survive. Black Rep stands today not only as a monument to Vaughn and her efforts but also as an emblem of a female-led Black Power campaign of the West and the successful intermingling of the economic and cultural fronts of Black Power that have ensured the theatre, and therefore movement's survival to this day.

Black Rep, originally named the Group Theatre, was founded by Nora and Birel Vaughn, who both had a long history in professional theatre and community engagement. Nora Vaughn's lifelong, theatre-based activism originated in her childhood, when she developed a love for the performing arts out of her emotional religiosity and exposure to the arts in school. Vaughn was born in 1914 in Utica, Mississippi. Attending Utica Normal and Industrial Institute gave Vaughn an appreciation for the value of Black institutions. Vaughn's father was instrumental in securing funds from Northern white individuals, exposing her to the tension between funding for institutional survival and submitting to white financial oversight.[33] The institute taught theatre, as well as trades, providing practical links between art and finances. The school was the earliest inspiration for Vaughn's theatre, and it also offered the practical expertise necessary for successful institution building. However, she would strive for communal funding, as had been historical tradition with Black property ownership since the end of slavery.[34] Nora married Birel Vaughn in 1935, started a family, and established the Group Theatre in 1938 in Vicksburg, Mississippi.[35] Like many Black Power leaders, as well as Black theatre, Black Rep had Southern roots.

Prior to 1960, most Black theatres operated in the South, reflecting the racial demographics of the prewar period.[36] However, the Black American exodus from the South marked the transplantation of the population along with their culture.[37] This burgeoning Black population sought homes as well as properties to house their theatrical traditions in these new regions. One of the most significant Black theatres in this period to be created and co-managed by Black women was the Free Southern Theater (FST), founded in 1963, and based in Mississippi. However, the theatre was short-lived due to lack of funds and mounting pressure from the white community to close their doors. When FST closed in 1980, the community participated in a public funeral procession and memorial, signifying that Black artists and the community valued theatre as a living organism.[38] Sensing more sustainable opportunities out west, FST managing director, Mary Lovelace, moved to the Bay Area to become chair of the art department at the University of California, Berkeley. Though she could not take her theatre company with her, Lovelace's new role demonstrated her continued commitment to art and institutionalism. Vaughn was forced to make a similar decision, though she was able to move and grow her theatre. This case exemplified the arduous undertakings of Black women to be both decision-makers in their homes and the builders of long-term communal institutions.

Vicksburg was the site of rampant racial inequity, especially in terms of property ownership and economic status.[39] Much of the Black population in Mississippi was underpaid and constrained from owning property.[40] These strongholds punctuated white recognition that property, capital, and culture led to equitable citizenship rights, and Black Americans pushed for ownership of all three. Though the Group Theatre was an established organization by the mid-1940s, they lacked a proper theatre building and, in keeping with the history of alternative Black theatre structures, were forced to perform in schools. They realized their theatre could not effectively function without a permanent space, self-sustaining funds, or full aesthetic autonomy. The Vaughns would need to somehow gain ownership of a rooted, thriving institution with the ability to uplift the Black community economically and culturally.[41]

The migration of Black Rep was directly linked to white supremacist violence in the South and was indicative of the larger Black migration to the West, accompanied by the mission to found separate Black institutions.[42] Vicksburg was not only entrenched in the Jim Crow South, but the city also had a long history of a strong KKK presence and led the country in number of lynchings.[43] Beyond the issue of needing capital in order to finance a theatre, the Vaughns also faced a hostile backlash to even their low-scale theatrical productions through demonstrations of violence and intimidation.[44] The lack of artistic autonomy in the South was overshadowed by mortal threats and severe restrictions on livelihood. The Vaughns were attacked three times in their home by the Klan, and they were issued a warning to "cease sharing Black Theater and stop teaching Black people awareness and Black Pride or be dealt with harshly."[45] In the last attack, Klan members fired their guns into the Vaughn home and one of the bullets flew into their daughter Mona's crib. For the Vaughns, this backlash proved that they were doing important work, and that they must migrate to continue and thrive on a broader scale.

Even when faced with the highest stakes, Vaughn knew the answer lay in culture and that her theatre would play a pivotal role in the Black nation building that defined this era. However, ownership of the theatre house was necessary for their plan to succeed. Vaughn convinced Birel to move west amid the Second Great Migration in the mid-1940s under the condition that their theatrical and social mission migrate alongside their physical move. Sean Vaughn Scott, grandson of Birel and Nora, and current Black Rep artistic director, noted that the progressive atmosphere is what drew his grandparents to Berkeley, stating, "They migrated here because of its history of providing a place for people to speak and to teach."[46] Berkeley was known for its flourishing free speech environment, which the Vaughns equated with a safer place to stage Black theatre and social improvement programs. It was also the site of burgeoning Black Power ideals and organizing.

The combination of Berkeley progressivism and Oakland's need for financial assistance made the area a perfect place to materialize the Vaughns' mission and cooperate with cultural and revolutionary nationalist figures and groups. The convergence of these two cities not only promised a more welcoming start, but also an expanding Black communal market, which would allow for, and almost necessitate, company development. Birel traveled to California alone in 1944 to canvas the area and begin building an economic foundation to support both his family and theatre. Birel secured a war industry job, building ships in San Francisco. The work was difficult and offered menial wages to mostly Black laborers, which often led to strikes.[47] As war production declined in the following years, conditions worsened for Birel and the Bay Area Black community. The key to Black Rep's survival lay in its ability to evolve. They were committed to observing the community and offering programs to address the changing systemic struggles of each new decade. The backbone of the theatre's longevity was structured by Vaughn's professional background, which set her on a pragmatic path and aligned with the Black entrepreneurial spirit of the era. The greatest obstacle, however, lay in finding a long-term structure to mobilize a deeply impoverished community for the long fight ahead.

After a year of working in the shipyards, Birel found the Group Theatre's first California venue in Downs Methodist Church in North Oakland.[48] Due to Black theatre companies often lacking funds for their own playhouse, they relied on existing structures in the Black community, including homes, schools, and churches. Black women used their resourcefulness and community leadership to transform these alternative structures, such as church halls, into theatrical stages. Historically, the Black church was a site of religious and cultural performance, and communal assistance through collectivity. Churches remained a starting point for Black arts institution building in the context of the Black Arts movement. Reverend Roy C. Nichols, head minister of Downs until 1964, had similar ambitions as the Vaughns in that he wanted to use his property to a political and social end for his community.[49] He utilized the church space as a stage for political gatherings and community meetings to devise social programs, which was indicative of what the Vaughns would do with their stage. Because churches had a long history of acting as cultural centers, and sometimes theatres, the theatrical nature of Black religious ritual was always found in the Black theatre.

Downs Church was right in the heart of the Oakland neighborhoods. As church membership boomed in the 1950s, the congregation outgrew their current church. The church would be forced to close because they could not afford a new property. In tandem with traditionally collective Black proprietorship, Birel, a craftsman by trade, spearheaded the building project for the church's new sanctuary in 1954.[50] According to Nora, "There is not a single block in there that he didn't lay."[51] After two years, the congregation declared, "The church was ours," signifying their ownership of the structure that manifested from their labor and materials and the comfort of having a rooted institution where they could come together in spiritual and theatrical performance.[52] Black Rep's future properties would remain communally funded out of necessity, as well as cultural and historical tradition. Furthermore, this project set a standard for future Black Rep stages, as Birel would construct their next venue with help from the community. His structures offered physical sustainability due to his expert craftsmanship and passion to build long-lasting communal infrastructure. When Birel was unable to construct the current home of Black Rep in the 1980s, Nora worried that there would be a glaring disparity in quality due to the resentments of white construction workers laboring to build Black property.[53]

Once Vaughn joined Birel in California, she asserted her leadership over the metaphysical, artistic mission shaping the institution she hoped to physically construct. Cultural heritage held especially by Southern Black women, such as Nora Vaughn, was key to how they activated a dormant spirit of activism in the Bay Area, employing ideas of "self-help, activism, and coalition-building."[54] For women, the fight to secure these

Black Rep's first theatre building in California at Downs Methodist Church.

institutions would prove exceptionally more difficult. Therefore, the success of female-run institutions, such as Vaughn's theatre, which survived beyond the 1980s death knell of most Black theatres, proved historic in housing the long-form revolution for Black and female empowerment.

The Vaughns operated the Group Theatre out of Downs Church from 1964 until 1967.[55] The church was an apt first venue for their theatre for several reasons. First, the longstanding tradition of church centrality within Black communities ensured the company could connect with the largest amount of people through Black cultural presentations. Aside from producing formal plays, Vaughn staged other forms of cultural performance, including fashion shows to bolster Black female self-confidence.[56]

Secondly, the church was located in the heart of Oakland which put them in tune with the community, often hosting political rallies, voter registration drives, tutorial programs, and Black history lessons within its walls.[57] This fact made Downs a prime platform for the Group's mission of communal development. Additionally, members of the church understood the value of owning property and renting out the church space to facilitate more collective ownership. The Black church was, therefore, a familiar, affordable, and welcoming alternative to mainstream theatre venues. Everyone in Downs contributed by crafting theatrical elements (including costumes and set pieces) and taking on acting roles in the Group Theatre.

The church's mission, however, remained tethered to early civil rights initiatives, not aligning with more radical platforms of revolution that the Vaughns were embracing as the next necessary phase due to the lack of poverty improvement. The church sits in Oakland's flatlands, in the impoverished sector of the city's Black population. However, those who ran the church were middle class, living in the hills and unable to take an accurate pulse of the realities of everyday poverty. The flatlands were majority white middle class before the war. After the war, whites moved into the suburbanized hills and the flatlands were now designated for economically destitute, Black residents. Whites owned surrounding properties, banks, and city zoning boards, all working in tandem to restrict Oakland's Black population to the flatlands, which would only continue to deteriorate within an inescapable low-income cycle.[58] The movement of the mid-1960s placed special focus on those choked by poverty. Seale and Newton operated exclusively among working-class Black America to stress nationalism from within and experience the most pressing issues firsthand.[59] Similarly, Vaughn, who aligned with this growing ideology, wanted her theatre near those it was serving on the frontlines of the revolution. It was necessary for theatre leaders to investigate and appreciate communal issues, as opposed to assuming what people needed, and evolve to meet those needs. Addressing the harsh realities head-on was a cornerstone of the new, radicalized Black liberation front.

Another issue was the content restrictions placed on theatres operating within church walls. Church officials often stipulated that the company could only produce religious pieces in the sacred space of the church.[60] After three years of stagnation and frustration, Vaughn reached her creative limits of producing staged religious stories and could no longer stifle her mission to produce plays written by Black playwrights with "purposeful, socially-charged messages."[61] Vaughn received a degree in Black theatre from Alcorn State in Mississippi, which was indicative of the era's wave of professionalization for Black women in theatre.[62] This training led to more stability in arts institution building, striking a balance between artistic expression and industrious financial campaigns. In her program, Vaughn's study of Black playwrights and methods of producing effecting Black theatre prepared her to be a facilitator of cultural nationalism. She now wanted to put her training and education into practice in the name of the Revolutionary Theatre.[63] Ready for a greater level of ownership, the Group Theatre formally parted ways with the church in 1967, though not the congregation who became financial investors to aid in the theatre's viability.

This period of property transition in the Group's history aligned with another traditional alternative to theatrical venues found in traveling Black theatre troupes, especially popular during the Harlem Renaissance. Even into the 1960s, many Black theatre troupes became transient due to lack of funding. It was often a step towards company dissolution as the funding cycle would not improve. The Group, however, shrewdly took advantage of this period of theatrical minimalism in the name of the larger cause. The Vaughns and other company members, mostly from Downs, used this time to build up their funds, remained local with performances, and still found ways to connect with the community through performance. One founding member from Downs, Wilbur Lamar, described the company in this period as "really nomadic, we didn't even have a home. All we had was loyalty to the commitment of our mission, but that was all we needed."[64] They did not have a formal stage to call home, but instead sought any unconventional venues open for public consumption of the culture. What the venues lacked in theatrical and technical elements, they made up for in accessibility to audiences in venues such as senior, recreation, and women's centers.[65]

When the Group Theatre could not find an indoor facility, they performed outside, which required no rental fee. Their experimentalism and pragmatism challenged conventional definitions of performance and stage which was indicative of the postmodernist style employed by many Black cultural nationalists. Stage spectacle was kept to a minimum to instead highlight the message. Margaret Wilkerson discussed this style as a trend in many Black theatres in California, especially seen in Bay Area theatres such as the Group and the North Richmond Workshop.[66] These theatres related theatrical minimalism to the fight for autonomy in several ways. Minimalism kept budgets low, providing allocation for more frequent productions. Artistically speaking, Wilkerson notes that these theatres muted set dressings to emphasize recurring messages that "the human spirit can triumph over material poverty."[67]

Though the Group was able to put their artistic mission into practice, their social undertaking halted until they could claim ownership of a private space and establish an institution. Most theatres, Black- or white-owned, need external funding in the form of grants. However, a theatre company must actively own or rent a building to receive grants, creating a problematic cycle for those who could not secure property without said grants. This point was punctuated whenever federal initiatives, such as Johnson's War on Poverty, fell far short in offering meaningful resources to aid impoverished Black neighborhoods such as Oakland.[68] Vaughn needed to meld creative approaches with business acumen to direct successful internal funding campaigns that offered true outreach to these neighborhoods, highlighting both historical tradition and the current moment of Black women actively leading nation-building campaigns.

In 1970, with collective funds from Downs, Birel surprised his wife with a new theatre building in an empty storefront at 1719 Alcatraz Avenue.[69] Similar to the Black theatres founded around Los Angeles in this period, a company's first or even second building was often not an equipped theatre house. However, this made it more affordable. They named the theatre the South Berkeley Playhouse and renamed their theatre company the Black Repertory Group, or Black Rep, expressing their feelings of security as they settled into their new artistic identity, mission, and home. The name also defined the type of theatre they sought to produce. A repertory theatre is a resident theatre company that cycles through a specific repertoire of plays. For Vaughn, she would be able to showcase Black playwrights, old and new. Older plays glorified Black cultural tradition and historical experience, while new plays celebrated a rising social consciousness by dramatizing the current moment and directing the future of Black theatre. Still, Vaughn was especially committed to presenting classic plays from the Harlem Renaissance and 1930s playwrights, such as Langston Hughes and James Weldon Johnson, to keep her audiences mindful of Black history.[70] These classic playwrights tended to attract larger Black audiences in this era and therefore garnered greater revenue to put back into the community.[71]

Once again, Birel was responsible for building the theatre out of this former furniture store due to the lack of funds for a construction crew. He made exceptional use of the limited space, and his emotional investment and craftsman expertise ensured the high quality of the project. Every seat was installed by Birel himself. The venue was a "cabaret-style" theatre, or small space, with the capacity to seat ninety-nine.[72] Though their stage was somewhat small, they had a full lighting booth offering the technical theatre elements that had been absent in their church and nomadic years. With their building secured, their ideology and mission for communal uplift could further materialize.

In the beginning, Vaughn's main goal was to provide the Black community with a home and resonating connections that were still grasped for in the wake of diaspora.[73] Vaughn expressed her desire to be a community, or nonprofit, theatre, as opposed to a regional or professional theatre. She wanted Black Rep to remain focused on the community, though capital was still key to the longevity of any institution.[74] She also believed the theatre was a means as opposed to an end. Her objective was not to produce art for art's sake or merely celebrate individual artistic expression. Vaughn's passion for theatre was surmounted by her mission to serve the Black neighborhoods, and she planned to use her theatre as an extrinsic tool to achieve these goals of local development. Overall, she never let her artistic passion distract her from the practicalities of business or the social goals that were observed in the era's Black Power tenets.[75]

Nora and Birel wanted to ensure that all ninety-nine seats were filled every night, both for financial reasons and to reach as much of the community as possible. The efforts put forth for the community would be reciprocated by community members through loyal patronage and fundraisers. This reciprocity exemplified historical traditions of Black property ownership with what Penningroth referred to as a "simultaneously economic accumulation *and* an investment in social ties" and the necessity of collective, communal ownership due to restrictive systems.[76] It also offered a character unique from white arts institutions with more mutually beneficial and democratic functions. Every person in the company and audience held equal value and was made to feel that they held partial ownership in the institution and its creations.

The South Berkeley Playhouse provided a physical space to carry out Vaughn's theatrical mission of cultural nationalism, stating that the "thrust of BRG is to instill cultural pride and self-confidence."[77] She noted that Black children in Berkeley knew very little about Black history and culture, and she decided that she only wanted their theatre to produce Black playwrights to raise that historical and cultural consciousness.[78] Black Rep's first season opened in 1972 with Ossie Davis's *Purlie Victorious*, which confronted the harsh realities of the Jim Crow South through satire, and Vaughn knew this classic would draw a large Black audience.[79] In this space, they also produced Langston Hughes's *Mulatto* and *Tambourines to*

Glory, James Baldwin's *Amen Corner*, Lorraine Hansberry's *A Raisin in the Sun*, and Phillip Hayes Dean's *The Sty of the Blind Pig*. Vaughn also tended to choose plays and musicals that showcased Black music as a necessary underpinning in Black culture education. Beyond a structured repertoire of production seasons, the theatre was also used for more informal, impromptu expressions of culture with community members participating in jazz shows, dance competitions, and original poetry readings.[80]

When it came to funding their theatrical endeavors, Vaughn was keenly aware of the double-edged sword of external funding. Capital was necessary to carry out her artistic and social programs, but it could also lead to overregulation of the theatre depending on who supplied the funds. The revolutionary plays that are often the focus of Black Arts studies were significant as artistic products, but these works were not fully actualized until produced, and white benefactors often refused to produce revolutionary artists. Therefore, Black theatre companies needed a self-funded institution to ensure these plays would be produced and that they made the decisions on where to funnel the revenue. In regard to white funding, Vaughn stated, "too much spoils the child."[81] She strove for a communal funding cycle and argued that grants corrupted both the artistic and social causes of Black theatre. Black Rep's goal of communal and self-funding was met for eight years.[82]

To perpetuate a positive revenue cycle for the theatre, as well as earn recognition as an institution celebrating Blackness and raising racial consciousness, Black Rep needed marketing and press attention. Western Black theatre initially drew little notice from the nation, even from Black press outlets. The early issues of the Chicago-based magazine, *Black World/Negro Digest*, founded in 1942, only included the East Coast and Midwest in their "theatre round-up." However, Black Rep was instrumental in shifting the publication's focus to the West when they hit their stride in their new location. Once the theatre established structural permanence and took communal root in the 1970s, the company was hailed with positive press and public attention.[83] This level of media furthered Black Rep's mission by advertising the theatre as a revolutionary avenue of Black nationalism, as well as presenting their model to a nation of rising Black-owned theatres.

Vaughn's theatrical institution produced full seasons of plays, but it also held year-round community programs like the Panthers, which they were finally able to operate within their building. Their early initiatives mainly centered around utilizing the art form of theatre to uplift groups from low-income neighborhoods, such as Berkeley's at-risk youth. Her efforts operated not within the confines of traditional play production, but instead in interactive programs offered to members of the community. These theatre programs were conducted in the spirit of Malcolm X and his emphasis on Black studies programs to build up the revolutionary and combat the damaging effects of poverty on individuals.[84] The theatre would not be able to pull the entire community up from impoverishment, but they worked to at least remedy the mentality of low self-worth that can exacerbate perpetual poverty.

Vaughn's commitment to youth underscored her objective of building an inheritance for the next generation. Gloria Sewell Murphy, a Black theatre critic for *Black World/Negro Digest*, acknowledged Black Rep's theatrical contributions in the Bay Area, stating in 1976 that the company "continues to approach its goals of creating a stage for the great playwrights of Black America, of teaching Black people about their heritage, of training and inspiring young people in the arts, and of serving the total Berkeley community by bringing them quality performances of plays reflecting a Black experience."[85] Murphy further discussed Black Rep's social service to the community, noting that the company is busy "conducting demonstrations, workshops on Black drama for local service clubs, recruiting and presenting Black youth in theatre arts, and presenting Black plays for various organizations."[86] Vaughn believed this practice was key to nationalism in that theatre had the artistic potential to empower the individual and connect Black Americans across generations and the world, sparking a mass-mobilized collective that could endure the lengthy revolution that lay ahead.

    To mobilize that collective, continue communal assistance, and remain self-reliant, the Vaughns had to contend with declining audiences. Black audience members were traditionally difficult to secure because economic hardship cast theatre as an economic luxury, leading the Vaughns to price some tickets as voluntary donations.[87] Black Rep was developed specifically for the Black community, and it was imperative to increase Black audience participation. Historically, nonprofit theatres struggle to become self-sustaining. Facing even more obstacles as a Black female-run institution, in that she was not taken seriously by white male sponsors or lenders, Vaughn employed her business expertise and found creative ways in which the community could still contribute and therefore participate in ownership of the theatre. Because they couldn't rely on profits from the box office, Black Rep regularly rented out their space. One reporter referred to this as a "rent-party as a means of tiding the company over when the theatre is dark and, equally importantly, of introducing the company to a group of people who normally would not come out to see a play."[88] The company was afforded the opportunity to perform through venue rental at Downs and therefore appreciated the potential for extra capital as well as the communal benefit of practicing shared property ownership.

Drawing on her background of professional training and community organizing, Vaughn knew networking and collaboration were key to financial survival and empowerment. Black Rep, therefore, joined professional Black theatre organizations, such as the AUDELCO group, which trained them in strategies for audience growth. They negotiated ticket prices on a "pay what you can" basis so that more people who lacked disposable income could attend. They relied somewhat on white audiences to make up the difference. The ultimate mission of nation building required packed houses of Black audience members who would be contributing to their own institution. However, in the beginning, the company needed financial security, and white people were more apt to attend theatre.[89] Therefore, in the early years of Black Rep, the groups performed Black plays for predominantly white audiences in Berkeley.

After eight years of operation and theatrical production, the South Berkeley Playhouse was condemned by fire marshals. According to the founders' daughter, Mona Vaughn Scott, the city was under pressure from white business owners on the same street who wanted that space for themselves.[90] Even when Black artists were able to claim property, there were often white officials and white-controlled institutions that used various means to revoke that ownership. In Los Angeles in this period, the FBI launched investigations in the Watts Writers Workshop and the Performing Arts Society of Los Angeles and were instrumental in the demise of both groups by sabotaging their spaces of artistic operation. The Watts Workshop secured their building, a damaged supermarket, in what became known as "Charcoal Alley" after the 1965 riots, and audience members remembered the charred walls.[91] Ironically, their building was supposedly burned to the ground by an FBI informant.[92] The fight to not only secure property but also keep it would be continuous for Black Rep and other Black theatres.

Institutional security was once again hurled into transition. A year into their search for a new home, Birel lost his battle with melanoma from working in the shipyards for so many years. Shipyard employers disregarded the health of their majority Black employees, despite the staggering diagnoses of skin cancer.[93] Amidst her grief, Vaughn remained focused on her goal of a permanently rooted theatre. The struggle to secure a venue was outweighed by the greater difficulty of keeping one. Vaughn's search echoed this period of movement transition and disillusionment on a national scale. As movements, Black Power and Black Arts seemed on the eve of destruction coming into the 1980s.[94] The decline of both movements was paralleled by the many Black Power theatres that were forced to close their doors after being founded at the height of the movement. As she searched for the new location, Vaughn observed the evolving social issues that Oakland's Black community faced, especially police brutality and poverty. The 1980s would bring new hardships, including the AIDS epidemic, crack-cocaine addiction, and mass incarceration, disproportionality plaguing Black urban communities all over the nation.[95] Vaughn devised new theatre programs to address these issues, such as campaigns for at-risk youth, health education, and drama therapy used for drug rehabilitation and societal reentry for those previously incarcerated. To reignite the reciprocal funding cycle, Vaughn needed a new building to house what was now an established Berkeley institution.

In 1978, Vaughn found her land, a vacant lot just several blocks away from their previous Alcatraz theatre. She became locked on this location because the lot was in Berkeley but still within view of Oakland, which was in desperate need of developmental assistance. Additionally, they could remain a nonprofit theatre operating for the people as opposed to moving into a predominantly white community where they would have undoubtedly received more funding and patronage but would consequently become disconnected from their community and the mission of Black nation building.

The vacant lot was owned by the city, which had no current plans for development or sale. Continuing a long history of the city's exclusionary zoning and racially restrictive covenants, Berkeley city officials were not keen on leasing or selling land to Black residents.[96] Vaughn took several years to fundraise because she knew it would be a financial feat to purchase the lot. She was able to schedule a meeting with officials regarding the lot on three separate occasions throughout 1983, but meetings

Nora Vaughn (left) placed this sign reading, "Future Home of the Black Repertory Group, Inc." in the city-owned vacant lot in 1978. *Courtesy of Dr. Mona Vaughn Scott.*

were cancelled each time by officials. Vaughn found other ways to garner their attention. She made several signs, one that read, "the future home of the Black Repertory Group," and placed them on the outside of the gated lot for the next nine years. She regularly sat with her signs next to the gate as a form of performative protest as cars passed by on the busy street. Her daughter, Mona recalls, "The power brokers at that time gave Mom so much resistance to building her new theater in the early 1980s that, after three dates that were not met and promises not kept, Mom picketed City Hall—right outside the Mayor's office! We display her picket sign that stated: HERE I SIT, TILL BLACK REP STANDS! Needless to say, Mom received the approval for construction the very next day."[97] According to Mona, the mayor was embarrassed by the public demonstration and pushed officials to meet with her. Despite agreeing to a meeting, officials planned to make the release of this land difficult. Officials underestimated Vaughn's negotiation and fundraising expertise, due to her being a Black woman. She used this to her advantage.

The city would not allow Vaughn to purchase the land outright and informed her that she needed to raise $100,000 before they agreed to the lease. As was the case with each Black theatre, the fight to gain property or financing was not an individual endeavor. It was a historically communal effort for the Black community. Though the Vaughns left Downs Church, the congregation remained tied to helping the Vaughns fulfill their mission, and many joined the Black Rep Board of Directors. Dona Irving, a longtime member of Downs, described the commitment of church members to the theatre's future:

> The hard-working board of directors, made up primarily of members of Downs church, has a commitment to the philosophy of BRG as great as Vaughn's. They convinced the city of Berkeley to lease a vacant lot on the corner of Adeline and Fairview streets to the group for fifty-five years at one dollar a year, and to construct the theater with the costs shared by the city, and the Department of Housing and Urban Development, and an ambitious fund-raising drive by BRG. BRG has use of the building with an option to purchase the facility in ten years.[98]

Church members' devotion to the theatre spoke to the communal ties that both sides refused to break. Vaughn organized a fundraiser, but most funds she used for the down payment came from a settlement she received after her civil suit against the shipyard company that contributed to Birel's death. His labor still contributed to the theatre building, though indirectly this time. In early 1987, empowered by her collective backing and business background, Vaughn not only secured a lease but also the deal of one dollar a year.[99] She negotiated the lease deal by citing the city's generous offer to a white theatre company, Berkeley Repertory Theatre (BRT), building a new theatre house the same year. However, the city sold BRT the land outright for one dollar, as opposed to a lease, highlighting the racial disparity of Berkeley proprietorship and the city's interest in maintaining a hold over the Black theatre group.[100]

Despite the city's motivations, Vaughn was poised to begin construction immediately. On October 11, 1987, the Black Rep found permanence in the new Cultural Arts Center that houses the Birel L. Vaughn Theater at 3201 Adeline Street in Berkeley. Once built, neighborhood craftsmen honored Birel's memory and helped Vaughn decorate the exterior of the building in order to collaborate on the structure that would in turn serve them.[101] The new theatre sat 250 and held more advanced technical

Large portraits of Nora and Birel Vaughn hang in the lobby of Black Rep's theatre.

equipment than the South Berkeley Playhouse. The layout also included a dance studio and a community room. Vaughn articulated her shock over what she was able to achieve for her community, stating, "Frankly, I never really thought it was going to be completed... It was a dream, but now it's a reality."[102] Though much of what Vaughn fought for had been won, there were still issues in their theatre's new home.

Current exterior of the Birel L. Vaughn Theatre housing the Black Repertory Group at 3201 Adeline Street, Berkeley, California.

The new performing arts center had proper equipment and space. Eight years after Birel's passing, Black Rep's new home was constructed by the city and could not compete with the physical sustainability of his Alcatraz construction. Problems were glaring, immediate, and indicative of white city officials and their apathy towards Black institutions. Heaters were improperly installed, cabinet doors and lighting fixtures were not installed, and sinks were mounted on the wall with no plumbing. A year into operation, the building's problems peaked. In 1988, a flood of water appeared around the first two rows of seats in front of the stage, referred to by staff and company members as the "swimming pool." City contractors neglected to survey the land and constructed a building unequipped to handle geographical issues. They ignored the fact that this location was a valley that collected water runoff from the hills and insisted on digging further into the earth to create a sloped auditorium.[103]

This drainage not only posed a hazard that threatened the integrity of the building, but it also had a negative impact on Black Rep patronage and subsequent revenue. At the time, the theatre charged nine dollars a seat. The two rows put out of commission due to damages had no less than forty-eight seats each. This meant that the company lost more than $85,000 in a nine-month season doing five shows a week. Even though it could not be guaranteed that the seats would fill, this problem negated the economic potential and demonstrated the city's indifference towards this theatre. Theatre board members petitioned the city with concrete plans to solve the issue at $20,000, which the city deemed unaffordable. One member wrote the city a letter stating, "The building... was meant to have been a source of pride, not only to the South Berkeley community but to the City of Berkeley as a whole. We have had enough obstacles placed in our path, and now we have to deal with incomplete construction, empty promises and health hazards. Enough is enough."[104]

Despite building shortcomings, Black Rep still had a physical site to convene, perform, and aid the community. When the Vaughns arrived in Oakland, the city was burdened with poverty. Reflecting on the state of the neighborhood, Vaughn stated, "there was no community—people (were) adjusting to a different culture."[105] The building had three stated purposes that emphasized the social potential of institutional ownership: "(1) improving the social environment and creating jobs for South Berkeley residents; (2) extending the retail activity and restoring the infrastructure of the Adeline/Alcatraz commercial strip; and (3) offering innumerable psychological and human benefits of the dramatic and other arts to the people of South Berkeley."[106] There were opportunities for the theatre to operate in service of the Bay Area community both through producing plays depicting Black life, culture, and history, and through developing assistance programs that operate out of their building.

In terms of cultural nationalism, Vaughn's vision involved producing works from Black playwrights, such as Langston Hughes and Ossie Davis.[107] Black Rep continued to produce older, long-respected works of Black playwrights written between the Harlem Renaissance and the 1950s, which set them apart from other repertory theatres of the time.[108] However, still wanting to address the unique issues of the day and provide opportunities for young Black playwrights of the community, especially young women, Black Rep explored new works as well. Vaughn prioritized Black cultural and historical literacy with her brand of cultural nationalism to ensure the community was aware and proud of their legacies.[109] Still, her cultural nationalism was never just about a selection of plays. Vaughn's brand of cultural nationalism was more deeply demonstrated by *how* she used the art form of theatre and performance for social change, her emphasis on employing Black artists for a cultivated Black audience, and her insistence on control over the theatrical space for uninhibited Black cultural expression.

Vaughn strongly believed she could offer critical leadership in creating a legacy to pass through the generations, just as Black women were historically responsible for passing down traditions of culture, ritual, and organizing. In defining Black Rep's legacy, for all their focus on the arts, Vaughn always felt the label on her company as a "theatre" incredibly limited their philosophy and efforts as an institution. She often stated in interviews, "We are not a theater. Never have been."[110] Vaughn strove for Black Rep to operate as a cultural center, housing the "Keepers of the Culture." She used the theatre to preserve Black culture as well as promote cultural utility in service of the community, ushering in a Black "cultural and economic renaissance in South Berkeley."[111]

Vaughn always planned to pass her theatre down to her children and raised them for the undertaking. In describing her mother's continuous mission for the theatre, Mona said, "The theatre is used as a means to uplift the individual and in turn uplift the community."[112] The collective was important, but Vaughn believed the individual needed to appreciate their position as a valuable revolutionary before they could contribute to cooperative, widespread change. Her mission reflected the Panthers in terms of increasing democracy by empowering the individual for the good of society. The revolution was staged not only in the traditional theatrical sense, but also in social performance through these various programs. The Birel L. Vaughn Theater became a gathering place for Oakland's Black residents; at the theatre, they could actively seek for their community to be kept along with their culture. Nora Vaughn built the Black Repertory Group as a local answer to the national call for Black nation building through the Revolutionary Theatre. Though somewhat unique in its locale, the Black neighborhoods of Oakland reflected other Black neighborhoods across the country in a common need for liberation from oppressive economic, cultural, and social structures.[113] As Black Power gained ground in the late 1960s, Black women continued to heed the call for theatrically institutionalization, especially in the historical center of Black theatre: New York.

THREE

THE TEMPLE OF LIBERATION AT 125TH STREET AND FIFTH AVENUE

The National Black Theatre of Harlem, New York

Very few cultural institutions have worked so hard and labored so long to build an innovative physical facility that represents the vital life force resonating inside the heart and soul of African thought. We believe that the space of ownership produces results of self-empowerment. Therefore, it is imperative that NBT, as owners, remain visible, viable, and strong in the Harlem community.[1]

—DR. BARBARA ANN TEER, FOUNDER
OF NATIONAL BLACK THEATRE

IN MARCH OF 1983, AN electrical fire leveled the building at the corner of 125th Street and Fifth Avenue in Harlem, New York. The building housed the National Black Theatre (NBT), founded by Dr. Barbara Ann Teer and established as a nonprofit tax-exempt corporation on October 24, 1968. She purposefully chose this cross street as a home for her theatre for both the uptown 125th Street atmosphere of revolution and the opulence associated with Fifth Avenue. World-renowned institutions line the avenue through the eastside of Manhattan, and Teer intended her theatre to embody cultural and economic wealth and redefine opulence in non-Eurocentric terms. During the '70s and '80s, she rented the third floor and, later on, the second floor of 9 East 125th Street to house her theatre, until the fire in 1983. For over a decade, she poured energy and money into establishing roots within this property to house the "Temple of Liberation for a Black Nation."[2] Even before owning the building, Teer made a visible impact on the Black community of Harlem. Though others may have searched for a new location following this structural devastation, Teer saw her opportunity to purchase the entire property and rebuild it in an Afrocentric image. Due to Teer's leadership in fundraising, the theatre company was able to officially purchase the building on September 20, 1983. Through ownership, her influence grew over the next decade. On May 31, 1994, one cross street of NBT's home was renamed National Black Theatre Way, and the other named Frederica L. Teer, after Teer's sister, demonstrating the NBT's widespread proprietary and cultural presence.[3]

The narrative of the National Black Theatre, and Teer's evolution to arts activist, is one of the most well-treaded histories of Black women within the Black theatre movement. La Donna Forsgren, Lundeana Thomas, and Jessica Harris have contributed formative works that document Teer's story, her significance, and that of NBT. Most work on Teer has focused more on the art of liberation as opposed to the address of liberation. NBT stands significant within the history of Black theatre ownership because NBT was unapologetically tied to celebrating Blackness, which Teer defined as "the unleashing of an overwhelming creative force," which was made possible by Teer's ownership of her stage.[4] She was also determined to cultivate long-term material change by revitalizing the Harlem community through Black acquisition of property and culture. Teer expressed her company's distinctiveness in this era of institutionalized Black theatre, stating, "The NBT is much more encompassing than just a theater where a group of people get together and perform plays [. . .] we are a multi-faceted institution, an educational institution, which uses the theatrical experience to help decrude [sic] ourselves and to help reverse the process of negative thinking."[5] Her sentiments were reminiscent of Nora Vaughn's assertion that Black Rep was "more than a theatre," demonstrating an ideological mission spanning from the West to East coasts. Today, the National Black Theatre stands as an internationally recognized institution. As a Black cultural center, they foster cultural consciousness and prioritize Black prosperity in Harlem and the restoration of Black communities both in and outside of New York.

The particular cultural and social history of New York City made it a pertinent location to establish a Black cultural institution that could outlast the historical moment of the 1960s. The city was the consistent epicenter of American theatre and flourishing Black cultural expression. The African Company, founded in New York City by William Brown, was the first Black theatre company in United States history. Despite structural issues, in 1821 they secured the first Black-owned theatre housed in an abandoned segregated hospital, called the African Grove.[6] Structural problems compounded with local police raids, and the first Black American theatre company went defunct within a few years.[7] The case of the African Grove Theatre was indicative of the tenuous history of early Black theatre venues but also indicative of similar tactics used by city officials in the Black Power era to shutter Black organizations, including theatres.

Many historians of Black theatre, including Errol Hill, Samuel Hay, James Hatch, Adrienne Macki Braconi, and Jonathan Shandell, have focused on New York as a prime location to challenge the nation's theatrical status quo as the site of white American theatre housed on Broadway, nicknamed "the Great White Way." Broadway was granted this epithet due to the lamps and marquee lights lining the streets of the Theatre District between 42nd and 53rd Street. However, for Teer and other Black artists, it held another meaning for Black artists who were excluded from performing on, working behind, or owning white stages.[8] The history of Broadway was bound up in racialized performance and was the birthplace of the most famous blackface acts of Al Jolson and Eddie Cantor in the 1920s. Furthermore, the length of Broadway theatres ran through predominantly white neighborhoods, so most autonomous Black theatres would be established in Black strongholds uptown in Harlem.[9] In her work on Harlem theatres, Braconi notes that Black artists of the Harlem Renaissance sought to merge "art, cultural activism, and social work," similar to some of the Black Arts movement goals.[10] However, the artistic gains made in New York during the Harlem Renaissance of the 1920s lacked physical proprietorship and the pervasive vision that property could lead to social uplift or a truly Black stage, liberated from Broadway and its Eurocentric and commercial significations.

In the wake of the preceding Black theatrical renaissance of the 1920s and 1930s, World War II marked a demographic shift in New York, as it did in California. Job opportunities in war production led to an increase in New York City's Black population from 6 percent in 1940 to 21 percent in 1970.[11] The population continued to climb after the war, but industry jobs were in decline. Postwar urban deterioration left Harlem in need of institutional assistance. Theatre historian Jonathan Shandell covers the history of the American Negro Theatre (ANT), whose story exemplified the growing ideological tensions of the war period and the coming civil rights movement.[12] Black artists in New York were trying to strike a balance between commercial success and cultural autonomy. The Depression-era Federal Theatre Project invigorated Black Theatre, especially in New York, but the project was halted in 1939 as focus turned to the war industry.[13] ANT was designed to be a spiritual heir. When ANT was founded in 1940, they pledged to "develop a permanent acting company trained in the arts and crafts of the theatre that also reflected the special gifts, talents, and attributes of African Americans" and to "develop racial pride in the theatre."[14] Alice Childress became an original member of the ANT and hoped it would be the theatre Harlem needed. However, as Shandell argues, ANT's focus on integration put them at odds with the growing movement of Black artists seeking autonomy and separatism.[15] Their 1944 Broadway debut of *Anna Lucasta* was deemed a "sellout" of Black theatre, and they couldn't secure their own theatre due to lack of revenue.[16]

By 1950, ANT was defunct, and Harlem was still left in dire conditions that continued to escalate in the next decade. The Harlem riots of 1964 demonstrated the desire to uproot the economic and proprietary status quo across the city. In 1966, the homeowner rate in Harlem was only 2 percent, compared to the overall rate of New York City which was 20 percent. Frustrations surrounding systematic community underdevelopment and police brutality led to demonstrations across the country, including the Philadelphia Riots in the same year and the Watts Riots erupting on the West Coast in 1965.[17] Despite desperation, the question as to the proper strategy to utilize gave pause. Harlem had a long history of championing the power of the Black consumer, which many Black Power figures argued would lead to a self-sustaining Black nation.[18] However, they did not have established Black-owned institutions that could offer economic or cultural support in exchange for patronage. Black Arts campaigns and organizations sought to change that landscape in the 1960s.

In the age of Black Power, the New York branch of the theatrical revolution needed to be located uptown in Harlem where the Black population was concentrated. Harold Cruse made a compelling argument for the city's centrality and significance, stating:

> Harlem has, in this century, become the most strategically important community of Black America. Harlem is still the pivot of the Black world's quest

for identity and salvation. The way Harlem goes (or does not go) so goes all Black America. Harlem is the Black world's key community for historical, political, economic, cultural, and/or ethnic reasons.[19]

For Cruse, all Black theatres of the nation were significant, but a Harlem theatre could be a true icon and provide the most productive model to unite scattered theatres as it was a historic site for artistic renaissances and political demonstration.[20] It was, therefore, imperative that a Harlem theatre take on the social responsibility to lead a nation of Black theatres instead of operating individualistically.

Initially, the community's sights were not set on a theatrical savior because their desperate economic circumstance cast theatre as an unnecessary luxury. Additionally, Harlemites were left cynical and suspicious of Black theatres after the failure of BARTS in 1966, a year after its founding. However, cultural nationalists in New York, like Teer, worked to dismantle theatrical classism and use Black theatrical institutions for reeducation, economic assistance, and artistic performance to spiritually link individuals. The stakes were high, and there had to be a guarantee that the sentiments of nationalism and the interests of local communities rose in tandem.

With New York being recognized as the nation's theatre hub, a number of Black theatres sprang up within the era of cultural nationalism.[21] However, they did not always carry the torch of revolution as NBT would. Robert Macbeth and Ed Bullins, who served as minister of culture for the Panthers, founded the New Lafayette Theatre in 1966, the same year the Panthers formed. Macbeth and Bullins secured their Harlem theatre space in the "old" Lafayette Theatre in 1967 at 132nd Street and Seventh Avenue. However, the company was heavily criticized for their emphasis on theatrical spectacle, as opposed to producing radical or politicized texts.

Though the company was located in Harlem, they were not able to produce shows in a consistent Harlem playhouse. One reviewer, Peter Bailey, seethed about the effect this had on the Black theatregoing community:

> Why don't they make their facilities available to other community activities? Why is that most provocative work, *The Black Terror*, by their playwright-in-residence, Richard Wesley, running at the Public Theatre in Greenwich Village rather than in Harlem? This play, which deals with real revolution, where decisions have to be made as to who will live and who will die, gives the characters a chance to state clearly their views on the woman's role in

The Movement, the relevance of European ideologies, such as Marxism, to Black Liberation, should have been done in Harlem where it would have been readily accessible to the people to whom these issues are crucial.[22]

The New Lafayette Theatre persisted through the criticism as a community arts institution, and their stability correlated with their location. Arts activists believed Black theatres had to be uptown in Harlem, as opposed to downtown in the center of white society.[23] Teer argued that "ghettos" especially embodied the spirit of Black communal culture, contending that it defined "the way we talk . . . the way we walk, sing, dance, pray, laugh, eat, make love, and . . . the way we look."[24] Her theory was reminiscent of Du Bois's concept of *second sight* in which he asserts that because of their twoness, Black Americans have a greater depth of understanding, experience, and character, and therefore, they have a distinct and valuable artistic voice.[25] Teer, similarly, believed that Black communities, especially in low-income areas, possessed an inherent veneration of collectiveness and that they expressed culture and identity with an intrinsic value. She referred to transformative expressions as "cultural sound" or "preacher rhythms," and said they had the power to deeply effect people and ultimately mobilize them for social change.[26]

By the mid-1960s, Black Power fervor was increasing rapidly in Harlem. In 1965, Malcolm X was assassinated just north of Harlem in Washington Heights, which galvanized the urgency of Black Power across the nation. The Congress of Racial Equality (CORE), an organization tied to the early civil rights movement, abandoned their more integrationist initiatives by 1967 and embraced assertive liberation campaigns.[27] This shift in ideology was demonstrated by their physical move from white Midtown to Black Harlem one year before the National Black Theatre was founded.[28]

The BPP New York chapter (NYBPP) was established the same year as NBT, and they had concerns similar to Teer's, establishing liberation schools by 1970 in order to undo generations of white-led education of Black students.[29] Though they were not tied directly to Black theatre, women's groups like Malaika highlighted Black women's roles in broadening the sphere of education from the domestic to a public and communal level.[30] Female cultural nationalists signified the cultural education of young Black people as a cornerstone of building revolution legacy.

The NYBPP held space for women to garner key organizing roles, including Frances Beal, who also founded the Black Women's Liberation

Committee to support Black women on a national scale. Teer, along with her sister and eventual partner in the theatre, Frederica L. Teer also occupied lead roles in the New York branch. Frederica was especially active in these organizations and volunteered her time and expertise to organize their free breakfast program. Frederica had an MA in social work and was highly politicized, which had a lasting impact on her younger sister. Both were raised to view the Black community as extended family, and they learned the necessity of supporting all family and that all success must be rooted in familial unity. Frederica's background prepared her to fight for economic freedom and uplifting the oppressed. She worked closely with CORE in the early 1960s and was instrumental in organizing the March on Washington for Jobs and Freedom in 1963.[31] With her theatre background, she also worked closely with Eldridge Cleaver, the cultural minister of the Panthers on the West Coast.[32] She would serve as executive director of NBT from 1976 until she passed in 1979.

The NYBPP was in the midst of defining themselves and their campaigns to best serve their distinct communities when the original Oakland chapter of BPP traveled to their city. The Oakland group was quickly pushed out by New York activists who perceived displays of misogyny from the group.[33] Those in New York felt these displays threatened the gender unity of their coalition, which made the New York Black Power Movement distinct. Though Teer still faced many obstacles as a Black woman trying to direct a revolution in New York, there was promising growth in a consciousness for gender equity.

The growing nationalistic mentality of the 1960s sought to affirm identity and foster racial pride and solidarity across class lines. The fight for economic justice during the civil rights movement fell short of helping impoverished black communities across the nation.[34] Regarding Harlem in this period, Teer said:

> Black consciousness is on the rise ... But these realities exist alongside an increasing crime rate, a proliferation of drug addicts, dirtier streets, more and more homicides and the organizing vigilante teams to get people home safely. How come, if everybody is so Black and proud, Harlem, the largest Black community in the United States is dying.[35]

For Teer, it was necessary to build these permanent institutions in the center of communities in need with the intention of operating on a local level and offering collective, revitalizing support. She was straightforward in her purpose for the theatre, stating, "We are in the business of transformation."[36]

The Black Arts movement, like Black Power itself, prepared Black America for the coming transformation and revolution. The major organizations acknowledged that the revolution would primarily be organized in areas of severe economic and social decay. Therefore, Teer viewed these neighborhoods as the most valuable participants for the theatre, both as artists and as audiences. She believed that Harlem was representative of the Black world, stating, "So let Mother Africa's divine plan to heal humanity begin now in our homes and our streets. Let the ground swell spread throughout the Harlems of the world."[37] Though she referred to "Harlem" in a globalized context at times, Teer also referenced the city's localized distinction as the "Renowned Cultural Capitol of the Black World."[38] These combined characteristics made Harlem an appropriate place to stage the revolution on the East Coast, just as the distinct atmosphere of Berkeley and Oakland provided a productive site for developmental theatre on the West Coast. Harlem antipoverty programs, such as Kennedy and Johnson's community development corporations and community action programs, were not able to shoulder the weight of the entire community. It was within this environment that Teer's theatrical and revolutionary ideologies would be nurtured, fomented, and eventually materialized.[39]

Dr. Barbara Ann Teer grew up in an all-Black community in East St. Louis, Illinois. In their histories on Teer, Thomas and Forsgren note that her background fostered her sense of art, activism, cultural pride, and business acumen.[40] She was exposed to Black culture and art during her formative years and had an exceptional view of Black women and their role in society. According to Teer's daughter, the only image Teer had of Black women was that they were leaders of not just families but entire communities. "Women indigenously hold the bowl of responsibilities."[41] Both her mother and grandmother were educators, which led to Teer becoming "overeducated," in her own words, attending no less than four universities and earning her bachelor's degree in dance from the University of Illinois.[42] She learned about business early on from her father and grandfather, who were both entrepreneurs. Above all else, they imparted in Teer the necessity of owning property. Her father owned several apartment buildings in East St. Louis and led communal development initiatives, providing an early model for Teer and her mobilizing spirit. He taught Teer that proprietorship spurred a positive economic cycle for individuals but also for underserved communities.[43] Teer's parents highlighted the value of institutions and studying under as many mentors as possible to have a well-rounded education and to become highly specialized and self-reliant. She would ingrain each of these lessons in her theatre, her fellow Liberators, and her children.

After earning her degrees, Teer started in the theatre as a dancer but switched to acting due to an injury.[44] However, Teer became a mainstream success, securing regular roles on Broadway stages. Still, she was unfulfilled. Her stage roles were limited to Black female caricatures as domestic workers or sexual objects.[45] Even when Black artists managed to break into mainstream theatre, it was often an empty victory because they were still overshadowed and controlled by the white owners of Broadway who would only present them in the likeness of how white audiences viewed Black people. Teer gave up her Broadway presence because she was ready to invest in a stage she could create for herself and her community. She specialized in actor training and argued that Black artists needed an internal transformation to raise their cultural, social, and racial consciousness. She referred to this process as "decrudding."[46] Patricia Collins centers self-representation and "the power to name one's own reality" in the growing consciousness of Black feminism.[47] Therefore, the theatre in Teer's mind was not as much about stage spectacle or even audience reception, but instead concerned with internal healing and spiritual connectivity. She wanted to build a space where all Black people, especially Black women, would feel safe, heard, and valued.[48] This process would begin with individuals but ultimately lead to collective catharsis and widespread cultural engagement.

A political awakening compelled Teer to finally cut ties with white theatres.[49] According to Forsgren, Teer recognized that reconciling her raising consciousness of gender and race with Broadway stages would require an egregious sacrifice of self.[50] There was no room for Blackness in white theatres. Teer was disturbed by the lack of Black people backstage and onstage. Her observation that "there exist many victims of the theater's fear of hiring qualified black personnel," demonstrated that the absence of Black theatre practitioners on Broadway was a conscious exclusion as opposed to any shortage of talented, employable artists.[51] She started wearing her hair naturally, which was a meaningful aesthetic in the era of Black Power. Directors refused to cast her, and her manager begged her to change it back.[52] However, she wouldn't change it, arguing, "I became conscious of who I was. Politically aware of what a black woman in America means. Cutting my hair helped me realize that I was in the wrong place, white theatre."[53]

La Donna Forsgren, a scholar of Teer, drew due attention to the gendered struggle that Teer, and other Black women, faced in the theatre and how she wanted to use theatre to elucidate the unique experiences and complexity of Black womanhood.[54] Although Black men in the theatre, like Amiri Baraka, had many obstacles obscuring their entrances to mainstream theatres, Teer faced even more barriers entering the white theatre as a Black woman. Her roles in mainstream theatre were pigeonholed in stereotypical roles that mocked her race and gender, adding another objectifying layer to what Black male actors had to contend with. According to Collins, Black womanhood has been historically collapsed, leading to misrepresentations of Black women in popular media.[55] In turn, the Black women archetypes presented in white-crafted plays shaped popular perceptions about who Black women were in the theatrical as well as social worlds. Teer, along with many Black female artists, was faced with compounding levels of theatrical and social dehumanization and mythologizing to overcome. Joining a Black-controlled theatre company held potential for more control over representation. However, Teer encountered problems of misogyny and colorism in several Black theatres. In 1965, Teer starred in a play at BARTS and was accosted by the male director who, Baraka observed, resented Teer's level of education and professionalization in the theatre.[56]

Another issue Teer witnessed within Black theatres founded in this era was white funding. Teer, along with Robert Hooks, founded the Group Theatre Workshop with financial aid from her father. However, several members, including Hooks and Douglas Turner Ward, wanted to accept more substantial grants from the Rockefeller and Ford Foundations who would ultimately control the location and naming of the company.[57] Teer, Turner Ward, and Hooks used the grants to turn the Workshop into the Negro Ensemble Company (NEC) in 1967, but Teer subsequently abandoned the group. Many Black artists took issue with this theatre for using Negro instead of Black and with the location of the theatre in downtown white neighborhoods. Teer could not support the new company, arguing "My philosophy was that we should not be called Negroes and we should not be located in Greenwich Village."[58] She was focused on this new era that made Black synonymous with Power, and she prioritized finding the right location for her optimum Black theatre that would be the most effecting for Black citizens.

Witnessing problematic operations within Black theatres only further solidified Teer's ideology and resolve to construct a Black theatre institution as a model for self-love and community pride. The timing of her putting this movement in motion in 1968 was critical as the civil rights movement was about to lose yet another leader. On April 4, 1968, Martin Luther King Jr. was assassinated. More Black activists across the nation became radicalized, with some reorienting their rhetoric and strategies to echo the call for Black Power. At the same time, Black artists were organizing within their cultural realms. Jim Williams, a Black actor in New York, published an emotionally charged essay that same year entitled, "The Need for a Harlem Theatre," which not only highlighted the intrinsic value of Black art in the city, but also offered the Black theatre proposal up as a prescription for the contemporary ailments of the neighborhood.[59]

Following her departure from the NEC, Teer started a performance training program when Zuri McKie, whom Teer directed in the off-Broadway production, *The Believers*, asked her for acting lessons.[60] Teer agreed and started recruiting Black artists who were invested in cultural revolution and organizing in Harlem. Though her migration was not as drastic as Nora Vaughn's, the two aligned in the shared emphasis they placed on carefully locating the site for greatest theatrical longevity and community intervention. In October of 1968, Teer and her artist revolutionaries started the National Black Theatre in a Harlem loft she shared with The Last Poets, similar to the setting of Georgia Douglas Johnson's parlor forty years prior.[61] The genesis of Teer's theatre company exemplified the long-standing tradition of Black theatre being relegated to homes as alternative theatre houses. It was in this loft, surrounded by other Black artists, that Teer was able to solidify her mission. She knew that the Western form of theatre did not accommodate the cultural character of people of African descent, and she wanted to formulate her own Black Arts institution that would not be influenced by anything European.[62]

By 1969, Teer's influence spread, and the loft was not substantial enough to accommodate the growing membership in Teer's group. One key figure who would join in this year of growth was Abisola Faison. Faison grew up in DC and made the move to Harlem in 1969 at the age of twenty-one with a passion for activism following the assassination of Dr. King. Her brother joined NBT first and convinced Faison to join. She arrived in Harlem with only $600 in her pocket and "a need to see what self-governance could look like."[63] It was her first introduction to theatre, and she was enthralled by the art. At this time, the art was still self-contained and experimental. This growing theatre group did not put on any public performances for their first year. Instead, Teer wanted performers to put ego aside to fully understand the potential of Black performativity.

Faison also underwent reeducation, which she received through the theatre company and through working in the offices of Bayard Rustin's organization. In the small space of this loft, Teer held required ideological classes every Monday to teach members about Black history and culture to undo years of miseducation.[64] Faison says she was completely transformed by the decrudding and wanted to contribute to implementing the social mission of the theatre. With her education and work experience in finance and social work, Faison was primed to become the long-time financial manager of the theatre and all of Teer's properties. The first assignment Teer gave Faison was the task of collecting data on abandoned homes in Harlem, which Faison found to be 70 percent of all homes standing in the city.[65] With these staggering numbers, Teer remained more determined than ever to ignite a cycle of Black property ownership in Harlem, and she started with the theatre.

As growth continued in 1969, Teer began looking for a proper theatre space. She rented their first theatre in an eight-thousand-square-foot bare room, located at 9 East 125th Street and Fifth Avenue. Though it could only be rented at first, Teer knew the value of outright property ownership from her father. While building up purchasing power for the theatre, she bought a brownstone in Harlem, and eventually several more, to begin investing in the community.[66] The structure was a 120-year-old jewelry factory with two attached buildings, the northside tower and the southside tower, where NBT's space was located. In keeping with Black property collective traditions, the group was able to rent the space with money pooled from members and Teer's own money that she earned directing a play at the American Place Theatre that year.[67] The American Place Theatre was significant to this era of Black theatre because, beginning in the early 1960s, the theatre produced the first works of Ed Bullins and Charlie Russell who became major Black playwrights. It indirectly helped fund the original space for Teer's theatre group, perpetuating Black theatre ownership, and it led to Charlie Russell becoming NBT's playwright in residence and instructor of the theatre's playwriting classes. The ability to retain a resident playwright provided a steady stream of Black play productions, avoided fees incurred from play permissions, and it created paid jobs for local Black theatre artists.

Under Teer's direction, NBT operated as a distinct Black theatre institution that reflected her personal brand of theatrical and communal uplift. She had artistic visions for an ideal theatre but broad concerns for the community at large.[68] Teer, like Vaughn, was not interested in being a subscriber to Baraka's school of revolution, but instead became a dogmatic philosopher in her own right. Several contemporaries deemed her a "lawgiver" of the Black Theatre movement.[69] Similar to Vaughn's journey, Teer wanted to be a performer but sought education and professionalization as an investment in her own career and in the mentorship of others. According to Thomas, this drive for knowledge and practical skill in the field primed her for her later role as a successful producer.[70] Her background also informed her ideology regarding theatre and its use for development. Teer described her search for a truly Black theatre in 1968:

> It therefore seems at this point our best and most realistic hope is to go back home, back to the Black community, and begin to build a "new theatre." A theatre that is not Broadway-oriented, a theatre where you can "call the shots" as you see them, and not be afraid of losing your job. A theatre where you will be free to experiment and to create. A theatre where you can relax and be "colored." A theatre where you can stop denying and begin identifying. Then, and only then, will you be able to create a power base which will allow you to become self-assertive.[71]

Teer viewed the Black community as a powerful consumer collective with the ability to support a Black theatre, as well as a Black nation. Therefore, she hoped that their audience demographic would be mostly made up of community members, stating, "if these same plays were produced by the same professional company in a black community, they would triple the amount of black theater-goers, thereby creating a power base."[72] She often reiterated the mutually beneficial relationship between theatre and community.

In terms of who Teer wanted to reach with her theatre, she produced for those "who don't even know what culture is, who don't even respect art, who thinks it's some sort of luxury or some leisure or some little thing that you do in your spare time."[73] She wanted to reeducate Black artists, as Black Rep did, arguing they should not allow themselves to be controlled by white directors and told the meanings of Blackness by those who neither understand nor appreciate its value. In Teer's mind, if Black producers continually try and fit into the Broadway establishment, then they will never attract a Black audience because it is not authentic. The audience played a pivotal role in institutionalizing and connecting to the broader movement of Black Power, and as Teer stated, "As long as we have no audience, we have no power."[74] Her emphasis on fostering the collective solidified the company's objective of nation building. She also wanted to affect her artists and audience to galvanize their revolutionary social actions. As she worked towards human and artistic authenticity, Teer also fostered a space for Black women. Though she wouldn't have referred to herself as a "womanist," she understood the care that stemmed from female leadership and that women needed more opportunities and safe spaces in theatre institutions. She not only made space for these women in the theatre-house but also in her home, holding weekly women's circles where women were encouraged to indulge in self-care and be vulnerable.[75] There were not many spaces in this time where Black women felt safe to be soft with themselves or others, and Teer intentionally built that space.

As Teer solidified her vision for the theatre, she was still in search of the ideal location because she believed her current theatre was not getting enough attention. Attention was vital to support the institution as well as the larger revolution. Teer rented a floor within the property, but her ultimate goal was to purchase the whole building which spanned an entire city block. The location was perfect for Teer and her mission. While Fifth Avenue was widely recognized as central to New York City, 125th street evoked thoughts of Harlem and uptown Black culture. Teer wanted her theatre to be found at that exact figurative and literal intersection. Continuing the tradition of shared property, the theatre was housed beside the Studio Museum of Arts and on the same block as The Last Poets, Roger Furman's New Heritage Theatre, and Michael Olatunji's Dance and Drum Center—all of which were all focused on showcasing Black art.[76] These seemingly separate cultural institutions would coalesce into a massive Black culture collective, collaborating and using each other's spaces for artistic and communal gatherings. The small retail space required construction to meet their theatrical goals. Just as Birel Vaughn had to convert

Dr. Barbara Ann Teer posing in front of the National Black Theatre building with the original sign. *Courtesy of the National Black Theatre.*

the Alcatraz retail space, Teer gathered community members and artists to renovate the space as a way of asserting communal ownership.[77]

NBT could only afford to rent one floor for the theatre and the second floor for administrative offices in 1969, but they worked to become more financially solvent in the 1970s. Frederica Teer, as executive director, took on a lot of the administrative and financial work at the theatre. Her primary intention was to ensure the viability of the theatre, but she was equally as intent on showing Black Harlemites that, despite their lack of resources and formal education, they are capable of becoming "effective managers, administrators of programs and confident producers in the business world."[78] She used her experience and acumen to train members of the theatre to democratize the industry and elevate Black theatrical professionalization. According to NBT's long-time executive director, Shirley Faison, Frederica played an instrumental role in constructing Barbara Ann Teer's ideas of autonomy and ownership:

> Freddie had an understanding of a lot of dialectics from communism to socialism to capitalism to Marxist, Lenin. Barbara began to speak of that early on, that artists must be entrepreneurial, they have to discover themselves, they have to produce themselves, direct themselves, write for themselves.[79]

Teer demonstrated her own entrepreneurial prowess when the 1983 fire became a catalyst to purchasing the institution. Teer's shrewd undertaking towards financial ownership of her theatre was reminiscent of Black theatre companies purchasing damaged spaces for lower prices in Los Angeles following the Watts Riots in 1965. Teer's definition of ownership was embodied by the theatre she created. She wrote in an article:

> NBT placed real estate and ownership as the foundation of a systemic funding source. The objective was to create a cultural leadership of entrepreneurial artists who would generate income by providing space for commercial and retail tenants, therefore using the income from real estate to subsidize cultural programs.[80]

Teer's ultimate plan for institutional permanence was for the real estate to subsidize the art. Both had to function congruently in order to function at all. The theatre had been operating in the southside tower but moved to the northside after the fire, and this is where they would continue operations through the rebuild with uninterrupted theatrical and social programs.[81]

The purchase price was $500,000, and the entire renovation would cost $10 million, but Teer saw this as an investment in what others would write off as dilapidated beyond repair.[82] This became an opportunity for Teer to demonstrate that the Black community was worthy of investment. The value was intrinsically present. She recounted this decision, stating:

> We now have the power to restore and reinvent. With this power, we can and will reshape America's crumbling mountains, replenish its drying rainforest, across our deserted deserts, down in the valleys of despair; we will repair its swamps and continue to perform radical and profound changes in the minds of its poverty stricken communities. It is time to create beautiful, nurturing, physical environments for our children to live and grow in."[83]

Despite her righteous goal, Teer had to fight for funding. She collected seventeen thousand signatures from the Harlem community, held local and church fundraising campaigns, and finally had a real estate friend help her secure a bank loan after she was denied at fourteen banks, despite her history of good standing with Harlem property ownership.[84] She was also able to garner $25,000 for "capital improvement" from the New York Division of Housing and Community Renewal who put a bond on the building, so they couldn't sell it to anybody else. On September 20, 1983, Teer became the only Black woman-led organization to own a city block-long property in Harlem.

After a few years of construction, the formal groundbreaking of the new building took place in 1989 and was marked by a public, outdoor event, in which all Harlem community members were encouraged to attend and celebrate this as a victory for all Harlemites. The event was also attended by New York State Governor Mario Cuomo.[85] On the structural founding, Teer asserts that the building now stood as a "first-class state-of-the-art Cultural and Education Institute. We became the owner/operator of a 64,000-square-foot piece of land and property in the center of the business corridor of 125th Street and Fifth Avenue (now called the National Black Theatre Way)."[86]

NBT, like Black Rep, rented out their spaces for the purposes of both revenue and for property sharing. They rent out three spaces, including the Black Box Theatre, the Black Box Theatre Lobby, and the Temple of Liberation. The five-thousand-square-foot Black Box Theatre hosts concerts, film screenings, recitals, and workshops, while the 2,500 square foot lobby is mainly for small seminars or receptions. The Temple of Liberation is the mainstage theatre. At eight thousand square feet, it can seat 250 patrons and is mainly used for theatrical productions. The broad usage of the spaces reiterates Teer's sentiment that NBT was more than just a theatre. They rent this space to local businesses which in turn supports Black business owners, and the revenue subsidizes theatrical productions and communal initiatives.[87] Most of the community's utility of the building is meant to leverage technology and space to build up and stabilize small Black-owned businesses and companies, which NBT refers to as incubation.[88] The NBT had a variety of retail tenants on its 125th Street side, including nationally known brands such as Anita Roddick's Body Shop. On the Fifth Avenue side, renters included an African American take-out restaurant, an art framing shop, a grocery store, and a church with over two hundred members. In addition, NBT rented out its own facility when its Theatre Arts Program and Communication Arts Program were not doing productions, workshops, or seminars. The Entrepreneurial Arts Program was the conduit for these in-house rentals to other theatre group productions for seminars, rehearsals, video shoots, conferences, workshops, office space, different religious groups, including Muslims, and for community events and receptions. These in-house rentals were designed to be a service to the community and to draw people to the theatre to see a one-of-a-kind, new collection of sacred Nigerian art.[89]

Once the building was secured, Teer could fully put her ideology into practice and institutionalize the movement. While wanting to be the cultural anchor of Harlem, Teer was always invested in reaching beyond Harlem with her mission of globalized Black Consciousness. There is, therefore, a historically metaphysical aspect to NBT that has fostered international collaboration with Black theatres around the world. She won a Ford Foundation fellowship in the 1970s to travel to Africa where she became evermore committed to designing the theatre in an Afrocentric, as opposed to Eurocentric, image. In 1973, NBT became the first Black theatre to travel to Africa as a company, and they performed at an international festival called FESTAC, also known as Second World Black and African Festival of Arts and Culture, held in Lagos, Nigeria, in 1977.[90] When Teer finally gained ownership of her theatre space, she wanted the physical building to reflect an African worldview and brought several of the Nigerian artists, as well as a Haitian architect, to Harlem to design the building. One Afrocentric aspect that was prioritized in the design was "sacred geometry," which relied on mimicking images of nature in order to understand it more spiritually.[91]

The building was now a physical embodiment of Teer's theatrical ideology. The goal was not to create a "Black Broadway." Instead, Teer wanted something separate and did not want it to appear as if they were creating their own theatre to honor Eurocentric culture or theatre. As one theatre pamphlet stated, "NBT Is More Than A Theatre: NBT goes beyond the narrow Western definition of theatre because it moves out of the conventional form of self-conscious art and introduces to the world the circular forms of God-conscious art." She stated, "You cannot have a theatre without an ideology, without a base from which all of the forms must emanate and call it Black, for it will be the same as Western theatre, conventional theatre, safe theatre."[92] NBT is, first and foremost, a theatre, but its commitment to cultural nationalism could not be reduced to the classic plays they produced in a Eurocentric, traditional sense of theatre. Instead, their mission of cultural nationalism invested in presenting Afrocentric performance, through their use of ritual, spiritually driven actor training, educational symposiums, and, of course, the art of the building itself.

Teer urged her theatre cohorts to celebrate the particularities of Africa. NBT embraced ideals also seen in Black Power organizations, including African aesthetics, spirituality, and emotionality, which were all very appealing to the Harlem community.[93] The objective was to make experimental theatre as opposed to traditional, or Western, which prioritized scripts and structured rehearsals to create uniformity in performance. Forsgren discusses Teer's use of ritual and revival in NBT's theatrical productions in the early 1970s, which involved emotion-driven song, dance, and audience participation.[94] Teer wanted "experiencing" rather than "acting" out of her performers, and referred to Broadway as a "Xerox machine," churning out the same theatre every night.[95] She celebrated unreproducible, extemporaneous theatre, which supported an anti-capitalist ideal shared by many Black Power activists. Teer was deeply tied to the idea of the "soul," as opposed to theatre materials, as the foundation of her theatre ideology. Despite the centrality of the soul, a balance was struck with the material needed to build the physical theatre and house these spiritual programs.

NBT was meant to be a Black institution built on the foundation of Black culture and history. The main goals of the theatre, which were philosophically in tune with both Black and cultural nationalism, were listed to:

> 1) Raise the level of consciousness through liberating the spirits and strengthening the minds of its people. 2) Be political, i.e., must deal in a positive manner with the existing conditions of oppression. 3) In some ways educate, i.e., "educate to bring out that which is already within." Give knowledge and truth. 4) Clarify issues, i.e., enlighten the participants as to why so many negative conditions and images exist in their community in order to eliminate the negative condition and strengthen the positive condition. 5) Lastly, it must entertain.[96]

Teer believed that the only avenue towards liberation would be paved by a unified Black community. Therefore, she pushed for nonhierarchical collaboration. Competition was highly discouraged, and everyone in the

NBT's lobby showcasing artwork and tributes to Dr. Teer.
Courtesy of the National Black Theatre.

theatre was required to work together, no matter their role in the company. Though Teer was interested in helping individuals, the idea of individualism was submissive to Black nationalism, which upheld the power of the collective. It was her goal to "eliminate the competitive aspect of the most commercial theatre. This goal was accomplished through an essential Black medium: the Black family structure."[97] Teer even refused to use the term *director* in the theatre.[98] Instead of directing, she wanted to apply the broadest definition of equity through group ownership of each production. Teer believed that culture was meant to nurture rather than to rule, stating in an interview that "culture" comes from a Latin term meaning "to care for."[99] For Teer, the theatre and community service was the most organic form of integration. She believed that a peaceful productive society thrives on cooperation and that competition breeds tensions and craves hierarchy which leads to an oppressed class. This is why she also chose to hold seminars on relationships between men and women.[100] Collaborative work, as found in the theatre, was more conducive to the mission of a liberated Black Nation.

The main programs NBT offered were designed to provoke the spiritual, artistic, and economic awakenings of Harlem. Teer's educational background led directly to her raised level of cultural consciousness and political being. Therefore, education was always in the foreground of the theatre. She utilized her spaces to house interactive dramaturgical lobbies that would inform audiences of the historical contexts of plays before they observe and participate.[101] The performing company hosted evenings of artistic communal engagement to educate audiences and democratize theatre. NBT Liberators broke barriers between actor and audience, which, as one pamphlet explained, raised the "level of consciousness, clarifies issues, politically enlightens, reeducates while entertains."[102] Due to the foregrounding of education and the amount of women co-Liberators, Teer developed a school within the theatre for members' children, who were all born in the 1970s. They provided a humanistic and Black-centric education for the children, which taught them how to be global citizens, storytellers, culture crafters, and future Liberators. Housing the school in the theatre also meant that women would not have to choose between career and childcare. The school ran until the 1983 fire when all the children would enter the public school system for the first time.[103]

Additionally, NBT held symposiums every Sunday, called "Blackenings." These symposiums were described as an "open forum where Black people can come and find out from the people directly involved in cultural-political- [or] economic activities what they are about."[104] The symposium format of these gatherings offered an alternative way to spend the evening with positive activities. These Blackenings worked for both spiritual and economic benefit. When community members attended these events, they could purchase wares, pick up health literature, or receive clothes and food through the theatre-sponsored drives. This practice created a mutually beneficial commercial cycle in which Harlemites could produce for their community, indulge in both necessities and luxuries they could not afford in other commercial places, and keep the spending and earning of capital within the community. The spiritual side of the symposiums was fed by speakers such as Kwame Ture and Nikki Giovanni, who encouraged the community to find their power in their collective force.[105]

For company actors, Teer's performance training techniques were rigorous. She insisted her actors train and make their way through five cycles of identity evolution before they were ready to perform in her theatre and effectively activate the audience. Once they reached the fifth stage of The Revolutionary, Teer said they were ready for full membership, which meant stage time alongside an investment of time and effort in community service in prisons and hospitals. "That's when the work really begins," she stated.[106] Teer was unique in her style of performance education. Though all Black theatres engaged in actor training, most institutions focused on artistic growth as opposed to raising the political consciousness of each performer as an individual. She believed that Black and cultural nationalism necessitated this particular evolution of artists and drew power from their engagement with humanism and immersion in an African Aesthetic. Teer wrote a lot of her own scripts for NBT production seasons as vehicles for her mission, including *A Revival: Change/Love Together/Organize!* (1972) and *Soljourney into Truth: A Ritualistic Revival* (1974), with the former highlighting historical Black revolutionaries and the latter centered Pan-Africanism.[107] The mission of NBT was so concerned with community that the opportunity to perform within the company was directly tied to the artist's commitment to building Black nationhood.

Though aspects of NBT are reminiscent of other contemporary Black institutions, Teer's ideology set her apart. Many artists believed the lack of Black theatrical institutions was a direct product of impoverishment. Teer disagreed, arguing that idea was manufactured for the purpose of negative conditioning through the Black community to limit them mentally and, therefore, socially and economically. She stated, "This shift led to NBT taking responsibility for creating an economic agenda designed to disintegrate the negative programming generated by the artist and to eliminate those value concerns of low self-worth."[108]

Culture was the key to this mental, and later economic, liberation. Teer believed that, though poverty had a lot to do with external causation, Black people could take back control simply by changing their mentality and gaining practical knowledge about opportunities for capital gain. Teer was acutely aware of the need for capital to establish and sustain a soulful theatre and its community, which is why she operated from a philosophy she defined as Culturnomics. Culturnomics epitomized Teer's marriage of spirituality and materiality. To connect her practitioners with this notion, she wrote a prayer to African Gods and implored both theatre and community members to recite the prayer with her:

> We humbly offer you this prayer for cultural restoration and economic codification. Let your spirit energy help us bring forth financial atonement. Let this soulful cultural healing and the natural resources of the planet be used systematically to bring forth the distribution and management of financial

wealth needed to uplift the whole of humanity ... In the name of our economic freedom and cultural autonomy, give us the strength to forgive all the many crimes committed against us.[109]

In order to reach the new level of consciousness, NBT offered Master Liberation classes, which were seven-hour workshops designed to help the individual understand their personal power and potential.[110] Another program historically offered by NBT is their Entrepreneurial Artist Program to educate people on business savvy and how to produce artistic events.[111] These forms of self-empowerment were meant to help those who lived in Harlem visualize a future of more economic and cultural privilege if they become active revolutionaries, and the theatre space facilitated this preparation and reeducation. She believed there should be a theatre on every block for widespread cultural and economic healing.[112]

Not everyone in Harlem or in the broader Black theatre community shared Teer's vision for the theatre and Teer's mission of unhindered cultural nationalism. According to Teer's daughter and current NBT CEO, Sade Lythcott, Teer faced criticism at times from other Black theatres of the community because she was so outspoken and perceived as radical with her ideals. These critics viewed NBT's mission and brand of theatre as too politically charged, and they feared it would harm the chances of Black theatre becoming mainstream.[113] In this sense, Teer deviated from Black Rep, which was still reliant on city funding and could not afford to be labeled as "political." This fact punctuated the main difference found in outright ownership, which NBT was able to secure and for which Black Rep still strives. Still, Teer was subject to her community. She did not want to capitulate on her belief that aggressive oppression must be met with aggressive liberation efforts, but most importantly, she did not want to lose touch with the community she was committed to assisting.

In an effort to connect with the Harlem community and gain more understanding of their needs, NBT sent out a questionnaire in the early 1970s inquiring about their feelings on identifying as Black in America and how they evolved over time. The survey asked questions about the current context and impact of the Black Power movement, such as "Have you noticed a change in your community since this new surge in Black Pride?"[114] The theatre wanted to remain as relevant as possible and adapt alongside the community as opposed to an individual entity.[115] The theatre spent time training around one hundred people in the NBT building

Current exterior of the building housing the National Black Theatre at 125th Street and Fifth Avenue, Harlem, New York.

to conduct this survey in the community. Teer revealed this questionnaire to be a part of a greater process, stating, "The questionnaire is the first phase of an attempt to revitalize Harlem..."[116] NBT was taking the internal pulse of the community to improve their programs, as opposed to BARTS leaders who merely assumed they understood the community's circumstance. By taking this action, NBT stood out as exceptional and ensured their long-term survival. Their mission was specific enough to make it a recognizable brand, but not specific enough that it would become antiquated.

NBT's building, theatre productions, and communal programs all cost exceptional amounts of money. The soul already existed, but funding was necessary to secure institutional permanence. Through her education and practical experience in the theatre business, Teer was able to not only sustain but expand the theatre's proprietary lines and all of the company's operations. For her, the key was a copacetic marriage between savvy funding campaigns and cultural and theatrical expression. Though much of the financial success came from Teer and her team, she wrote her gratitude into the company's religious prayer, highlighting this economic and artistic merger:

> We thank you for the challenge of having to generate millions of dollars, for it was this challenge that opened up the way for us to experience the consciousness and healing force of CULTURNOMICS. This challenge has taught us to use a mathematical theology to tap dance on the keys of the computer, the way we used to dance to the rhythm of the drum. It has taught us to reach out and establish global partnerships, collaborations and Internet access, linking us into future digital technologies and opening us up to receive energy and information from all the super highways of the world.[117]

Teer surrounded herself with people who knew the business side of culture and did her best to rely on those within the community as opposed to outsourcing assistance for the theatre.

Over the years, the list of funders for NBT grew. In 1986, Teer secured funding from the National Endowment for the Arts Challenge America Grant, which was specifically designed to fund projects that bring the arts to underserved populations due to factors such as economics, geography, or race. As an individual powerhouse, Teer received two honorary doctorates in recognition of her theatrical institution, one from the University of Rochester in 1994 and the other from University of Illinois in 1995.

By 1970, NBT had their mission and their building, but it would still be decades until they felt secure in their permanence. Though the Black

Panther Party began to dissipate in New York by this time, NBT was carrying forward nationalistic social and cultural programs for the Harlem community and broader Black communities who were now traveling to witness the internationally recognized transformative art housed at NBT. They approached each new decade with reverence for their original mission and a pragmatic attitude, ready to adapt to new contexts and communal needs. New York proved a critical space to foster and fortify Teer's intended theatre movement. Black theatrical organization and production historically thrived in this city, and it was overall a place for Black cultural transformation. However, the Du Boisian notion of Harlem as a state of mind, rather than a place, was also evidenced in this movement. The new renaissance was regionally pluralistic but nationally present. Roughly ten years after Teer began her theatrical mission, when Black Power organizations started waning, the origination of another Black theatre began to stir on the southern coastline of Texas.

FOUR

THE ENTERTAINERS, ENRICHERS, AND ENLIGHTENERS AT 3535 MAIN STREET

The Ensemble Theatre of Houston, Texas

People understand that they aren't just buying tickets to see a play, but they're buying into an institution, into an idea.[1]

—EILEEN MORRIS, CURRENT ARTISTIC DIRECTOR
OF THE HOUSTON ENSEMBLE THEATRE

IN EARLY SPRING OF 1985, George Hawkins's car broke down on the way to his theatre company's first house, which had been condemned by fire marshals months prior. As he began his walk to the theatre, he happened upon an abandoned auto repair shop right on Houston's Main Street. Burdened but not defeated by his luck, Hawkins saw this an opportunity to open a theatre house on Main Street, which was an up-and-coming theatre district with its true direction yet to be determined. Hawkins planned to stake an early claim to this area to prime it as a site for Black developmental theatre that would have a widespread impact on Houston's Black community. He stated that he wanted an "off-Main mentality to develop" and for this street to be indicative of "off-Broadway, but an indigenous inner-city theatre district."[2] "Off" Broadway, as opposed to "on," was a significant distinction because he did not feel that they could function organically or authentically as a Black theatre if housed in a theatre district transplanted from the "Great White Way." The theatre needed to be close enough to Houston's theatre center to garner attention and patronage, but they also had to avoid being commercialized or co-opted while remaining communally connective to foster social development. Today, there are only a handful of Black theatres in the nation that hold outright ownership of their theatre building. One of these few is Hawkins's Ensemble Theatre housed in a repurposed auto repair shop at 3535 Main Street in Houston, Texas.

Ensemble was founded in 1976 by Texas-native George Hawkins. This Houston theatre was established after the peak timeline of the Black Power and Arts movements and outside the city centers of the East and West Coasts that hosted many of the significant Black Power organizations and theatres of the period. However, Houston's history of race relations runs somewhat parallel to Harlem and Berkeley with its concentrated Black populations and culture, and its early demonstrations against subjugation. By the early 1970s, the city was a burgeoning hub for radical thought, action, and art. In the wake of the Black Power downturn, the Houston atmosphere encouraged innovative strategies to revitalize revolutionary fervor and institutionalize a revolutionary stage in a hub of the Black South.

The humble beginnings of Hawkins's theatre were similar to the Black Repertory Group and the National Black Theatre, first performing in his home, churches, dilapidated spaces, and on the road. On July 4, 1985, George Hawkins signed the lease for the auto shop on Main, which included a purchasing option after five years. Hawkins passed in 1990, before he could purchase his dream theatre on Main Street in Midtown. However, he knew that ownership of this space was pivotal to the theatre's future as a permanent cultural institution, stating, "At the old building, we had so many talented artists but couldn't give them enough work due to limited facilities. Now we have the artists, the program, the space—and the challenge to raise the money to make it all work."[3] Though Hawkins would not be able to see this mission through himself, he invested time and money in organizing a highly trained group of mainly women supporters and collaborators who would carry on this endeavor. Ensemble differs from Black Rep and NBT with its Black male founder, but Hawkins placed the theatre's operations in the hands of Black women. Coming to the end of a long illness, Hawkins passed his torch to the women of Ensemble, notably current Artistic Director Eileen Morris, past Artistic Director Marsha Jackson-Randolph, and Board President Audrey Lawson, who secured its future with effective funding and artistic campaigns. Together, they actualized Hawkins's dream, carrying the temporary space into permanent ownership in 1995. When asked in a 2009 interview what the most significant event in the history of company was, Morris responded with recognition and reverence for Black proprietorship: "Purchasing the building and burning the mortgage."[4]

Ensemble is geographically distinct within the Black social and theatre movements of the era, leading to the creation of an institution that was in conversation with the other theatres of the movement but still unique in character. Houston is hailed as the theatrical epicenter of Texas, hosting the earliest companies and some of the most sustainable. Two theatres were founded in 1838 before the city built a single church. Texas Revolutionaries, such as Sam Houston, who fought with the purpose to secure the future of slavery in Texas, became involved in the earliest theatres, denoting a long state history of racially exclusive stages.[5] Though existing on the edge of the new frontier, Texas was intermingled with the large, urban theatre scenes of New York and Chicago, hosting touring companies and shows in its major cities following the Civil War.[6]

Despite the focus of Black theatre scholarship on Harlem, the greatest number of black theatres were historically concentrated throughout the South. Out of the 216 Black theatres in operation before 1960 though, few had a long tenure.[7] The theatrical debut of Black actors on the Texas stage dates back to the antebellum era when enslaved people were forced to perform variety shows, such as the Cakewalk, for enslavers and their guests on makeshift plantation stages.[8] These forced performances in slavery states of the South persisted as the only form of allowed Black performance for a century after emancipation. However, as soon as Black settlement developed in Texas towns such as Houston, theatrical ventures quickly followed.

Prior to the Black Arts movement, Black theatre in Texas was produced for the white gaze. As Black theatre emerged in Houston, it tended to follow national trends of minstrelsy. Newspaper advertisements for Houston "Black" theatre troupes date back to 1845 with the mention of the Ethiopian Minstrel Show. However, the reports are difficult to interpret because so many white vaudevillian minstrel troupes marketed themselves as "Black" performers.[9] The first documented Black theatre organization in the state of Texas was the Thespian Society for "Cullud Genman," located in Houston. Founded in 1866, only one year after emancipation, this company played mostly minstrel shows to entertain white aesthetic tastes and appease their expectations for a "Black theatre." Minstrel shows thrived in Houston in the 1920s, and especially the 1930s when racial tensions peaked amidst economic destitution.[10] In 1931, Houston joined the ranks of the Negro Little Theatre Movement with their own branch. The Houston Negro Little Theatre was funded with $20,000 given to the Houston Recreation Department by the Works Progress Administration to establish a Black theatre troupe. However, they were not able to secure a theatre for rental space. Instead, they began performing plays in the basement of the Carnegie Library Branch, reminiscent of Du Bois's Harlem Little Library Theatre. The basement was too small for productions, and water had to be bailed out of it before every performance. The company outlived Du Bois's but ceased operations by 1955.[11]

The Black artistic and social revolutionaries of Texas organized later than their West and East coast counterparts, largely due to their demographics. One reason for the surge in revolutionary and artistic demand on the Texas front in the 1970s was the rapidly increasing Black population. Texas ranked among the top two states, including California, for receiving the majority of Black migrants who moved at the tail end of the Second Great Migration in the late 1970s.[12] Though moving from the South to the Midwest and West was the most common trajectory during the Second Great Migration, the migratory pattern began reversing in the 1970s through the 2000s.[13] The attractively low property rates in Texas especially drew Black Americans from the increasingly oppressive rates in California. In this sense, Texas presented a more viable option for Black property ownership than California or New York.

The city of Houston remains consistently at the forefront of the nation as "the most diverse city in America" since the ethnographic changes of the 1970s.[14] In all, over one hundred thousand Black people migrated to Houston in the 1960s and 1970s, increasing the Black demographic to over 25 percent of Houston's population.[15] Despite lower property rates, Houston segregation and local policy led to decaying Black neighborhoods in need of development. The Third Ward, located in Midtown, historically and presently hosts the largest concentration of Houston's Black population, and it is historically marked with impoverishment.[16] The growing population invigorated Houston's Black community to mobilize an assertive front against racially discriminatory practices and police violence, and to raise political, collective, and cultural consciousness among Black Texans.[17]

Racial strife in Houston was consistently met with resistance of equal fortitude, often with Black women at the forefront. In 1939, Lulu B. White became president of the Houston Chapter of the NAACP. Her mobilization of the Black Houstonians led to the Houston branch becoming the largest in the South by 1943. The leadership positions of White in the NAACP and Houston Urban League CEO, Sylvia Brooks, were indicative of the broad Black female leadership in Houston and the state of Texas.[18] Houston was also the site of the original case that kicked off the landmark Supreme Court ruling on *Smith v. Allwright* (1944), knocking down all-white primary elections, and hosted nationalized civil rights demonstrations such as sit-ins and protests of theatre segregation in the early 1960s. Civil rights activists in Houston fought against police brutality and conservative political policies that cut public housing and federal subsidizing of schools and free lunch programs.[19]

Despite being at the forefront of the modern civil rights movement, organized Black Power arrived late in Houston in 1970 and had trouble getting off the ground. The Houston chapter of the Black Panther Party was called the People's Party II, which was headquartered on the corner of Tuam and Dowling. This cross street was the site of a 1970 shootout between the Houston Police Department and the People's Party and the future site of Houston Ensemble's first theatre house nine years later. The shootout ended in the murder of People's Party leader, Carl Hampton. In 1969, Hampton moved south, from California to Texas, with the goal of establishing his own Black Panther chapter in Houston after observing the original model in Oakland.[20] His migration, in general, reflected the migratory patterns of radical politics and theatrical tradition during this era. However, his recruitment efforts and property acquisition in Houston proved difficult for several reasons.

Hampton's strategy was reminiscent of the Panthers, starting with college students at the University of Houston. Unlike the Panthers' success at Merritt College, Hampton had trouble finding Black students who were interested.[21] Adding to the local organizing difficulties, the Black Panthers put a national freeze on new membership due to infighting, public and media scrutiny, and fear over mounting government surveillance.[22] Black Power was a national movement, but the Black Panther model of the East Bay area in California would not necessarily work in all locales. These organizations, like the theatres, had to individualize themselves to operate within their particular social, cultural, economic, and political climates.

1970 marked the first year of the People's Party, and under Hampton's guidance, the party secured a rental property in the Third Ward of Midtown, where help was most needed and where Hawkins sought to build his theatre later that same decade. The People's Party distributed clothing and food to community members, but Houston race relations began devolving in April of 1970 when two white Houston officers beat a young Black man, Joe Connor, to death.[23] Houston police chief, Herman Short, issued the following statement as a warning to party members: "The law will be enforced in the 2800 block of Dowling as it is everywhere. There is no place in this city where a policeman can't go."[24] His statement reflected the ethos of white law enforcement which refused to recognize or respect Black private property in Houston and instead used property as a means to surveil. On July 26, 1970, Houston police took position on the roof of St. John the Missionary Baptist Church. When Hampton went outside to investigate, a shootout between snipers and Hampton ensued, resulting in Hampton's death.[25] The People's Party continued to operate, but their reach became more limited due to the negative attention. The explosive confrontation of police brutality and economic disparity reflected the race riots of New York and California on the eve of their Black theatrical renaissances.

The regional history and culture of the South crafted a distinct landscape for Black social, economic, and theatrical radicalism.[26] The concentrated Southern Black populations spurred the creation of many theatres. However, the heightened racial tensions in these same areas hindered sustainability. Even the ideological model of BARTS was inspired by a theatre founded several years prior in the Deep South: The Free Southern Theater (FST). FST was founded by Doris Derby, John O'Neal, and Gilbert Moses in Mississippi during Freedom Summer in 1963. Though not located in Texas, it proved significant both as its own theatrical entity, and as a model for other Black Southern theatres. Just as the surges of Black theatre on the East and West coasts were the product of migration, mass mobilization during the civil rights movement inspired some Black Northerners to move south and participate. Theatre practitioners in the North, such as Moses, brought with them an acumen for running professional theatres. Both Derby and O'Neal were working for SNCC when they met Moses. In their original mission statement, the founders wrote, "Our fundamental objective is to stimulate creative and reflective thought among Negroes in Mississippi and other Southern states by the establishment of a legitimate theater."[27]

Despite FST's revolutionary position as an early, Black-run Southern theatre, the company played to white audiences and performed plays written by white dramatists in their early years. FST was forced to shutter by 1980 due to the lack of funds and the lack the autonomy, authenticity, and militancy called for by the impending wave of cultural nationalism.[28] Though it was located in Mississippi and fell short of burgeoning artistic radicalism, many Southern Black theatres were inspired by FST's efforts, especially because there were few Black theatres with longevity to view as models in this period.

The Texas branch of the Black Theatre movement spread statewide in the 1970s. The larger cities of Texas soon had representative Black theatres catering to unique issues, demographics, and artistic tastes, including the Black Academy of Arts and Letters in Dallas (1977), which subscribed to the era of cultural nationalism and is still in operation today.[29] The diverse landscape of Texas added another nuance to Black theatre groups that was not seen in other regions. Several of the theatres founded in this era became racial coalitions between Black and Hispanic theatre practitioners, including the Janus Players (1969–1974) and Dallas Minority Repertory Theatre (1973–1979), both in Dallas.[30] Despite the varied state of Black theatres in Texas, overall, these institutions remained within larger urban centers. The main reason for the urbanized theatres was that a large portion of Black Texans living in rural areas had moved to the cities by the time of the civil rights movement and rural areas were in need of infrastructure.

Two notable semiprofessional Black theatre companies were founded in Houston prior to Ensemble during the Black Arts movement. In 1969, one year after Barbara Ann Teer founded the National Black Theatre in Harlem, Barbara Marshall founded the Urban Theatre in Houston's Third Ward neighborhood.[31] Though the theatre was founded during the movement and located in a neighborhood in need, Marshall's mission diverged from both the Black Power and Black Arts movements. She set out to establish a "multiethnic theatre" that was not concerned with cultural nationalism or economic or social uplift of the Black community.[32] A year after Marshall founded her theatre, Reverend Earl Allen founded the Black Arts Center Repertory Theatre. The Black Arts Center produced more politicized works, such as the dramatization of Malcolm's X's autobiography, and it was the first Black theatre company to own their own building. However, the building conditions were so poor that actors, including George Hawkins, refused to perform there after a few years, and the building burned down in 1980.[33]

Despite the difficulties of establishing permanence in many of Houston's Black theatres, the city's brand of theatre in the context of Black and cultural nationalism was distinct from the East and West coasts, and it proved successful in its own right. By the time Ensemble was founded in 1976, hundreds of movement theatres were already established, and many had expired across the nation.[34] Therefore, the timeframe of the 1970s is generally regarded as the fatal moment for both Black Power and Black Arts movements. Despite the visible decline of the Black Theatre movement in the late 1970s, the movements were not dead but instead in transition.[35] The same can be said of Black Power and the way the movement and Black theatres related to each other in this new period. Black Houstonians were still in need of revolutionary institutions in the 1970s, and the artists of these institutions had to be pragmatic, creative, and business adept to survive.

The failure of a formal Black power organization to take hold of the growing racial disparities in Houston underscored the need for a different kind of institution. George Hawkins's professional background, pragmatism, and Black-centric cultural mission primed him to lead a theatrical institution of Black liberation in Houston and connected him to the national movement. Hawkins was born in Dallas but made Houston his new home when he attended Prairie View A&M College. College facilitated Hawkins's future success as a theatre founder by sparking his love for performance art and providing him applicable business knowledge and training. He graduated with a degree in business administration, and he earned a second degree in accounting from Case Western Reserve University in Cleveland, Ohio. After receiving his education in business, he continued his theatre studies at two notable Black theatre companies, Beale Street Repertory Theatre in Memphis, Tennessee, and New Freedom Theatre in Philadelphia, Pennsylvania (1966). He returned to Houston in the 1970s and was working as an accountant for Pinnacle Oil Company when he started devising plans for a theatre.[36]

As an actor, Hawkins was pigeonholed into roles such as enslaved characters and butlers, similar to Barbara Ann Teer and Nora Vaughn.[37] He really wanted to nurture young Black artists and appreciated the compounding obstacles Black women faced in the theatre. In Hawkins's mind, the only way to empower these artists was to provide a space for them to train and express themselves artistically.[38] When asked in an interview how Hawkins was able to fund his early productions and tours, Eileen Morris stated that it was "nominal," but his ultimate goal was not deterred:

> George just wanted to get the work out there and make people aware of what he was doing because his goal became having a home base for the theatre and that's why he kept trying. All of the places they performed were just a set up to get ready for his home base where he could be there and set up shop and do plays in a contemporary setting.[39]

With his professional degrees, Hawkins was primed, as Teer and Vaughn were, to head an artistic institution that could effectively function as a Black-owned business for Black cultural consumers. Highlighting his goal for the theatre to be a highly collaborative and mutually uplifting space, he named the troupe the Black Ensemble Theatre.

Though Hawkins's Ensemble existed outside of the coastal urban centers that housed many significant Black theatres, the company's evolution mapped both national and historical patterns. The first venue to stage Ensemble performances in 1976 was at 2010 Wentworth Street, Hawkins's house, which paralleled NBT's beginnings in Teer's loft.[40] Once he solidified a group of performers and honed their process in his home, Hawkins knew he had to produce this art for larger audiences. Before securing spaces within the Black Houston community, his early efforts to establish the Ensemble as a name in Texas Black theatre resulted in a traveling troupe, resembling that of Langston Hughes's Suitcase Theatre.

Just as Hughes fit his entire theatre into a suitcase, Hawkins packed his car and took his theatre on the road. Morris recalled that "he had this long black Cadillac that someone had given him and he used the trunk of that car to haul the whole—the costumes, the props, and he adapted that play, the Br'er Rabbit story, and they toured that play for a couple of years . . ."[41] Hawkins needed to maintain his full-time accounting job in order to fund the theatre. This aspect was also indicative of the long history of Black artists who were forced to seek economic stability with supplemental jobs outside of the theatre. Though Hawkins's theatre was homeless in these early years, he kept it alive through mobility and was even able to create a new play from stories steeped in enslaved African American folklore.

For his first season, Hawkins produced only one play, *Br'er Rabbit*, which was a common show performed in minstrel style in the early twentieth century.[42] One-show seasons were common for Black theatres early on because it cut down on production costs. Low cost production was also necessary due to the fact that many of the *Br'er* performances were free to the public, including the premier in September 1977 at the Houston Public Library.[43] By providing free performances to Houston's Black community in the early years, Hawkins made it easier to establish a name and following for the theatre, and he made an elitist art form more accessible to those who normally could not afford to attend the theatre. However, this also meant that Hawkins only spent money and incurred debt in the first few years before jump-starting a cycle of revenue that was needed for maintaining and growing his institution.

Choosing *Br'er* as the company's first show portended the future of Ensemble productions dedicated to folk culture and Black storytelling traditions intended for Black audiences. However, *Br'er* was outdated and contained offensive dialog and dialect for modern Black audiences. In an attempt to still reach his contemporary audience with folk art, Hawkins found ways to adapt and modernize the 1930s script by making it a musical and diluting most the outdated dialect. His efforts to make old folklore relevant in a new context were successful, and the script was the most well-received version since the 1930s. Ensemble continues to perform the script annually.[44] By modernizing the language, minimizing the stereotypical dialect, and adding depth to otherwise one-dimensional archetypes, he turned this play into an educational tool in the spirit of Black nationalism to connect Black audiences with deep roots of history and culture. The success of this show solidified the creative and nationalistic identity Hawkins wanted his theatre to possess. In all, Hawkins wrote two musicals and six plays in his career, all focused on Black history and culture.

As Ensemble traveled and performed in various cities, the company often rehearsed and performed in church basements, similar to Black Rep at Downs Church. Most Black theatres in Houston hosted patronage from Black churches, which meant that most of these theatres had at least one religious show in each season. Houston's Black churches historically pooled resources to gain collective ownership of property in the city. Emancipation Park was founded after the Civil War in honor of

Juneteenth Day and emphasized this collective support with the *Houston Post* remarking:

> In Houston, the effort was led by the Reverend Jack Yates, a Baptist minister and former slave. His church, Antioch Missionary Baptist, and Trinity Methodist Episcopal Church formed the Colored People's Festival and Emancipation Park Association. In 1872, they pooled $1,000 to put down on ten acres of open land as home for their Juneteenth celebration.[45]

The park operated as a separate space that allowed the admission of Black Houstonians in a city that was overrun with Jim Crow laws. The city allocated funds to all-Black parks and all-white parks. However, there was a sizeable funding disparity. For example, in 1929, the city of Houston allocated $200,000 to white recreational spaces, and $5,000 to Black facilities.[46] Therefore, Black institutions, communal organizations, and public accommodations had to be internally funded.

The historic Antioch Church that helped secure ownership of Emancipation Park later became a major supporter of Hawkins and Ensemble. Ensemble's first play in the Antioch church space was Douglas Turner Ward's *Day of Absence* in 1976.[47] Black churches tended to be wary of producing shows that were nonreligious or too political within their spaces. Antioch's approval of the production of Ward's 1965 play was radical as the show was highly politicized and caused a social stir when it premiered with Black actors performing in white face as a social commentary about the integral role Black people occupy in the American context.[48] The church saw both the artistic and social merit and wanted to support Hawkins in his broader mission for the community. Investing further in his development as a theatre practitioner, Hawkins traveled to Europe in 1978 for ten months to study theatre in London. He returned in March 1979 with a new philosophy centered on purposeful art and developmental theatre.[49]

After gaining enough of a community following, and a stable income from his accounting job, Hawkins was able to shop around for a rental space. His budget was small, and he would only be able to secure a dilapidated building that was not intended to be a theatre. However, unlike the spaces he had been producing in, this new property would ultimately be a space dedicated solely to theatre. He signed a lease for Ensemble's first

George Hawkins posing in front of the original Ensemble building on Tuam Street. *Courtesy of the Ensemble Theatre.*

theatre building in 1979. The property was an old pet store at 1010 Tuam Street in Houston's Midtown.[50] The 1100-square-foot property had to be converted from a storefront to a theatre house, similar to Black Rep in their converted furniture store and NBT in the jewelry factory. It was a mere few blocks away from the People's Party headquarters where Hampton was assassinated less than a decade prior. Unable to sign a full year contract, Hawkins opted for signing a month-to-month lease in May 1979 with a five-hundred-dollar loan from a friend.[51] To remain solvent, he also kept his staff small early on but always worked with women in the theatre. Early on, Debora Ledet managed the box office and ran the theatre operations alongside Hawkins.[52]

Hawkins was able to self-subsidize for a time because he would produce his own scripts (often under the pseudonym of Carl Anderson), such as the first production at Tuam, *Surprise, Surprise . . . A Love Story* (1979) and those of local and regional playwrights, for both economic and artistic reasons.[53] By producing his play or the play of a local artist, Ensemble did not have to pay royalties to established white playwrights. Economically, this marked another level of ownership and economic collaboration among Black artists. Artistically, Hawkins could remain tied to cultural nationalism by producing Black playwrights writing on Black history and experience for an audience made up of Houston's Black community. Hawkins actively supported Black women playwrights of Houston, such as Celeste Bedford Walker, by producing their plays. Colson was known for presenting unapologetic Black historical perspectives and experiences, as in the Ensemble productions of *Once in a Wifetime* (1980) and *Camp Logan* (1992).[54] Another part of his artistic mission was to elicit Black joy, which is why he staged theatrical soap operas, like his own *Who Killed Hazel Patton?* (1980), staged in multi-night "episodes," and upbeat musical variety revues, like *Monday Night Follies* (1980).

Despite Hawkins's efforts to highlight the talent of local Black playwrights, Hawkins noted that it limited exposure. It was very difficult to garner national attention or widespread production of a play produced in a regional theatre outside of New York. He stated, "That's dictated by success on Broadway. If a show doesn't have a big success in New York, it just doesn't get the exposure to make it a hot property, a play everyone wants to see when it comes to the regional theatres."[55] In a catch-twenty-two, Ensemble was not able to garner larger audiences for a well-known Black play, such as August Wilson's *Fences* in their 1989 season, because they could not afford the rights. The Alley Theatre, a white theatre company and the first professional theatre in the state of Texas, produced it that very season.[56] Still, Hawkins was able to afford rights to several known Black playwrights, especially when they served the purposes of his mission to simultaneously entertain and instruct his audiences. In observing that Black comedies pulled larger audiences, Hawkins ventured outside the local repertoire to produce comedies in his 1981 season that also contained important messages about historical oppression and future liberation, such as Douglas Turner Ward's *Happy Endings* and Ted Shine's *Contributions*.[57]

Though Hawkins secured a rented space for Ensemble in 1979, the venue was not without major problems. Like Birel Vaughn, Hawkins would have to renovate and convert the building himself. Theatrical facilities, such as a green room and dressing rooms, were makeshift and usually set up on the actual stage. Harold J. Haynes, who went on to found his own company, Encore Theatre, in 1994, described working with Ensemble at this location: "It was so hot in there. I mean, it was like one hundred and ten degrees ... you had to go across the stage to get to the restroom which was a small tin building."[58] Hawkins was forced to purchase window air conditioning units, and they were frequently stolen. He also built a tin shack right behind the theatre building which housed one restroom and doubled as the dressing room and only "backstage area" for the actors. Therefore, performers had to usually hide during intermission. Though the theatre lacked in physical stability, the security of Ensemble grew as ardent community supporters organized for production assistance. Over a dozen people joined together to form Friends of Ensemble (FOE) and would assist in marketing campaigns, ticket sales, concessions, stage crafting, and designing costumes. The group was mainly made up of women.[59]

Despite the shortcomings of the physical venue, the reach of the theatre was undeniable with its growing number of backstage supporters and patrons. The theatre served about ten thousand patrons every season while at Tuam Street. The small brick building could not facilitate an audience as large as Ensemble was pulling in in its first few years. People would occupy "standing only" areas in the back of the audience or purchase tickets to sit on the piano bench in order to see these plays.[60] They needed the extra ticket sales to make rent each month, and, with these sales, they were able to sustain themselves for five years. Hawkins rented out his Tuam theatre space to garner revenue for the company and to promote other Black theatres, such as the Inner City Repertory Theatre of Los Angeles (ICRTLA) in 1981.[61] C. Bernard Jackson, the artistic director of ICRTLA, argued that this movement:

> is not about making it on Broadway or prepping actors to go into commercial films. Our main function is to find ways to make statements, to relate our concerns to people of color ... People urge us to move closer to

Hollywood where we would get more attention, but our interests are still to serve the people of the area.⁶²

Hosting nonlocal theatres in Houston strengthened the national networking and collaboration necessary for Black theatres to sustain themselves and granted them at least temporary ownership over widespread stages. Additionally, hosting ICRTLA, specifically, strengthened Hawkins's steadfast position to become a prominent Houston-based theatre without Broadway ambitions.

Hawkins intended to remain localized and self-reliant, but financial crisis hit Ensemble by 1980. In the years that Hawkins self-subsidized, he became notorious on the Houston theatre scene for not paying employees on time. Some artists and technical designers quit mid-production, and as soon as actors received their checks they were said to have rushed to the bank to cash it first because they knew Hawkins's account could not cover everyone.⁶³ Additionally, overdue bills loomed constantly over the company with the threat of losing functioning utilities. Hawkins's unyielding support of Black artists was evident, but his inability to cover costs of employment threatened the vision. For Black women especially, the position of uncompensated labor was all too familiar. Sacrifices were made by many in Ensemble's early years, but they were made with the hope that the institution would ultimately institutionalize and reciprocate financial support. No one made deeper sacrifices than Hawkins himself for the ultimate mission of elevating the community out of the conditions he currently resided in. Though Black Power uplift centered on empowering collective means, some leaders were forced to sacrifice their individual standing for the survival of an organization.

Like Nora Vaughn, Hawkins was ambitious and wanted to self-subsidize the theatre without corporate sponsors or a board of directors. He was keenly aware that financial overhead would seamlessly translate into artistic censorship. Hawkins was able to operate for his first few years without a board, but by 1981, he relented in order to stabilize and grow the theatre. However, he would build the board with precise intention. He was known as a "thought leader," viewing artists and administrators with a thoughtfulness and care for what creates productive and positive group dynamics. He decidedly chose board members, especially women, who would help the theatre thrive.⁶⁴ Indeed, the board was able to secure government and corporate funding. Corporate funding came

George Hawkins and Eileen Morris. *Courtesy of the Ensemble Theatre.*

in several forms. Traditional corporations, such as Gulf Oil and Eagle Insulation, contributed. Additionally, community organizations, such as Pull for Youth and the Contemporary Art Museum, recognized the theatre's commitment to community, arts, and the next generation.[65] Government funding ranged from the local to national level, including the Houston's Cultural Arts Council, the Texas Commission on the Arts, and the National Endowment for the Arts.

The newly available funds marked a shift in the economic stability of the theatre and rewarded those who had worked without wages for years. Hawkins hired staff for the theatre, including himself, who would all be paid now for their contributions to the theatre's mission. In 1982, he hired Eileen Morris, who was eager to fill whatever role was needed in the company over the years. She moved back to Houston after attending college in Illinois, and her sister told her about a man building theatre sets outdoors. After meeting Hawkins, she immediately took on a volunteer role for the theatre. Though her theatre positions were more fluid, from stage sweeping to managing director, her dedication to the theatre's mission and future was stalwart.[66] Morris quickly became Hawkins's fellow thought leader and was instrumental in steering the early and continued direction of the theatre company. Despite the ability to make himself and Morris paid employees of the theatre (holding the roles of both artistic and executive director, respectively), Hawkins continued to put his wages towards the theatre and his artists. Consequently, he kept up a minimalistic standard of living in an efficiency apartment and had no money for medical attention when he became deathly ill at a young age. Morris's excitement regarding the theatre and its purpose pushed her to not only take on the responsibilities of co-running the theatre with Hawkins, but to also opt out of pay as he did. Morris worked for Ensemble for nearly a decade before receiving regular paychecks.[67] Her sacrifices helped stabilize the theatre.

Hawkins envisioned a reciprocal relationship between the theatre and Houston's Black communities. The theatre's mission statement asserts that "The Ensemble played the role of social liaison between the Houston community and the black theatre experience."[68] Hawkins was concerned with the state of Houston's Black neighborhoods, especially the Third Ward neighborhood. He believed the remedy lay in the production of proudly Black cultural expression, a building to facilitate community programs and organizing, and a Black-owned business that would funnel money back into the Black community at large. They continued making a concerted effort to feature local playwrights, both for affordability of production rights and to offer exposure to local Black artists. Hawkins also regularly produced plays written by Black women, such as Lorraine Hansberry, Judi Ann Mason, and Christine Houston, and highlighted the Black female talent at Ensemble, such as Debora Ledet, Dannette Johnson, and Fannie Belle.[69] Hawkins believed, like Teer, that artists, especially actors, who experience more struggle in life have more to offer artistically. He celebrated the opportunity to showcase actors at Ensemble that came from backgrounds of poverty and oppression, stating:

> The more a person experiences life, the better he can portray it on the stage. We're always glad when an actor comes from a childhood in one of the wards, because we know his background. The majority of our plays deal

with struggle, hope, and dreams. People from the ghetto can relate easily to those themes, having grown up with them as reality.[70]

Hawkins resented the circumstances these actors came from, but he also recognized, as Teer did, a particular value that these artists could offer the world through artistic expression and connection.

Though Ensemble was first and foremost a theatre, it aligned with Black Rep and NBT in its extensive entrepreneurial and communal initiatives, and its artistic and cultural mission cannot be reduced to their production seasons alone. Hawkins aligned with that of other theatre founders in his particular passion for investing in artistic inheritance by uplifting the younger generations through theatre. In 1983, the theatre established a four-week intensive training program for high school students. As a part of the program, Ensemble members went into Houston schools to tell students about their programs who may not hear about it otherwise. The program ended with a showcase of student-created works. Like Black Rep and NBT, Ensemble nurtured the next generation with programs directed at improving the circumstances of underprivileged youth with vocational training and positive artistic and identity expression. The program also brought in steady money which led to Hawkins and Morris taking home a paycheck for the first time by the late 1980s. The training programs are still offered today for young students during breaks from school.[71]

Beyond their youth programs, Ensemble now hosted full production seasons on their stage. In 1984, the company produced Langston Hughes's *Tambourines to Glory*. Hughes's play was considered a classic of Black drama, and many Black theatres produced it in times when they needed a guaranteed large Black audience. For that reason, it was the inaugural show of Black Rep. However, Hawkins had to produce the play with a noticeably small budget. By this time, Ensemble had a name in the community and garnered regular attention from Houston's major press outlets, notable the *Houston Post* and *Houston Chronicle*. The most notable critiques came from Everett Evans of the *Houston Chronicle*, who gave the theatre mostly positive reviews through the 1980s and 1990s. Reviewers, including Evans, criticized Ensemble for cutting corners in a glaring manner.[72] Garnering harsh criticism, the theatre risked losing media exposure which endangered audience attendance. Marketing for Ensemble, as with other Black-run theatres, was too expensive and difficult to secure. Therefore, good press was key to creating a positive economic cycle for the theatre. Hawkins not only had to make rent each month, but also keep the building up to both city and operational theatre standards, in the face of constant threats of being shut down by the fire marshals.

After several years of continuous threats, the 1010 Tuam theatre was shut down in 1984 by fire marshals for not being "up to code" in a fate similar to Black Rep just six years prior. Officials demanded that the facility undergo major construction projects in order to pass inspections, including rewiring the whole building, reconstructing bathrooms, and additional exits. They also wanted to limit the size of the audience to only forty-nine seats, which would not allow the company to earn enough revenue from ticket sales to recoup production costs. Because Hawkins could not meet the construction requirements of the fire marshals, the building was officially condemned.[73] Even though Black Rep was founded over a decade before Ensemble, both were in transition at the same time due to the fire marshals. After a fight, Hawkins secured a temporary stay for his theatre at the Tuam address.[74] Though Ensemble was allowed to continue with their production season, a great amount of effort now had to be geared towards finding an address of permanence.

Hawkins needed time to find another building and secure the necessary funds, but he did not want to disrupt artistic operations. Amidst the crisis, the women of Ensemble took on more active roles in the company. They found ways to keep the theatre running and formally recognize the labor and talent of company members. The rest of the season was stocked with exciting Houston premiers of Black-written plays, and Ensemble established the Giorgee Awards Gala to honor all their resilient, talented artists during their 1984 season. The awards were started by Cecilia Williams and chaired by Darlene Buhl, both prominent women involved in the theatre.[75] Hawkins's original purpose of the theatre was to give Black artists a place to work, but it was also important for them to be recognized and gain accolades, as they were denied acknowledgement in the white theatre world. These awards were not only a testament to individuals and their work but also a reward for those who did not give up on the Ensemble in its most tenuous time of uncertainty. Despite the intrinsic significance of artistic recognition, funding was still needed. Over time, the awards gala became the largest fundraising event that kept Ensemble afloat.[76]

At this same time, Hawkins promoted Eileen Morris to managing director of the company with a grant he received from the city. Hawkins saw in Morris something innately valuable, which she didn't even see in herself, with her ability to listen meaningfully, lead diverse group of people, and her understanding that sacrifices were required to make art. She and

Current exterior of the building housing the Ensemble Theatre at 3535 Main Street, Houston, Texas. *Courtesy of The Ensemble Theatre.*

Hawkins shared similar ideologies about the power of Black theatre and cultural nationalism. Collectively, Morris and the other Ensemble women ensured the theatre would persist in its production of revolutionary art and acts of racial and communal uplift. Though they remained afloat, they were operating on borrowed time until a more permanent property could be secured.

While Hawkins was directing shows for the 1984–85 season, he was on the hunt for a new property. He first set his eyes on a building off Main, but a white theatre company, Stages, was also in search of a new home, and they nabbed the lease. Hawkins did not feel the sting of disappointment long once he saw the potential of the old auto repair shop on Main Street. He went under contract for the 25,000-square-foot space in 1985.[77] He successfully secured the building and his company's future in the same year that the funeral was held for the Free Southern Theater. The era's Black theatre model of the South was dead, and Hawkins inherited the mission of becoming the new model for the region.

A brand-new building with theatrical potential was exciting yet financially daunting. What would become the now famous Ensemble home had to be repurposed, like so many Black theatre houses. As soon as they locked in the building, the race to secure funding was on. The dream on

Main was lofty, but Ensemble already had almost a decade of legacy building on the Houston theatre scene, and they were now pushing for sustainability. In terms of practical funding campaigns, the first step Hawkins took was reorganizing the board of directors to highlight leadership with business backgrounds. This board, run by Audrey Lawson, campaigned for individual, corporate, and government funds. They established three tiers to classify individual contributions: gold medal, silver medal, and patrons.[78] The varying levels offered loyalty discounts for season tickets as well as for meals at Black-owned restaurants, which in turn helped other Black-owned local businesses. The theatre also began hosting regular individual giving campaigns to engage the community, which were organized by women board and theatre members, who were entrenched in the Houston community. Though they still rely somewhat on corporate funders today, they have hosted individual giving campaigns several times a year since 1985. By sourcing their funds more internally, the theatre has not been beholden to a corporation. Instead, it is a communal effort mainly coming from individual Black donors and can, therefore, cater to their community interests and artistic aesthetics.[79]

Hawkins, ever persistent in avoiding disruptions to his theatre seasons, rushed to make the space on Main production ready. Their first show on the new stage premiered in April of 1985. By that summer, Hawkins was able to resume his tradition of renting out extra theatre space to other local Black theatres, including Houston's Chocolate Bayou Theater Company (1979–1994) who began the same year as Ensemble.[80] In terms of the kind of the theatre he wanted to produce, with his space now secured, Hawkins was similar to the Vaughns in that he did not feel compelled to produce political plays that would be perceived as inherently or overtly militant.[81] Hawkins argued, "By presenting the works of Black playwrights we perpetuate our culture and increase people's understanding of it."[82] For Hawkins, as well as the Vaughns, associating cultural nationalism only with plays about oppression and radically pushing against it actually reduces cultural nationalism's aims. Nationalism was about centering Black culture and signifying its artistic and social value. In line with that nationalistic ideology, he prioritized plays that presented Black authenticity and represented the range of Black experiences.

Some Black reviewers took Hawkins to task over these artistic choices, arguing that he was doing a disservice to the Houston community as well as Black theatre. Despite lacking aggressive social commentary, the Ensemble brand of theatre was for, by, and about Black Americans and inherently political because it functioned in spite of overwhelming oppression. In terms of patron demographics, from its inception to today, the Ensemble audience remained 90 percent Black, supporting audience participation in adherence with cultural nationalism.[83] Despite the racially homogenized makeup of the audience, Hawkins wanted his theatre movement to also be individualized because he appreciated the distinct character and experience of Black Houstonians. He joined the national ranks of Black theatres but never lost a localized lens, which ensured the support of the company's future on Main Street.

In October of 1989, Ensemble produced Leslie Lee's *Hannah Davis*, a piece about siblings who diverge on how best to "present Black" in the white world. Hawkins emphasized this message in an interview with the *Houston Chronicle*, stating, "It shows that each individual has his own identity, his own way of acknowledging his cultural background."[84] The sentiment of nationalism required the self-acknowledgement of Black cultural and identity markers, but Hawkins recognized that people would interpret or relate to that process in individualized ways. Hawkins was concerned with striking a balance in what kinds of Black plays would be produced in terms of dramatizing the revolution versus dramatizing the everyday Black experience. By maintaining his perception of the community as individuals with nuanced character and evolutionary natures, Hawkins ensured that Ensemble would be able to cater to a broad spectrum of people over a long period of time, changing for the people for which they perform. He foregrounded cultural nationalism in his efforts to nation build in Houston's Third Ward.

When Hawkins still ran the theatre, he traveled to North Carolina's Black Theatre Festival in August of 1989 because he believed strongly in collaboration among Black artists and wanted to participate in the national movement that carried on past 1980. He found the experience both enlightening and validating of his mission back in Houston. He stated:

> I met a lot of new playwrights and a number of established ones who are writing again. Some of them are writing less revolutionary texts, a bit more mainstream. I think there's more diversity in what Black playwrights are saying today. I came away with a suitcase full of new scripts.[85]

By bringing a suitcase of plays back with him to Texas, Hawkins participated in a new kind of theatrical migration. The Second Great Migration had ended by the time Hawkins founded his theatre, but there was still migration on a metaphysical and artistic level. In his 1989 interview with the *Houston Chronicle*, Hawkins asserted there was a "resurgence" of Black playwrights that matched the energy and mass artistic production seen in the 1960s. Despite the arguments that the Black Arts movement was past, Black theatre practitioners on the ground level regularly engaged in local and regional theatres, national festivals, and a transnational networking of plays and staging.[86]

In the late 1980s, Ensemble facilitated cross-state collaboration and modeling for the next generation of Black theatre practitioners. Dr. Vernell Lillie, who was a professor of Africana studies at the University of Pittsburgh, had a theatre company made up of students. Wanting to professionalize the company, Lillie traveled to Texas to interview Hawkins and other members of Ensemble to understand "how the theatre was founded, who were the people involved, what kind of plays did they do ... what kind of audiences, all of that."[87] She saw a realized vision with the Ensemble stage and wanted to learn from their model. With collaboration on the rise, it was clear that the movement had much further to grow.

Though founded in the 1970s, following the establishment of Black Rep and the National Black Theatre, the Houston Ensemble Theatre was still in the process of institutionalizing by 1990 when it underwent a major transition. As the theatre entered its fifth and final year of the original lease, tragedy struck Ensemble. On July 21, George Hawkins died at the age of forty-three. He made almost no wages from the theatre and had no health insurance after having to resign from his accounting job to devote his time and energy to the theatre. Therefore, when he got sick, he suffered with the illness for about six months before he passed because he couldn't afford a hospital stay.[88] When Hawkins died, he had no children as heirs, like founders at Black Rep and NBT did. However, he had a significant legacy to be inherited. And, as with Black Rep and NBT, he left the theatre in the hands of the women who committed themselves to sustaining the theatre and the revolution it staged each season of unruptured operation. Indeed, mortality raised a shared question that spanned the coasts: Even if they survived through everything else, could the theatres and their missions outlive their indelible founders?

FIVE

BEYOND THE MOVEMENT

Inheriting the House of Revolution

> Black communities have always had black theaters ... we will continue to need them, even when, if ever, this land is free of racism. Theater serves as the mirror of life experience and reflects only what looks into it; everyone yearns to see his own image once in a while.[1]
>
> —ALICE CHILDRESS

A LICE CHILDRESS VIEWED BLACK THEATRE as a transformative, yet persistent, force. A national movement was born from the 1960s call for innovative and radical action, and its growth continued despite constant affronts. Black Power and Arts movement leaders battled for decades against state violence, government dismantling, and morale fatigue from both revolutionaries and sympathizers. These forces took their toll, causing several Black Power organizations, such as the Black Panther Party, to recede by 1980. For many Americans, the Black Panther Party was an emblem of the entire movement, and its demise distracted the public from seeing the survival of the movement in other spaces. According to Childress, humanism was the greatest impelling force in the artistic branch of the self-determinist movement, which fortified it for a slow yet steady, long-form revolution.[2] In her mind, the humanistic need for theatre arts kept the Black Theatre movement alive. The fight was exhaustive, but the art was revitalizing.

The Black theatres of Berkeley, Harlem, and Houston survived the death knell of 1980. The founders of these theatres ensured that movement tenets remained in their spaces, committed to enrichment of the self, communal aid programming, and self-represented theatre productions. Their use of art was also successful in mostly staving off government attention and participant fatigue. However, there were natural forces that even the strength of these theatres was not impervious to. The theatre founders began to pass by the 1990s, abdicating the helm of what they built. Yet, even after such substantive loss, the theatres persisted by design. Each founder was keenly aware that the movement was bigger than one individual. Black Power was centered on individual efforts being used communally for a collective power, and they built their theatres within that vision. Theatre is inherently collaborative, and Vaughn, Teer, and Hawkins each made preemptive plans for who among their collective would inherit their theatres to carry the movement forward, even beyond death.

The Black Power movement, alive and well, can still be located today within these theatres and their current modes of operation. All three theatres persist today not only in existence but in their nationalistic potency. The women heirs now run their institutions with a deep reverence for the founders' artistic and social intentions, the institutional legacies, and the cultural identity of their particular theatres. Each theatre, occupying vastly different regions across the country, had to remain adaptable to evolving social, political, economic, and cultural landscapes over the last several decades. Their ability to remain tethered to Black nation building on three separate coasts despite these changes speaks to the power of institutional permanence and the nationwide survivability of Black Power through theatre.

Establishing transgenerational legacy ensured that the Black Repertory Group would stand as a long-form movement, not simply a moment. Nora was the genesis for many communally beneficial programs, and her daughter, Dr. Mona Vaughn Scott, took up the mantle after Nora's passing in 1994, the same year of Alice Childress's passing, signifying the loss of valuable movement leaders in this decade. Vaughn Scott represented the new generation of revolutionary artists as well as the unruptured line of Black female succession. In college, Vaughn Scott followed in her mother's footsteps by first receiving professional training in Black theatre. Her commitment to continuing her mother's social programs led to Vaughn Scott receiving her doctorate in social work from Stanford, despite facing discrimination as a Black woman in graduate school in the 1960s.[3]

Sean Vaughn Scott (standing) with Dr. Mona Vaughn Scott.
Courtesy of Dr. Mona Vaughn Scott.

This combination of studies afforded her the ability to actualize cultural nationalism by merging developmental theatre with social development in South Berkeley and Oakland.

Vaughn Scott was also connected to powerful and prominent figures in this era that kept her directly tied to the Black nationalist movement. Before taking her current position as executive director of Black Rep, she worked with Kwame Ture when he was organizing in DC in the early 1960s. She also developed a working relationship with Dr. Nathan Hare, who taught Ture at Howard University and wrote letters of reference for Black Rep to receive grants for their exceptional work in the movement.[4] Politically, Vaughn Scott's husband, Richard Scott, was connected with the Kennedy family, serving on Bobby Kennedy's Senate office staff. Her connections allowed her to remain connected with the changing movement and collaborate with a broader network of activists when Black Rep needed assistance. Even as the Black Power movement waned in several corners, Vaughn Scott's institution remained an active site of cultural nationalism.

Funding still presented issues for Black Rep in the 1990s, their first decade in the new building. City officials underestimated Vaughn Scott, as they had her mother, and they tried to take advantage of Nora's passing to revoke the theatre's lease. Vaughn Scott fought the city in court and won her case to maintain the one-dollar-a-year lease, though the city still held out on allowing Black Rep to purchase the theatre.[5] Officials consistently made promises to invest in the Black communities of Berkeley and Oakland. However, their established organizations, such as the Adult Minority Employment Project, the Neighborhood Youth Corp, and the Oakland Economic Development Council, had few if any people of color serving on the relevant committees.[6] Therefore, government initiatives were always short term and failed to address the most pressing issues people faced in their day-to-day lives.

These shortcomings emphasized the continued need for nationalistic uplift from within the Black community. Black Rep was a true grassroots movement, led by Black people for Black people, and they were most concerned with practical community improvements, cultural pride, and longevity. Even though they partially operated off local government funding out of necessity, the Black Rep board of directors were business-savvy and community-conscious enough to push programs that would work for the betterment of Black Oakland.

Under the leadership of Nora, and later her daughter, many programs placed emphasis on aiding Black women whose plights, at times, were neglected by male Black nationalists. Because Black women were historically tasked with maintaining the health of their families and whole communities, Nora and her daughter were committed to intracommunal healthcare as a necessary service in building a strong, sovereign nation.[7] One of the first programs Nora established was their Health Education through Theatre (HETT) initiative in 1977. She designed the program to increase health literacy by raising awareness of health regiments to prevent diseases that disproportionately affect the Black community, such as heart attacks, high blood pressure, and hypertension. In the 1980s, the Black community faced a new, dire health concern. In 1986, the theatre company established the HIV/AIDS HETT program to raise awareness about the AIDS epidemic, how it spreads, and prevention. The increase of drug abuse in Oakland ran parallel to the epidemic, rendering community members especially vulnerable to contraction. The AIDS epidemic affected the most vulnerable Americans, including those in the LGBTQ community, those in low-income areas, and people of color. Due to this fact and the stigma of the disease, the government refused to assist afflicted citizens or even provide basic health information regarding the disease. Consequently, many efforts to apply for grant funding for this program were met with rejection.[8] Though the company had already created the program, their efforts were hampered prior to securing their permanent venue to host sessions, and Vaughn Scott would be tasked with carrying this initiative into a new era of health awareness.

In 1999, after being stable in their building for over a decade, Vaughn Scott was able to formalize Nora's HETT program. Community members were given incentives, usually free season tickets to the theatre, for attending seminars hosted by the company. These sessions included informative skits and free blood pressure readings, which were also regularly offered during intermissions at their weekly performances. This program offered a health education and care system that were affordable and accessible for financially and health vulnerable community members. Black Rep's efforts were recognized and financially supported by a $10,000 Pfizer Health Literacy grant in 1999.[9] Vaughn Scott, like her mother, recognized the power of the collective and sought to represent all in the Black community through her programs.

As another part of this program, Vaughn Scott coordinated an innovative initiative in which youth created their own theatre skits to educate their peers and the community. While writing their sketches, the youth collaborated with Dr. Barbara Staggers, Director of the Youth Clinic at Oakland Hospital, and an expert in Adolescent Medicine. This particular program earned Vaughn Scott a $10,000 grant from the Junior League of America San Francisco chapter. She was given even more of a boost with a $75,000 grant from the Office of AIDS Education through the Alameda County Department of Public Health.[10] Black Rep used this money to conduct a study on the effects of drama education on HIV/AIDS prevention. Vaughn Scott expanded her healthcare by championing HIV/AIDS prevention for the homeless population. She also ensured that Black Rep cast HIV-positive actors to hamper the stigma through performance and aid the mental health of the actors through role-play drama therapy. In 2013, she received a Gilead Corporation grant for promoting HIV/AIDS awareness in the community as well as prisons.[11] She further advanced the mission of uplifting Black women by becoming president of the board of directors for the HillCare Foundation, which was tasked with aiding low-income women of color with teen pregnancies in order to reduce prenatal and infant mortality rates in Alameda County.[12] Though Vaughn

Scott secured external funds for health literacy, her healthcare work was nationalistic in nature as she built it from the ground up, and she facilitated it all through her institution of cultural nationalism.

Vaughn Scott placed special emphasis on developing Black Rep's youth programs, due to her mother's great passion for helping children. In considering legacy, Nora wanted the theatre to support the next generation of artists and revolutionaries and always characterized parenting her own children as "raising revolutionaries." She took the same approach with the youth of South Berkeley and Oakland, establishing herself as a communal matriarch.[13] In 1968, Nora developed a drama workshop in collaboration with Berkeley's Neighborhood Youth Corps for area teenagers who were in need of a creative and positive outlet to deal with the day to day hardships in their neighborhoods.[14] Students were able to act out frustrations while also receiving training in the theatrical arts, leadership, and guidance on staying in school. UCB also participated by hosting tours for the high school students and small workshopping classes.[15]

Vaughn Scott continued the programs but changed them over time to address evolving youth issues. Her knack for adaptation ensured longevity for her model of cultural and economic nationalism. With her educational background in theatre studies and social psychology, Scott incorporated psychodrama to practically carry out her mother's mission. She studied and utilized the findings of Dr. Jacob Moreno, known as one of the founders of psychodrama, to introduce troubled children to role-playing and self-expression through performance. Another respected scholar of the field, David R. Johnson, defines psychodrama as, "the intentional use of creative drama toward the psychotherapeutic goals of symptom relief, emotional and physical integration, and personal growth."[16] Drama therapy allowed Black artists to act out their internal identity struggles and begin to break down the double consciousness that distorted Black and Black female self-perception, providing mutual catharsis for actor and audience.[17] Role-playing fostered identity reconciliation, and in turn, deeper racial pride—a priority within Black nationalism. With so many Black families still lacking the necessities for survival in the 1980s, mental health was severely neglected by governmental institutions and, therefore, needed coverage in the Black nationalist model. Vaughn Scott appreciated the need to build the community up physically as well as mentally. As she continued developing theatre therapy programs, she also joined the First Black Mental Health Conference held in San Francisco in 1981.[18]

Early on, Black Rep implemented a New Arts Program to showcase young local artists, which continues today under Vaughn Scott's leadership. Young playwrights receive feedback and guidance from professional playwrights who work with Black Rep. At the end of the program, they see their play fully realized in a production put on by the company. Students of this training program write their own plays based on prompts that explore both the struggles of their everyday lives, such as poverty and violence, as well as uplifting endings that allow the children to see the potential for a better future and how they can control their own destiny. The theatre also hosts annual theatre camps in the summer for youth in the area.[19] Students of the camp often come from single-mother households who struggle with work schedules when their children are out of school in the summer months. Mothers are able to work during the day while their children are given positive educational activities, creating works that are showcased at the end of the summer. In recent years, Black Rep began rolling out a literal red carpet for the children to walk before entering the theatre for performance night. This program is designed to bolster literacy, cultural pride, and self-efficacy through creative development, especially for Black girls and young women who, according to Nora, hold a significant position in Black Rep's legacy.[20] Vaughn Scott and her mother shared the hope that this model for Black and cultural nationalism would be taken up by the youth and carried across time and spatial boundaries.

The New Arts program also focuses on children who are held in the Alameda County Juvenile Detention Facility and at-risk students in the Oakland Unified School District's Workability Program. They are bused to the theatre to see plays free of charge, and they receive training as a form of early professionalization in theatre as a trade. D'Alan Moss, an East Bay comedian, was interviewed about the effect Black Rep's youth program had on him, stating, "Before I started with the group I was an insecure—a teenaged thug. But when I joined, I learned to articulate and work in front of people. The 'Black Rep' has taught many of us that most of us would be nowhere if we had not come here first."[21] Dr. Ruth B. Love, who heads Leadership in Education Equity at UCB and served as an education advisor to President Barack Obama, recognized Vaughn Scott's commitment to youth education in a testimonial she wrote praising the "creativity she brings to the activities and programs inspire and inform the young minds and spirit of children and youth."[22]

In 2007, Vaughn Scott drew on her past connections with the Kennedy family to formalize the violence prevention program and wrote a letter to Senator Ted Kennedy in the hopes that he would join the initiative. She explained the theatre's goals to Senator Kennedy, stating:

> We want to put on a realistic violence prevention conference focusing on collaborative and comprehensive community-driven solutions. We run the 43-year old [Black Rep] Community Cultural Center & Theater founded by my mom, Nora Vaughn, with the intent to showcase those who have not been readily showcased and to empower at-risk and disenfranchised youth."[23]

She wrote on the dark reality that there will soon be "no child left," and described the neighborhoods as "war-zones." Her efforts of nation building would be futile if the epidemic of gun violence continued claiming lives of the nation's next generation. Whenever Vaughn Scott requested external assistance, she always required that it be delivered without threat to racial pride or undermining their other efforts in building up economic nationalism, stating that "the kind of help that is not paternalistic—help that respects the person's contribution in seeking a comprehensive solution to 'the violence-problem.' " In her letter, she also thanked Kennedy for supporting her previous social initiatives, including a correlative project out of George Washington University showing that the increase in valuing and supporting women decreased recidivism rates in men.[24]

Another current issue the theatre addresses, which disproportionately affects economically vulnerable Black girls and women, is human trafficking. In September of 2013, Black Rep became an active site of public awareness regarding trafficking, especially of children. The theatre hosted educational symposiums with performances and speeches from survivors and specialists who study trafficking. The theatre also offered a space where mentoring and support services could be offered through their facility and volunteer counselors.[25]

The institutional security of Black Rep increased with Vaughn Scott's fortifying efforts. With that permanence, their influential reach went beyond improving the South Berkeley-Oakland area, as much of Black America remained in need of economic assistance. As executive director, Vaughn Scott strove to balance her mother's original goals: a "community theatre" with local concerns and a widely applicable model for a Black cultural center and institutionalized economic nationalism to reach the broader, metaphysical Black community. Witnessing Black Rep's efficacious cultural production and nation building, Black repertory theatres sprang up in major urban centers across the nation. The companies that still exist today are the St. Louis Black Repertory Theatre (1976) and the North Carolina Black Repertory Theatre (1979). North Carolina Black Rep founded the National Black Theatre Festival (now known as the International Black Theatre Festival) in 1989, which, in 2009, honored Black Rep with the Longevity Award for forty-five years of uninterrupted service and defying the low average lifespan for most Black theatres.[26] Though their building facilitates their ability to carry out social change, the Black Repertory Group continues to challenge localized and structural limits in defining artistic nation building in the modern era as well as Black theatre of the West and of the nation.

As the stamina for Black Power declined by the early 1980s, Black theatres fell across the country.[27] It was at the end of this decade that Black Rep emerged in exception and formally secured their building and, therefore, their future as a sustained institution facilitating active output of cultural nationalism today. Just as the fight for racial equity in America continues, so does the fight for the theatre. Vaughn Scott continues to spearhead campaigns to buck against the constant, external threat from city officials to cut funding and starve the company out of material existence. Still, Vaughn Scott relies on the same survival tactic as her mother: community support. Through support from both the local and national Black community, Vaughn Scott continues to lead Black Rep's artistic endeavors and communal and financial programs that, in turn, remain desperately needed to reciprocally aid the Bay Area Black community. As "Keepers of the Culture," their sights are set on both past and future by preserving and presenting Black histories and cultural footprints. Vaughn Scott argues that "the building is the starting point for keepers of the culture," though struggles persist. The continued struggle for autonomous Black Theatre was not regionally exclusive to the West Coast.

By the late 1980s and early 1990s, the National Black Theatre garnered widespread national and international recognition as an established institution and a powerhouse of Black theatre at the same time that Black Rep's recognition was on the rise. Ronald Reagan recognized the National Black Theatre in 1989 as a "cultural treasure," and said that it is "one of the 63 most important art institutions in America," denoting the widespread acknowledgement of the theatre's standing. However, he was also instrumental in cutting federal funding of the arts in the 1980s while president.[28] The cuts shook the financial stability of the theatre, which would worsen in the 1990s due to the city's efforts to further revoke funding from the theatre. Anonymous calls were placed to the police to give them cause to enter the theatre and create "issues" to justify the removal of city capital.[29] By 1989, there were less than ten Black theatres operating, including the National Black Theatre, compared to the 112 Black theatres in 1970.[30] Some Black artists in the New York theatre scene attributed this decline in the 1980s to the white audience's aversion to Black theatre, as they tended to be the most common ticketholders.[31] The conundrum of many Black Power theatres was the issue of low Black audienceship due to affordability.

Despite the high stakes of operating as a Black-run theatre in this tenuous atmosphere, by 1998, NBT still owned their performing arts center and expansive commercial space. The facility fostered an atmosphere of shared property ownership and allowed for more outside, communal entities to rent the facilities.[32] In May 2000, Dr. Teer held a hopeful vision for her theatre's lasting impact, stating, "let all the wealth which abundantly flows from this cultural and financial healing be used to erase the cosmic patterns and false beliefs of our emancipation and let the true declaration of our personal freedom be affirmed."[33] Still, financial hardship persisted, and in 2000, Teer partnered with two Liberian entrepreneurs, Richelieu Dennis and Nyema Tubman. Within several years, the pair were deeply in debt and took out a $6.5 million loan that was meant to subsidize theatre renovations. Instead, Dennis and Tubman leveraged the building as collateral and spent the money elsewhere. Teer took action to protect her institution in April of 2008 and sued her partners in court.[34] However, no one could have predicted her sudden passing just a few months later in July. The case was posthumously decided in Teer's favor just a few weeks after her passing.

Following Teer's passing in 2008, Sade Lythcott and her brother, Michael Lythcott, took up their mother's mantle, with Sade named CEO of the theatre and Michael the chair of the board. Lythcott was not prepared to inherit the theatre and, despite growing up in the institution, she was not sure she wanted it.[35] Despite her inner conflict, Lythcott ultimately found her own approach that still honored her mother's legacy. She began to see herself as a "change agent" who saw "the power of art and activism."[36] She found herself committed to continuing her mother's mission and further developing the institution as the Temple of Liberation.

Sade Lythcott. *Courtesy of the National Black Theatre.*

With her children at the helm, the theatre was renamed Dr. Barbara Ann Teer's National Black Theatre Institute of Action Arts to reflect Teer's everlasting ownership of a now world-renowned Black cultural institution which activates citizens through art.

Beyond inheriting the theatre, they also inherited the financial and legal issues. Lythcott released a statement in 2011, "Unfortunately, nefarious business practices and eventual abandonment by our investor group, Nubian Heritage, now threaten our property and our community programming. Yet we refuse to allow our community to be victimized."[37] The incident led to a legal battle and a struggle for Lythcott and her brother to maintain ownership of their mother's theatre. Sade and Michael also strategized how to stabilize the theatre from within. Though Teer was able to keep the theatre afloat for decades, she was never able to strike equitable financial stability between the real estate and the art. Sade and Michael decided that the organization should be split between them, with her taking the art side and her brother, who is business-adept, taking the business side. They wanted both the artistic side and the business side to separately receive enough care and attention to heal before being merged back into a cohesive, balanced entity.[38]

NBT, like other Black organizations struggled to maintain their financial success in the new millennium. In 2009, the country suffered an economic recession, and Black institutions, especially theatres, suffered disproportionately. Financial crisis struck NBT as they entered their fortieth season. Executive director Shirley Faison was interviewed by the *New York Amsterdam News*, a Black press, on the effect of the crisis on NBT. Faison asserted that the arts have a positive impact on the economy, especially when institutionalized in a property owned by those within the community, and therefore it must be especially supported during downturns. She encouraged the Harlem community to invest in the institution that would in turn support them by creating jobs and generating revenue for the community. She explained:

> For example, if you drive, you have to park your car (parking garages). You generally eat out that evening (restaurants), you may have a little time before the show to shop (boutiques and surrounding business). Through this lens, it becomes obvious that contributing to the arts stimulates the community's economic viability.[39]

In order to self-sustain during this period, the theatre had to cut the number of shows in their production season. They also created Join the Drive to Keep Black Theatre (Soul) Alive, and as Faison said, "stay committed to sustaining and maintaining the artistic vision of Dr. Barbara Ann Teer as we grow and develop ourselves and the next generation of entrepreneurial artists to bring dignity and respect into the community in which we live, work and serve."[40]

Economic distress persisted with mortgage debt threatening the NBT theatre house until 2012 when the Manhattan Borough President, Scott M. Stringer, stepped forward to aid the institution. His respect for the theatre's longstanding self-subsidized operations inspired him to ensure the theatre had a long future ahead by personally mediating a new financing deal between NBT officials and the bank. In regards to Stringer's assistance, Lythcott stated, "We've worked so hard to reach this day and the fact that the Borough President played such a huge part in resolving this was the final piece of the puzzle. We are overjoyed that we can now get on with our mission, and our community is richer for it."[41] In that same year, Lythcott was gifted a key to Harlem to acknowledge her cultural contributions to the city. She co-chaired the Coalitions of Theaters of Color (CTC), a New York-based Black theatre networking entity, similar to the Black Theatre Alliance that ended in 1984. CTC was established to "address the inequity of funding to chronically underfunded theaters of color."[42] This merger was another effort to offer collective support to NBT, as well as other theatres of color in New York.

Another source of revenue for the theatre was the continuation of Teer's rental programs for communal use of the theatre's spaces. Though most of the hosted gatherings were in the realm of performance, Teer did not want to semantically limit all that her property had to offer for community use. However, after the Lythcotts took over, certain organizations sparked controversy after renting the spaces for purposes that didn't align with the theatre's mission. NBT executives were forced to issue a "Stance on Sacred and Safe Space" in 2015. Written by Sade Lythcott, the statement stipulates that the institution has an open-door policy to help all community members and organizations find public space to express their concerns and beliefs. It also stipulated that any discriminatory or bigoted rhetoric will not be tolerated on their property. The theatre sought to find a balance in their dual identity as a company and a community arts center. They rent out their spaces and avoid censoring artistic expression, but they work simultaneously to protect their economic interests and the community from any hateful dialogue being presented on their stages.[43]

Sade Lythcott's campaigns to raise more awareness of the theatre and its power continued to revolve around emphasizing the physical theatre. In 2018, she gave an interview at a Google launch party discussing NBT's history and their building. She discussed her mother's decision to relocate the theatre to the most famous address in the world on Fifth Avenue, and states that their mission remains the same today as it was in 1968: "To activate citizens to become activists in their daily practice. The theatre exists as a beautiful intersection of art and civic engagement."[44] She argued in favor of a new, diverse audience that now attends NBT productions, insisting that it does not dilute the group's radical mission. In fact, it increases collaboration across many lines. People venture to Harlem, who perhaps never would have, where they have new cultural and social experiences, and the theatre hosts post-show "town hall meetings" in which productive discussions take place. However, the theatre pulls no punches on their art material. It is still heavily tied to social resistance and Black liberation and focuses on subjects such as police brutality, Black identity struggles, and mass incarceration. Lythcott prescribes audience members from outside of the community to "lean into the discomfort" because that makes them a part of the "artmaking" and the larger cause.[45]

In this same interview, Lythcott also stated that one of the most pressing issues as of 2018 was gentrification in Harlem. Properties are being bought out, renovated, and sold at greater costs, increasing property rates and pushing community natives out of their homes. Therefore, she insisted that there is great value in "owning a piece of the neighborhood and community" in which she was raised, just as her mother stressed property ownership. She also describes the company as being so successful that they are currently "homeless." This sense of homelessness was the result of NBT expanding its physical presence in the community with new buildings, which are still currently under construction.[46] The $185 million redevelopment project of a 21-story high-rise includes new hotel, residential, and retail space to keep the block of property in the community's name. It was designed to be a mix-use building being built now to house a higher-volume business.[47] Additionally, they designed a "flexible" 250-seat temple space and 99-seat studio theatre.[48] NBT board member and capital campaign co-chair, Cleo Wade, expressed the theatre's excitement for the project, stating:

> "The National Black Theatre is born from and for revolution—revolution in culture, theatre, and the arts. This space has been and will continue to be the home of intentional innovation, radical imagination, and a deep and tender care for the community it reflects, is inspired by, and serves. Today we break new ground for groundbreaking ideas that will provide an everlasting gift for generations to come."[49]

The new house of the National Black Theatre is set to open its doors in 2027. NBT was going to temporarily be housed in the Apollo Theatre, but the arrangement fell apart due to COVID. Their executive offices are currently housed, instead, in the basement of Dr. Teer's brownstone home that was renovated to accommodate its growing staff in 1975. Though construction is a lengthy and expensive project, exacerbated more in the last several years, Lythcott is excited for the changes, stating that "the new building is an opportunity to earn the name of National Black Theatre on a level that hasn't been seen yet. We're creating work all around the country, more iterant than ever. Dr. Teer had the blueprint, but we get to build it."[50]

Lythcott has much to say about the legacy of NBT and the significance of the building, stating:

> Bricks and mortar, the owning and operating of these institutions are the key to the vitality and longevity of Black theatre. Black arts institutions provide the most viable platform for us to display honest interpretations of the full spectrum of Black life without censorship or commercialization. Let me put it to you this way—if you are a person without a home, no matter how many people allow you to stay for varied limited lengths of time, in various zip codes, from the most exclusive to the most basic of couches, are you not still homeless?[51]

Building ownership was essential for NBT, as it was for all Black theatre companies. The marginal success of Black artists on Broadway still happens on an individual basis. The success of a few does not necessarily benefit the overall community. Lythcott refers to them as "refugee artists" who sometimes find a welcoming home to stay in, but it is not permanent, and it is not truly their home. In order to stop Black theatre from becoming too commercialized, the collective must be put before individual ambitions. Coalitions and institutions are just as pivotal to nation building as they were in 1968. For Black theatres to survive today, Lythcott encourages all institutions to collaborate and assist each other and to craft connections between the older and newer generations. The stakes remain high for Black theatre survival, and the external pressures are difficult enough to overcome without the addition of internal divisions.

October of 2019 marked the fiftieth season of the theatre company in their home at 125th Street and Fifth Avenue. They referred to this landmark season as "Liberation: A Journey Beyond Walls."[52] The structure is the first step to liberation, but it is a part of a larger process that is meant to go beyond the limitations of one building. The broader goal is to liberate Black culture and communities across the nation and world, requiring the theatre owners to go outside of their bounds and spread their influence. Because NBT has always been invested in international work, Lythcott was committed to seeing that aspect grow along with the local structure. Engaging Afro-Swedish actors, NBT of Sweden was founded in 2018 with Josette Bushell-Mingo as its artistic director. The company was formed from the 2016 all-Black ensemble. In 2017, Josette Bushell-Mingo, well known performance actor and artist, and a group of Afro-Swedish artists while visiting NYC, toured NBT and spoke to the executive staff of the National Black Theatre. Additionally, NBT has collaborated with Afro and Indigenous theatres in Australia, South America, and the Caribbean.[53]

Collaboration and global projects would not have been possible without the localized anchor of NBT's building and institutional revenue. Lythcott echoed her mother's prioritization of theatre ownership as the key to revenue, stating that "Ownership would allow the real estate to subsidize the art, which was a model that would disrupt the standard practice of nonprofit theater funding."[54] However, Teer noted that despite the generation of profit, "NBT remains committed to advancing the development of its community because we believe that community-based theater is a promising way to realize the economic potential of the great cultural resource called 'Soul.'"[55] The revenue helped NBT reach a different level of liberation. NBT could continue activating Black citizens around the world to lead to widespread liberation beyond their walls. The theatre currently hosts four major programs to carry out this work. The Communications Arts Program nurtures artistic spirituality, while the Theatre Arts Program provides space and support for young theatre artists to perform. Practical business training is offered through the Entrepreneurial Arts Program in order to prepare the next generation for Black theatrical autonomy and ownership. Lastly, the Tourism Program educates audiences on local, national, and global stages about African aesthetics and cultural traditions.[56]

NBT became and remained the only Black theatre in New York City that owns property spanning a city block.[57] The institution endured, reflecting the historical survival of the Black community, despite economic crises and systemic oppression. In 1968, the theatre was an institution the community of Harlem needed. Today, the institution holds many accolades to boast about:

> NBT has broken ground as the country's first revenue-generating Black art complex, as the longest-running Black theater in New York City, as

acquisitor of the largest collection of Nigerian New Sacred Art in the Western Hemisphere, and as one of the oldest theaters founded and consistently operated by a woman of color in the nation.[58]

It remains a necessary entity today, as institutional struggles continue and transform with modern issues such as gentrification. Two months before her death in 2008, Teer wrote in an essay, "The human sacrifice of millions of burnt skinned, spirit faced people, who were the 'Ground breakers' for the new vision of the western world, and were then and are now, the major contributors toward the materialization, unification and globalization of that vision."[59]

The theatre has received widespread recognition for its influence through financial grants and awards. Today, NBT is partially supported by grants from the Upper Manhattan Empowerment Zone Development Corporation, Council of New York, City of New York Department of Cultural Affairs, New York State Council on the Arts, Columbia Service Society, Theatre Communications Group, MetLife, and individual contributions which range from $5 to $1,000. The Upper Manhattan Empowerment Zone Development Corporation funds eight performing arts institutions including the Apollo Theatre and NBT. It allocates 25 percent of its funding capacity to these facilities.[60] In 2022, the theatre was the recipient of a $10 million award from the New York State Council of the Arts (NYSCA) Large Capital Improvement Grants for Arts and Culture. During their tenure, NBT has received fifty-eight Black Theatre Excellence Awards from AUDELCO for promoting Black theatre on the national level and their continuous efforts to increase Black audienceship, with more than ninety thousand in attendance each season.[61]

Just as Lythcott was the legal heir to the theatre corporation, the next generation of Black artists are all heirs to the legacy of the National Black Theatre. Teer's vision was far-reaching. Her creation was meant to be inherited, as she prayed, "Let the fruits of our labor, bring a cultural and economic healing to our children. Take away their illusions of limitation, lack, materialism and exploitation, thoughts which have stopped their cultural and spiritual growth."[62] Teer overcame racism and misogyny to establish "the oldest continually run Black theater in New York City and one of America's longest continually operated theaters run by women of color."[63] She sacrificed money and personal needs in order to ensure that those who came after her would reap the benefits of the institution she established. Similar to Vaughn Scott, Lythcott inherited her mother's mission to ensure these benefits would persist. This positive cycle of institutionalization through generations secured a future for Black theatre and the Harlem community who now had a cultural center to call home. The work of nationalism in Harlem would continue, anchored by the National Black Theatre.

Inheritance anchored NBT and Black Rep as models of Black theatre and twenty-first century cultural nationalism of their respective regions, while Ensemble, on the third coast of Texas, made the national character of the continued movement undeniable. By 1990, Ensemble was Houston's most established Black theatre. Morris had a mission to keep it thriving after Hawkins passed. The board agreed without hesitation with Hawkins's wishes for Morris to take on his position as Ensemble's artistic director. Morris's history with Hawkins and Ensemble, along with her dedication to the theatre and its mission, made her the obvious choice to become artistic director after Hawkins's passing.[64] She stated in an interview with the *Houston Chronicle*, "The Ensemble is a vital necessity for the future of the Black arts in this city. It has to survive."[65] She equated the survival of Houston's Black community with survival of the theatre, and her background prepared her for the practicalities of that difficult task.

Like Hawkins and other successful theatre owners of the time, Morris was highly educated and trained in the theatre industry, earning her theatre degree from Northern Illinois State University. She devoted years of service to this theatre because she was fundamentally committed to the growth of Black cultural institutions, as evidenced by her establishment of the Afro American Club for Actors at her high school of mostly white students. At her university, there were few opportunities given to Black theatre students. However, a small group of Black graduate students took them under their wing to perform Black plays and engrained in her a new level of appreciation for Black theatre and its mechanics. In this program she learned all the elements of play production from acting, designing, and directing to the business of theatre.[66]

Before joining Ensemble, Morris demonstrated steadfast commitment and professional development in support of Black theatre nationwide. She served on several boards and panels, including the Cultural Arts Council of Houston in Harris County, Pennsylvania Council on the Arts the Multi-Cultural Arts Council of Pittsburgh, ProArts, the National Endowment for the Arts, Shakespeare in American Communities for Arts Midwest,

Eileen Morris. *Courtesy of the Ensemble Theatre.*

and the Theatre Communications Group. She later held various offices, including president of the Black Theatre Network from 1994 to 2004, and currently serves on the board of The Midtown Management District.[67] Her commitment to seeing Black theatre thrive remained unruptured, and she used her professional acumen to foster longevity in Black institutions.

When Morris inherited the theatre, she prioritized the continuation of Hawkins's intergenerational work by including a space to operate his youth programs in the new theatre renovations. This program offered "educational workshops, artist-in-residence experiences, and live performances for students both off-site and at the theatre, and the Young Performers Program" to all children of the community ages six to seventeen.[68] It ran continuously as Morris would not allow the four years of renovation in the mid-1990s to interrupt these programs. She secured a space for the young theatre artists to produce and perform in the South Main Baptist Church.[69] In this period, Ensemble extended its reach to college students who were preparing to enter the workforce and who historically sought out social involvement. The theatre's close proximity to Houston Community College afforded them accessible recruitment opportunities, similar to recruitment strategies of the Houston People's Party and Black Rep in Berkeley. Ensemble was not only concerned with preparing young people for their futures, but also with rectifying the history of theatrical exclusionary practices. They still hold auditions once a year for retired citizens who have never had the opportunity to be in the theatre before in order to keep seniors mentally stimulated and support a group that is too often disregarded.[70]

Morris was not the only woman to take up the legacy of Hawkins and Ensemble. Board president Audrey Lawson, along with company member Mildrid Bright, inherited Hawkins's financial mission and led the capital campaign for Ensemble's $4.5 million building renovations that concluded in 1997.[71] Lawson was a social worker and a powerhouse of civic service in Houston. She was instrumental in the establishment of Houston's enduring Black churches, charter schools, inner-city youth programs, and Ensemble.[72] She was primed to lead a multi-functional institution with the ability to tackle various community issues. With the capital the company put towards their new home, the company went from 1100 square feet on Tuam to 25,000 square feet on Main. The building includes the George Hawkins main stage, which seats two hundred audience members, the Audrey Lawson Arena seating up to 125, and a performance center large enough to accommodate five hundred patrons.[73]

When the company was in the midst of renovations, they did not have as much money for productions. The company, therefore, had to forego productions in the arena for several seasons.[74] They were renting out the entire space but could not use it for theatrical or social purposes due to the extra costs. In the spirit of collective power, the theatre fostered collaboration with community and theatre organizations on the local, state, and national level such as the Museum of Fine Arts in Houston, Lone Star College, Houston Community College, Texas Southern University, and Prairie View University. [75] In general, there was more collaboration with college theatres than other community theatres. These connections, and Ensemble's established reputation, inspired New York's New Federal Theatre to travel to Texas to attend several annual fundraisers for Ensemble's renovations in the mid-1990s.[76]

In establishing their economic and theatrical profile, Ensemble was classed as a nonprofit regional theatre, meaning they were a professional theatre operating outside of New York. Despite the theatre being nonprofit, everyone's economic interests were protected with Ensemble becoming an equity theatre in the late 1990s, meaning that they are union protected, and actors are guaranteed a specific wage.[77] Before earning equity status, Hawkins was always open about the fact that he never took home a paycheck and remained in a constant cycle of debt. Not only has this company become economically stable in their building, but their theatre production budget has also grown. In the early 1980s, their budget for their annual theatre season sat between $3,000 and $4,000, with the Texas Commission on the Arts and the Cultural Arts Council of Houston as the largest funding entities of the theatre.[78] As of 2009, that budget reached $1.85 million.[79]

Though a portion of seasonal production money is granted through Houston Endowment Inc., Morris argued that the greatest force of theatre solvency is the community.[80] In adherence with the NBT and Black Rep models, one way in which Ensemble was able to sustain themselves was by renting out their space to various Black community organizations, a tradition they continued from Tuam Street. When Morris discussed the company's financial stability in a 2009 interview, she emphasized the correlation between property ownership and a positive economic cycle, stating, "the facility itself—the renovation—we wanted to make sure that we had a space that could be rented out because we knew that was going to be one of our revenue generating things."[81] Hawkins allowed a struggling white community theatre, Stages, to rent out space in the theatre when their lease fell through, during Ensemble's first season of operation.[82] Hawkins, and later Morris, prioritized the need for money to keep the institution afloat, to directly fund Black community initiatives, and to eventually operate independently from white funds.

Due largely to the work of Morris, and board women such as Lawson and Bright, the company officially paid off their mortgage in 2004.[83] Ensemble presented an early model that proved sustainable, leading to a large number of Black theatre foundings. Beyond property ownership, Morris prioritized board organizing in modeling sustainability for other theatres, stating:

> Board development is an important tool. Institutions must identify individuals with passion for the vision, proven professional expertise, and access to resources that can help advance the mission. In February 2012, The Ensemble's Board of Directors took note of the funding climate change that had forced many reputable cultural institutions to face economic hardships.[84]

She knew that the longevity of movement building hinged on savvy, experienced, and creative leaders. Other Black theatres took note of Ensemble's approach. In this way, Ensemble was localized, yet their social and artistic missions could not be contained within Houston's city limits.

Another aspect of Ensemble's success was tied to loyal patrons and contributors. In terms of patrons, the growth in subscribers has only occurred in the last decade. In 2006, the theatre had five hundred subscribers. Within three years, they reached 2,300 and are now in the many thousands with tiered subscriptions.[85] The development of subscribers allowed the community to buy into Ensemble's mission and own a piece of the theatre as well. One of Hawkins's major goals was to sustain this theatre, and in doing so, he created artistically and financially stimulating careers for theatre contributors. Many who joined the Ensemble in its early days remained with the theatre, with some tenures reaching the present. For instance, Ray Walker has worked as the company's technical director for over thirty years and is still there today. Additionally, Black actors found a mutually beneficial relationship with Ensemble. The company needed young aspiring actors to affect audiences, and these young artists needed a jump start to their early careers, such as Byron Allen who is well established in the television and film industry in Hollywood.[86] The longevity of employees secured consistency and direct connection to the original mission of the theatre.

Of the consistent members, Eileen Morris remains the most steadfast. Morris carried the company through renovations and successful first seasons in the new space. She shared Hawkins's goal in prioritizing property ownership, stating:

> Owning our own facility not only increases our earned revenue stream, but it serves as a place into which we invite the entire Houston community—from rental of the spaces, to mainstage performances and youth programs. We never lose sight of the fact that ownership enables us to "be the change we wish to see" in the City of Houston.[87]

Morris was the true inheritor of Ensemble. Her vision and indelible commitment to the theatre aligned with Hawkins's, and her work was instrumental in securing the theatre's finances, property, and communal establishment. However, after serving the theatre for seventeen years, Ensemble's board of directors dismissed Morris in 1999. The board stated that they wanted a more diverse show list and audience, which ultimately meant producing white plays with Black or multiethnic casts. Morris did not agree with this new direction because she knew that it violated Hawkins's theatrical Black-centrism.

Morris's dismissal garnered a lot of negative attention, even on the national stage. Ensemble was so well known at this time, that the news of both Morris's termination and the theatre's new mission reached the African Grove Institute in Los Angeles. President Victor Walker denounced the board's decisions.[88] This institute was founded a year prior in 1998 as a Black theatre advocacy group, with the following mission: "AGIA hosts regional and local seminars throughout the United States with the goal of strengthening African-American theatre companies by helping them identify and overcome artistic and financial problems."[89] Therefore, they had a stake in the future of this Houston theatre that had been carrying the mantle for cultural nationalism since the movement started its decline. Even August Wilson was upset by this and pulled his rights from for the Ensemble's production of one of his plays in their upcoming season.[90] Ensemble produced a large number of August Wilson plays under Morris's direction, and he called their 1997 production of his *Two Trains Running* the best version he's seen produced.[91] Despite being beyond the height of the Black and cultural nationalism movements, the push for Black theatres to remain tethered to movement ideals was pervasive.

By 2006, the board was disappointed in the lack of growth they expected would come with their reorganization. Despite being granted $250,000 by the Houston Endowment for the Arts in 2003, the board went through two artistic directors in seven years and were unable to increase communal investment. Morris was brought back in 2006 for the thirty-year anniversary of the theatre. Instead of advocating a "new direction," which had garnered little growth for the theatre in Morris's absence, the board was concerned with celebrating their thirtieth year of operation. They wanted signs of thriving growth, such as growing the number of subscribers, expanding community and educational outreach, and a return to the theatre's strong roots of intentional Black theatre. Morris's return to lead Ensemble was a return to the theatre's roots of Black artist recognition and communal uplift. The theatre kicked off their thirtieth year by honoring Ensemble alumnus Danny Glover, who began his theatrical career at Black Rep in Berkeley, with a Lifetime Achievement Award.[92] She also created programs, such as "Theatre Speaks" workshops, that address pressing community issues, such as housing insecurity and women's rights.

With the recession, the theatre's funding was depleted. However, the individual giving campaigns surprisingly held on. In a 2009 interview, Morris discussed the economic hardship of 2009 and a few instances where people in the community had been laid off yet still donated a few dollars to the theatre during these drives because they believed in Ensemble.[93] Morris points to "collaboration" and community support as a key aspect of sustaining the theatre during economic downturns, stating:

> Our staff has partnered with organizations for food drives, used museum art as marketing collateral, volunteered to serve meals to the homeless, and given performances for professional organizations and social clubs. The result has been an increased interest in our programming and increased community presence at our productions.[94]

Though organizing campaigns for corporate funding remained important, Morris puts more emphasis on campaigning for internal funding because it created a healthier cycle of support and revenue coming into the theatre simply from more community members attending shows.

By 2009, Ensemble reached a new level of prominence during a transitional period in American racial politics. The theatre needed to sustain its production seasons as well as its longstanding community initiatives. Hawkins's original goal was to provide Black artists with a training space, a residency program for young artists of the community, and employment opportunities to Black Houstonians. As of 2009, they employed 210 artists per year, which was up from twelve members when the company began over thirty years prior.[95] Hawkins was not localized in his training, attending universities and becoming involved in Black theatres in other parts of the South, the North, and England.[96] Therefore, his theatre would not just be on the local level either. They tour their plays around the state and nation to spread their influence. The company was asked to perform at the National Black Theatre Festival in 2009, the same year that Black Rep was honored with their Longevity Award, which demonstrated the festival's recognition of Ensemble's contributions to Black theatre and gave Ensemble a platform to perform in front of Black theatres from across the nation. In that same vein, Ensemble tours shows today, but not out of necessity or the lack of a theatre house. Their property anchors them, but their influence is now more widespread. As a byproduct of the funds incurred at their theatre house, Ensemble is able to perform at other venues around the country, especially in the South.

Ensemble is housed in the first Black-owned theatre building in the Southwest and remains the biggest in the region today.[97] The Ensemble theatre house has four spaces for rent on their property: the lobby, the greenroom, the arena stage, and the performance centre. They rent their spaces out for business meetings, fundraisers, and special occasions. For events that require vendors, Ensemble provides a list of preferred vendors.[98] There are many Black-run Houston businesses included in the list, demonstrating Ensemble's commitment to lifting up other Black entrepreneurs in their current position as a thriving Black economic and cultural center. This exemplifies collective uplift, which stands in opposition to traditional American norms of success through individualism.

Despite economic difficulties, the company continues to produce rich theatre seasons of Black culture and to find innovative ways to use their owned space to perpetuate funding and communal uplift. Much of the company's success and support is due to the women of Ensemble. Hawkins was always focused on the uplift of Black women, and Morris carried the initiative forward. In 2018, Morris was awarded a $250,000 grant from the Helen Gurley Brown Foundation, which is meant to fund women of theatre leadership excellence. The grant is provided through the BOLD Theatre Women's Leadership Circle, and Morris has been awarded the same grant every year since first earning it in 2018. The grant is used by Ensemble to hire more women directors and designers, support a masterclass of theatre leadership training for women, and to fund Black female playwrights. Out of the six shows Ensemble offers each year, three to four are guaranteed to be authored by women to ensure their voices are heard in this theatre.[99] Currently, Ensemble audiences trend at 50 to 60 percent women.[100] Ensemble also facilitates intersectional campaigns through their theatre with their "OUT at Ensemble Theatre" events. These are mixers for LGBTQ and allies for the purpose of networking and dialoguing about coalition building. The theatre also continues their efforts to uplift the youth with their young professional events, called Act One, which connect young theatre professionals with young professionals in other industries at mixers held in the theatre's lobby in order to foster collaboration and collective assistance.

As a Black-owned theatrical institution founded towards the end of the classically defined Black Theatre movement, Ensemble looked different from Black Rep and NBT. However, today, the theatre presents a similar image to its coastal counterparts by functioning as a permanent cultural nationalist theatre championing Black proprietary and cultural ownership for Black nation building with Black women at the helm. The fact that Ensemble does not fit neatly within the geographical or chronological bounds of the Black Power and Arts movements exemplifies that these theatres were not confined to a limited timeline or place, nor were they condemned to meet a premature end. Just as the Panthers were reaching their final years of organized operation, the birth of the Houston Ensemble Theatre was a testament to the power of innovation and art in relocating the movement to cultural institutions. By the time of its inception, there were cases of both successful and failed Black theatres, and the surviving theatres were already undergoing rebirth and establishing new stable structures to house their art, communal work, and movement legacy.

The passing of time, movement institutions, and movement leaders was both organic and systemic. Vaughn Scott, Lythcott, and Morris battled on multiple fronts so that their inherited institutions would not have to be mourned or forgotten. Each had a passionate, personal investment in these theatres. However, they also carried backgrounds of arts education and business experience, similar to the founders, to function as pragmatic entrepreneurs. All three theatres have won the Longevity Award from the National Black Theatre Festival, and AUDELCO has awarded each for surviving the death of a founder, formally recognizing the rarity of that level of persistence. Instilled in each of them was a transgenerational appreciation for the keeping of culture, collective, and property. With their past preparation and their mission ahead, these women put artistry into nation building.

Though Black Rep, NBT, and Ensemble each had a different genesis and regional context to operate within, their commonalities overwhelmingly outweigh their differences. Stalwart female revolutionary artists grew these theatres to be accessible and adaptive as the needs of their communities and the threats against them changed with time. All three powerhouses function with a dual nature as legacy theatres of past struggle and model theatres for future endeavors of liberation. Through the process of inheritance, each theatre proved contextually transcendent and was marked by the endurance of transgenerational activism. They provided blueprints for structuring post-1980s Black Power survival and an avenue for the next generation to continue the movement in the face of new changes and challenges in the twenty-first century.

CONCLUSION

Co-Opted, Compromised, and Commercialized: Historical Legacies and Living Revolution in Today's Black Theatre

If art is the harbinger of future possibilities, what does the future of Black America portend?[1]

—LARRY NEAL

ON JULY 13, 2013, THREE Black women, Patrisse Cullors, Alicia Garza, and Ayọ Tometi, started the Black Lives Matter (BLM) movement in response to police brutality and the 2013 acquittal of George Zimmerman after he shot and killed seventeen-year-old Trayvon Martin in 2012.[2] Though police brutality and hate crimes have been historically perpetrated against Black Americans, Cullors, Garza, and Tometi created a new campaign with new rhetoric designed to call attention to the ever-present hierarchy of value assigned to human lives in America. They were also determined to highlight the intra- and intercommunal negation of value assigned to the lives of Black women and transwomen of color. The particular rhetoric used in this budding moment within the Black liberation movement was an assertive refutation of the purported era of a "post-racial" American society. They negated the myth of color blindness and implored the public for visibility and color consciousness. In 2014, following the police murder of eighteen-year-old Michael Brown in Ferguson, Missouri, the country erupted in street protests and marches, mobilized networks of civil rights advocates, Ku Klux Klan and white nationalist demonstrations, and media coverage of it all.[3] The image of twenty-first-century unrest was distinct, yet familiar. It was the birth of a new moment and the revitalization of an older movement.

This mobilization within a renamed revolution came fifty years after the Black Power peak in the mid-1960s. The original movement was not dead by 2013, but instead existed within the network of Black theatres across the nation who embodied the movement since its beginnings. As Cullors, Garza, and Tometi set a new stage for the Black Revolution, three other Black women wondered how best to fit their already established theatres into the transforming context and conversation. In 2013, Mona Vaughn Scott, Sade Lythcott, and Eileen Morris aimed to spark more attention for their theatrical institutions in the midst of a changing nation with new issues to address. By the time BLM was a recognizable hashtag on social media in 2014, these institutions had been anchors for Black American uplift for fifty, forty-six, and thirty-two years respectively.

To create a responsive front, leaders had to understand the nature of the current context. Some issues persisted from the original movement, such as poverty, but other racially oppressive systems were newly constructed answers to the ever-changing reform movements that dismantled ancestral systems of slavery and de jure Jim Crow. Particularly poignant in this current period is the criminalization of Black Americans, especially men, which has deeply historical roots in post-emancipation period but escalated since the 1980s with the War on Drugs and War on Crime campaigns, leading to mass incarceration.[4] As citizens of all demographics contend with the question of what it means to be Black in America today, Vaughn Scott, Lythcott, and Morris lend their stages to these tough conversations and questions while continuing to hold their communities together within their well-rooted theatre houses in Berkeley, Harlem, and Houston.

Despite their longevity, the security of these Black theatres is not guaranteed in the twenty-first century. Gary Anderson, artistic director of Plowshares Theatre Company and founder of the Black Theatre Matters website, conducted a national survey in 2016 and 2017 to assess the health and status of Black theatre in America. The assessment of seventy Black theatres across different regions showed that only 16 percent of companies owned their building, and nearly half operate on budgets under $50,000.[5] He concludes that institutional endangerment reflects the lagged momentum in America's racial progress with a sizeable population that generally subscribes to myths of post-racialism. The continued negation of systemic racism and racial disparities has made "Black Theatres endure under a deliberate system of imbalance" and remain in "separate and unequal" institutions.[6] With sand-submerged heads, white society still sidesteps educational opportunities, such as bearing witness to Black theatre where they might be forced to confront uncomfortable truths of unfinished work.

The new millennium was also met with the passing of the generation that had personal connections to the previous movement, including the original founders of these three theatres, Alice Childress, Larry Leon Hamlin (founder of the International Black Theatre Festival), Harold Cruse, and Amiri Baraka. As a previous generation passed, the younger generation developed their own cultural standards and a new Black Aesthetic to define the new century. Black Rep, NBT, and Ensemble survived decades of uninterrupted service because they constantly adapted to function relevantly within evolving social, economic, political, and cultural ecosystems. Cultural flourishment often accompanies socio-political movements as an assertive affirmation of meaningful presence. Black artists were eager to connect to this new movement, and the public response was not always supportive. Rapper Kendrick Lamar received criticism for shouting out Black Lives Matter during one of his shows in 2014.[7]

Not far removed from the start of the "new Black Arts movement," there is still a lack of literature devoted to analyzing the burgeoning aesthetic and artistic mission. Currently, the largest work is Margo Crawford's *Black Post-Blackness: The Black Arts Movement and the Twenty-First-Century Aesthetic*. The most significant takeaway from this present Black Arts movement, as discussed by Crawford, is the resurgence of Baraka's term for the Black Aesthetic, the "changing same," meaning that Black art is about simultaneously "moving forward and staying grounded."[8] In other words, the past and present Black Arts movements are connected through their shared artistic concern with what it meant to be Black in that period, but equally preoccupied with what Black art and life will look like in a "post" era. In that same vein, the Black theatres that survived prepared themselves to innovate and evolve, so they could avoid antiquating themselves as relics of past aesthetics, only pertinent within their original context. Through conscious effort, responsive updating, and purposeful community engagement, their cultural and communal performances remain relevant.

The theatres themselves always felt compelled to address the current context given their long history of responding to dehumanization with art as a restoration of human dignity. They weighed in on the conversation engaging as many willing community members as they could, though their strategies differed. In 2013 and 2014, Black Rep and Ensemble focused on creating various fundraising campaigns. Their resistance was embedded in their survival and continuous work to demonstrate how and why Black lives, culture, and physical and mental well-being, matter. Both theatres were also especially interested in expanding their youth programs to educate Black children on difficult realities and help them find ways to cope and thrive within a nation that threatens their success at best, and their existence at worst. Other organizations directly confronted the issue by writing and producing plays, like New York-based New Black Fest's *Facing Our Truth: Ten Minute Short Plays on Trayvon, Race and Privilege* (2013).[9] In February of 2014, one month after the death of Amiri Baraka, the National Black Theatre hosted a five-day event of community engagement seminars, art installations, and performances to honor Trayvon Martin.[10] NBT wanted to confront the problem of police brutality and killings directly because the stakes equated to survival. Outright ownership of their building made them more secure to do so. Their facility was a safe space where community members and youth could express their anger and come together in productive discourse and action.

The successes and survival of these theatres provided, in one sense, an answer to the Black Arts debates dating back to the 1920s when the call first rang out for a Black Nationalist theatre. Few other organizations, institutions, or art forms were able to carry as many Black Power tenets into the twenty-first century. Therefore, it is imperative to understand the extent of each theatres' successes and obstacles. These theatres have housed the revolution for the last forty to sixty years, and many arts activists are fighting to keep it located in these anchoring structures. Even after overcoming strategically positioned hurdles and surviving for decades, the future of these theatres still has to be secured with great intention and planning. Black theatres across the country face threats of extinction from various fronts. One threat stems from the fact that theatre, in general, has declined in popularity and that movie theatres are considered a more sound investment. Ebony Showcase Theatre, which operated in Los Angeles since 1950, was closed in 1993 to convert it into a movie theatre despite ample community protests.[11]

Other persistent threats that are poised to attack the economic self-sufficiency of Black theatres include the shortage of funds as a result of economic recession, the gentrification of Black neighborhoods that raises property rates, and the redirection of funds to white-owned theatres who co-opt Black-written plays or plays with all-Black casts.[12] In Ensemble's case, white-owned Alley Theatre in Houston has produced Black written plays since 1976, when they premiered *The Sty of the Blind Pig*, the same year Ensemble produced its first play. They continue to produce August Wilson plays who stipulated no white directors for his plays, asserting his ownership and cultural nationalist sentiments that stand against this trend.

Though Alley's intention, especially in recent decades, is to shed a theatrical light on multiculturalism and portray Black stories more authentically, they are snuffing out what Hawkins referred to as the "indigenous theatre."[13] As Childress lamented over fifty years ago, white production of Black plays takes the financial capital out of Black pockets and the cultural capital out of Black hands and institutions. Additionally, this outsourcing positioned Black art on the periphery and granted a measure of white ownership rights over Black artistic labor, expression, and thought. Sade Lythcott penned a warning about this trend of removing Black theatre from its home:

> Home is a concept that is often taken for granted in this ongoing debate about the state of black theatre. We have unwittingly created an ecosystem of refugee artists—left to fend for themselves and cleave to whatever opportunity comes their way. The only way to really address these issues is to examine their roots. Are we seeking out or supporting the safe havens and spaces where we can express ourselves freely and fearlessly? The danger in making these discourses singularly about black theatre and not institution building is that the more black playwrights that get produced on Broadway or in other commercial venues—venues that might not care even a little bit about our culture and who we are as a people—the more the collective consensus is that there may no longer be a need for black cultural art institutions. As a result our institutions are on the brink of extinction and the expression of a richly complex beautiful culture is officially becoming an endangered species. And you, my refugee artist geniuses with your craft are left wandering.[14]

Amidst the growing threat of rehoming Black plays, economic crisis struck. In 2008, the year that Dr. Barbara Ann Teer passed, America's housing market crashed, and the country entered into a recession. When the economic bubble burst, Black theatres across the nation faced impending expiration with the depletion of funding.[15] However, new crises were beaten back by equally robust fronts. Project1VOICE was founded in New York in 2009 to help Black theatres escape economic expiration and continue to assert the notion that Black theatre is deeply consequential to the Black community and America at large. The organization raises awareness of Black-owned theatres, and they are especially interested in highlighting Black women as pioneers and warriors for Black theatrical and communal survival.

Preceding the founding of BLM by just one month, Project1VOICE organized an international benefit in June of 2013 to save Black theatres. Seventeen theatres across the country, and one in South Africa, staged playwright Charles Fuller's *A Soldier's Play* (1982) at each theatre on June 17. Project1VOICE was honoring emancipation from legal bondage with the chosen date and emancipation from cultural hegemony. The project was meant to draw audience attention as well as "promote volunteerism, attract corporate and foundation funding, and seek in-kind goods and services." It also asserted, "Help keep African American theater strong, vital and alive by attending this historic and highly anticipated event in your area."[16] Both the National Black Theatre and the Ensemble Theatre in Houston participated in this event. Though the play was divisive among movement heads, with some criticizing it for perpetuating stereotypes, it also created a moment of Black theatre connectivity. The project had a global presence with coordinated performances at each of these local theatres that have too much legacy to recede quietly. Intercommunal projects are effective in increasing local awareness. However, knowledge and recognition of these institutions must spread on a broader scale for networking and collective economic support.

Organizations like Project1VOICE were not the only new connective entities for theatres. One advantage of operating these theatres in the new millennium is the democratic marketing of social media, which raises public awareness of the theatre's artistic and social commitments and allows for networking at no external cost to the theatre. This strategy allows for another connection to the present social movement as BLM leaders conduct awareness, fundraising, and organizing campaigns online. The vast connective power of the internet has made more of the population aware of Black social and artistic struggles and missions than ever before. Black theatre festivals, such as the International Black Theatre Festival (1989) and New Black Fest, founded in 2013 in response to Zimmerman's acquittal, are another key to supporting and raising visibility of Black theatres across the nation. Festivals also serve as a concentrated demonstration of the power of collectivity and collaboration between Black artists and arts entrepreneurs. Despite broader connections, there were still limits to the accessibility of these theatres, their art, and their social programs that persist today. Though they wanted to reach everyone within the metaphysical Black community, these theatres generally serve their immediate communities, leaving surrounding Black rural communities unbenefited. It is difficult to establish a successful community theatre outside of urban and suburban areas, and rural theatres that already exist must allocate most of their limited funds to maintaining their local position.

Another economic threat is posed by theatre grant trends from the National Endowment for the Arts (NEA), the largest federal funding entity for art. NEA grants are instrumental in keeping theatres alive not only through their funds but also through their review process which notifies private arts funding entities of investment-worthy groups and creates a broader funding cycle. However, the NEA mostly funds mainstream, white-owned theatres.[17] In 1998, August Wilson spoke at the National Black Theatre Festival about the egregious neglect of Black theatre from granting institutions. White theatres became anxious about losing funds to Black theatres and started producing plays that feature marginalized artists, diluting cultural nationalism in the name of cosmetic diversity quotas.[18] This method of co-opting Black art was, as it has always been, popular and successful. Though the NEA started funding several Black theatre institutions across the nation, more money was allocated to white theatres in the same areas.[19] White theatres were rewarded for presenting Black theatre under their direction over Black-directed theatres whose entire purpose was to present this art in an indigenous context.

The list of NEA recipients includes many theatres that are predominantly owned by white men, such as Berkeley Repertory Theatre just down the street from Black Rep, and Ensemble's Main Street neighbor, Alley Theatre. While Black Rep has received no NEA grants in their sixty years of service, Berkeley Rep, established in 1968, has been granted over $1 million since 1998.[20] Similarly, while Alley Theatre has received around $550,000 in NEA grants since 1999, Ensemble has only been gifted two grants with one in 1998, and one in 2019, totaling less than $30,000.[21] NBT has yet to receive any funding from the National Endowment for the Arts, despite their recognition and location in America's theatre capital.

Not only does this funding strategy endanger Black-owned theatres and take money out of circulation in the Black communities by defunding their institutions, but it also makes Black theatre inaccessible to Black audiences who cannot afford inflated theatre prices. In his 2016 survey on Black Theatres, Anderson states that "institutional sustainability is linked to the financial stability of African Americans in this economy," and argues that there is a "moral debt" to be paid to equalize support of culture-specific institutions.[22] Furthermore, this funding and investment disparity signifies, once again, the value hierarchy. The negation that Black theatre matters as much as white theatre is a broader affront to the value of Black culture, especially since theatre is such an encompassing signifier and site for the history of Black cultural and artistic traditions. Lythcott predicts that if Black theatre is wholly removed from these institutions, it will be regarded as a genre of theatre instead of an entire culture of complexity and intrinsic value. She warns Black artists not to lurch after commercialized glory, but instead warrior on for preservation of the culture.[23] To combat this threat, funding must go directly to these Black institutions for in-house art and communal uplift.[24] Though individualized artistic journeys still hold value, these theatres will have to present a united front reminiscent of that in the Harlem Renaissance and later in the Black Arts movement.

The most recent threat to these theatres came in 2020 with the global COVID-19 pandemic. As with health crises of the past, Black communities were some of the most vulnerable and underserved in the pandemic response. Black Rep, NBT, and Ensemble persisted with virtual performances until they could open safely. Unruptured art and community protection were their greatest concerns.[25] Though virtual performance did not hold the same transformative power as live performance, each theatre adapted to any available mode to keep producing their art for the community. While Black theatres were forced to close their doors, the call to action against racial injustice became more urgent as they faced a deadly new disease and the resurgence of an older racialized epidemic.

Though the new movement against police brutality formed in 2013, the murders of George Floyd and Breonna Taylor in 2020 by police officers reanimated the movement due to the especially heinous circumstances surrounding each death. Police violence, especially against Black Americans, has become performative in a sense as more incidents are filmed and streamed for audiences across the nation and world, harkening back to the theatrical ritual of lynchings. Though these disturbing images are vital to awareness campaigns, white audiences become little more than voyeurs if their involvement remains limited to watching videos of Black suffering. Black theatre practitioners and owners were now not only faced with financial fallout from the pandemic but also with the question of how to respond to a community filled with both grief and rage. A new organization emerged to call attention to the inaction and silence of white theatres in regards to their Black counterparts. We See You WAT (White American Theater), a BIPOC collective of theatre artists, published an open letter and list of demands in 2020 addressed to America's white theatres. Among their demands, they called for equitable casting and compensation practices, cultural competency, and investment into security agencies that are not associated with police.[26] Despite more verbal commitment to antiracism in a number of white theatres, Black theatres continue to lead the charge in organizing and actively engaging with social issues.

For theatres like Black Rep, NBT, and Ensemble, revolution is a slow and steady war in which failures lead to a rebirth through pragmatism rather than to the death of operation. Historians have reported the demobilization and subsequent death of the Black Power revolution in the early 1980s. It was also purported by many Black Arts scholars that the Black Theatre movement ended in the same period.[27] However, the trajectory of arts activists on the ground was one of sustained stamina and forward motion. Despite the broad consensus among scholars to mourn a "dead" movement, these theatres did not suddenly emerge in the twenty-first century. They are historical anchors and present links between the original movement and today's BLM movement in terms of Black radical thought and manifesting. Still, the argument that the whole of the Black Power movement has since demobilized serves a dangerous narrative that could affect how the present fight for liberation unfolds.[28] This narrative invalidates the cause and discredits effective methods, ensuring they lose support. If this social movement proved successful, even in survival, perhaps the whole system they challenged could be dismantled.

Black Rep, NBT, and Ensemble are the physical sites of the continued movement. They embody nuance and regional variation, but in the broad sense, they converge on many fronts. Convergence and overlap are indicative of a movement as opposed to these theatres operating as incidental anomalies. The leaders of these community-based theatres followed national trends and early models of Black theatre, ever cautious with their knowledge that, historically speaking, institutional permanence was rare. They also each stood as answers to one of the Black Arts debates by establishing a balance of localism and nationalism. They were specific enough in their mission to signify movement cohesion, yet unique enough to deal with local atmospheres and make necessary change over time.

Additionally, these theatres had to present a united front of Black theatre networks to survive and thrive. Most Black theatres that are still in existence today hold membership in national Black theatre organizations such as Project1Voice, the National Conference on African American Theatre, the National Black Producers & Actors Leagues, the Black Theatre Collective, and the Black Theatre Network. Several of these organizations host annual conferences to connect Black theatre practitioners throughout the nation to offer collective support and guidance. In this way, Black theatres redefined property ownership as collective, as opposed to individually based, as the community did historically.

Another shared element of these three theatres was that their productions celebrated and elevated Black artists, onstage and off. Even if they were not overtly political in performance, they have remained true to cultural nationalism for over half a century. The lack of gains in political nationalism, a major cornerstone of Black Power, was offset by strides made in cultural nationalism and economic self-determinism. Additionally, each theatre's season of performances and community programs places special emphasis on the dissemination of Black history. Woodie King Jr., the founder of the New Lafayette Theatre in New York, argued that "African American theatre of tomorrow must exist as a result of one's knowledge of the past. We must be aware of the pioneers and their contributions."[29] The education of Black history and experience through plays and community workshops stirs up racial pride and intellectual emancipation.

Ultimately, Black women are the heart of what connects these theatres. Each was highly trained and long prepared to lead a revolution, both artistically and logistically. Within their theatre houses, Black women made space for the most marginalized voices, elevated self-determinism to be gender conscious, kept culture and community through productions and programs, and empowered, professionalized, educated, and raised the next Black generation. The founders all invested in the next generation who eventually inherited the theatres as well as the cause. The movement was bigger than any one leader as Black theatre belonged to future generations and to the masses.

By converging in these ways, Black Rep, NBT, and Ensemble present the image of a cohesive, nationalized movement spanning the "three coasts," offer a structured formula for future Black theatres to model themselves after, and exhibit recognizable markers for scholars seeking to understand the movement in this form. By nature, a movement that has faced constant attack and surveillance, such as that of the radical liberation of Black America, will at times become covert to avoid detection. As scholars of the Black Power and Black Arts movements, we must continue to search for ways in which these movements have persisted as long-form, multigenerational revolutions, which tend to present differently than in their inception due to innovative strategies. We otherwise mute the efforts of these revolutionaries, invalidate their effectiveness, and participate in threatening their houses and, therefore, the stage for revolution. In an interview with Mona Vaughn Scott, the long-time revolutionary stated that "the hardest thing about fighting a revolution is longevity."[30] Revolutions traditionally and historically play out as short, excited bursts of radical thought, action, and cultural production. They burn brightly and extinguish quickly. How can revolutionary action be sustained over decades? Each of these theatres stands as an answer. As Black cultural entities and internal nation builders, they are radical and affecting. Repression of this movement success brings the movement into disrepute. By elucidating the histories, missions, and connectivity of Black Rep, NBT, and Ensemble, it is made clear that these theatres are legacy sites of Black Power, Arts, and Feminism. It is a movement still intact and postured to liberate Black America in the new century, if due attention is paid.

These structures do not stand as memorial markers of defunct movements. Instead, they operate and function to keep the culture alive and well. It is not enough to acknowledge the impact of these theatres during the Black Power and Arts movements, or even to recognize them as signifiers of a continuous movement. The next step is to understand the unrelenting endangerment of these institutions and to meet these threats with a more robust campaign from all communities to redistribute cultural funding, to re-signify the value of Black culture, and to ensure Black theatre survival by actively supporting the expansion of their revolutionary stages.

The movement for Black liberation is currently housed, neither dismantled nor demobilized, at several addresses. A vast list of programs and campaigns remain in operation to serve and uplift the East Bay Black community at 3201 Adeline Street, in Berkeley, California. Black theatre is alive and well in the same city where it all began in the nineteenth century at 125th Street and Fifth Avenue in Harlem, New York. And the idea of proprietary and cultural ownership has become a reality located in one of the largest Black-owned theatre centers in the nation at 3535 Main Street, in Houston, Texas. However, a movement cannot be contained within four walls. It starts with a building, establishing a foundation, image, and name for themselves, setting a model, and insisting on the stakes of their existence. Nora Vaughn, Barbara Ann Teer, and George Hawkins and Eileen Morris always planned for their brand of theatre to break the conventional fourth wall and engage with their audience on a reverberating level and to demolish racial, gender, and proprietary barriers to house a significant and powerful Black nation.

In 1968, during the height of the Black Theatre movement, Larry Neal presented the future of Black America as a question mark while asserting that the answer undoubtedly lies in the possibilities of art. The story of these theatres does not merely offer an opportunity to present Black Power through a theatrical or feminist lens. Instead, it invokes a more holistic appreciation of how the widespread application of Black Power ideology, the distinctiveness of women leaders, and theatre as a revolutionary art form ultimately converge and function reciprocally. Each field, therefore, is ultimately broadened and re-signified through this scholarship.

On their own, Black Power and theatrical performance operate with autonomous and potent value. When merged, and with Black women leading, they stand as stalwart pillars that support the structures of past, present, and future movements. Theatre, by nature, embodies social and cultural power because the inner workings of theatrical performance as an art form necessitates participation, shared experience, and raised consciousness from the audience. These histories demonstrate how that nature can either be exploited by the majority to culturally subjugate others or how it can be utilized by marginalized groups to liberate minds and dismantle those structured hierarchies. The house of theatre operates as the optimum site for staging enlightenment of the self, the emancipation of empathy, and the mobilization of the collective.

The aims of the Black Theatre movement for collective uplift through autonomous cultural performance could not be achieved without artistic institutionalization and proprietary gain. Revolutionary playwrights needed a stage to actualize their mission of activating audiences and a positive economic cycle generating in the community. Since their start in the 1960s and 1970s, Black Rep, NBT, and Ensemble remained constant in their commitment to Black social, cultural, and economic uplift. However, it was not until the procurement of their brick-and-mortar theatres that they could carry each mission through with investments of Black communal funds, time, and labor. These theatres embody the aim and spirit of Black Arts institution building in this period, yet they remain exceptional in their longevity due in large part to their lineage of Black female leadership, savvy entrepreneurial practices, and ability to evolve with their communities. From their physical addresses, theatrical and social programs can be staged, and a cycle of economic betterment can begin.

By 1990, each theatre had finally built their permanent house—a house in which Black women are leaders, Black nationhood is attainable, and Black culture and art are sustaining. These theatres stand today, not as relics of a past movement, but as permanent addresses to locate Black Power, proving that building up and maintaining arts infrastructure will continue to be necessary as long as there is a struggle for racial uplift and economic and cultural capital. Today, the public can enter these theatres and actively engage in Black nation building. The pulse of the Black Arts movement remains steady with moments of acceleration that send possibilities once again coursing through the community. If today we are to answer Larry Neal's question, we must first possess reverent knowledge of historically Black performance houses and steadfastly pursue the present possibilities of the living powerhouses of theatre if there is to be a future liberation of Black America.

NOTES

INTRODUCTION

1. Childress, "But I Do My Thing," 9.
2. Amiri Baraka, "The Revolutionary Theatre," *Liberator*, July 5, 1965.
3. Jonathan Shandell, *The American Negro Theatre and the Long Civil Rights Era* (Iowa City: University of Iowa Press, 2018), 44.
4. Alice Childress, "Trouble in the Mind," in *Selected Plays by Alice Childress*, ed. Kathy A. Perkins (Evanston: Northwestern University Press, 2011), 57.
5. Allen J. Matusow, *The Unraveling of America: A History of Liberalism in the 1960s* (New York: Harper and Row, 1984) and Charles M. Payne, *I've Got the Light of Freedom: The Organizing Tradition and the Mississippi Freedom Struggle* (Berkeley: University of California Press, 1995).
6. Jeanne Theoharis and Komozi Woodard, *Freedom North: Black Freedom Struggles Outside the South, 1940–1980* (New York: Palgrave Macmillan, 2003); Jacquelyn Dowd Hall, "The Long Civil Rights Movement and the Political Uses of the Past," in *The Journal of American History* 91, no. 4 (2005): 1233. Additionally, the scholarship of Martha Biondi and Robert Self foregrounded sites such as New York and California, both of which were previously considered geographical outliers in a common narrative of the civil rights movement that identified as its main stage the Jim Crow South.
7. Hall, "The Long Civil Rights Movement," 1235. The idea of the long movement has been met with criticism, most notably from Sundiata Keita Cha-Jua and Clarence Lang, who argue that the framework denies distinctions of varying historical contexts and is, therefore, ahistorical.
8. Mumia Abu-Jamal, *We Want Freedom: A Life in the Black Panther Party* (Cambridge: South End Press, 2004), 34.
9. Peniel E. Joseph, "The Black Power Movement," in *Black Power 50*, eds. Sylviane A. Diouf and Komozi Woodard (New York: The New Press, 2016), 1. Joseph defines the period from 1966 until 1975 and designates the division over Marxism as the reason for the movement's demise. Spencer notes a later demise occurring in 1982 with the closing of the Oakland Community School, their last program. Robyn C. Spencer, *The Revolution Has Come: Black Power, Gender, and the Black Panther Party in Oakland* (Durham: Duke University Press, 2016), 177.
10. Sundiata Keita Cha-Jua and Clarence Lang. "The 'Long Movement' as Vampire: Temporal and Spatial Fallacies in Recent Black Freedom Studies," *The Journal of African American History* vol. 92, no. 2 (2007), 270.

11. Robert O. Self, "The Black Panther Party and the Long Civil Rights Era," in *In Search of the Black Panther Party: New Perspectives on a Revolutionary Movement*, eds. Jama Lazerow and Yohuru Williams (Durham: Duke University Press, 2006), 39. For a history on the Black Power Movement, see Jeffrey O. G. Ogbar's *Black Power: Radical Politics and African American Identity* (Baltimore: Johns Hopkins University Press, 2005); Peniel E. Joseph, *Waiting 'Til the Midnight Hour: A Narrative History of Black Power in America* (New York: Owl Books, 2006); Charles V. Hamilton and Kwame Ture, *Black Power: Politics of Liberation in America* (New York: Knopf Doubleday Publishing, 2011); Peniel E. Joseph, *The Black Power Movement: Rethinking the Civil Rights-Black Power Era* (New York: Routledge Taylor and Francis Group, 2013); Spencer, *The Revolution Has Come*; and Tom Adam Davies, *Mainstreaming Black Power* (Oakland: University of California, 2017).
12. Robert L. Allen, *Black Awakening in Capitalist America: An Analytic History* (Trenton: Africa World Press. 1990), 215.
13. Komozi Woodard, *A Nation within a Nation: Amiri Baraka (LeRoi Jones) and Black Power Politics* (Chapel Hill: University of North Carolina Press, 2005), 67.
14. Maulana Karenga "Black Cultural Nationalism," *Negro Digest* 1968 13(3), 5. Scot D. Brown, "The US Organization: African-American Cultural Nationalism in the Era of Black Power, 1965 to the 1970s," (PhD diss., Cornell University, Ithaca, 1999), 11.
15. James Smethurst, *The Black Arts Movement: Literary Nationalism in the 1960s and 1970s* (Chapel Hill: University of North Carolina Press, 2006), 17. Richard H. King, *Race, Culture, and the Intellectuals, 1940–1970* (Baltimore: Johns Hopkins University Press, 2004), 266. Maulana Karenga, "Kawaida and Its Critics: A Sociohistorical Analysis," *Journal of Black Studies* 1977 (8), 125.
16. W. J. Wilson, "Revolutionary Nationalism versus Cultural Nationalism: Dimensions of Black Power Movement." *Sociological Focus* 1970 3(3), 45. For more essays on cultural nationalism, see Earnest Mkalimoto, "Theoretical Remarks on Afro-American Cultural Nationalism," *Journal of Ethnic Studies* 1974 2(2); Helan E. Olivieira and D. France Olivieira, "African-American Cultural Nationalism," in *Cultural Portrayals of African Americans: Creating an Ethnic/Racial Identity*, ed. Janis Faye Hutchinson (Westport: Bergin & Garvey, 1997); and Mia Bay, "The Historical Origins of Afrocentricism," *Amerikastudien* 2000 45(4).
17. Robert C. Toll, *Blacking Up: The Minstrel Show in Nineteenth-Century America* (New York: Oxford University Press, 1974), 25. White and Black actors would both apply burnt cork to their faces to darken their skin and draw exaggerated facial features as a mockery of Black appearance. These Black caricatures engaged in lowbrow humorous acts and stereotypical activities that whites audiences associated with the Black community.
18. William J. Mahar, *Behind the Burnt Cork Mask: Early Blackface Minstrelsy and Antebellum American Culture* (Urbana; University of Illinois Press, 1998), 337.
19. Thomas F. DeFrantz and Anita Gonzalez, eds., *Black Performance Theory* (Durham: Duke University Press, 2014), 10.
20. Ashley D. Farmer's *Remaking Black Power: How Black Women Transformed an Era* (Chapel Hill: North Carolina Press, 2017), 94. Kimberly Springer, *Living for the*

Revolution: Black Feminist Organizations, 1968–1980 (Durham: Duke University Press, 2005), 44.

21. For histories on the Harlem Renaissance, see Nathaniel Huggins, *The Harlem Renaissance* (New York: Oxford University Press, 1973); David Levering Lewis, *When Harlem was in Vogue* (New York: Oxford University Press, 1981); and Cary D. Wintz, *Black Culture and the Harlem Renaissance* (Houston: Rice University Press, 1988).
22. For monographs on the Black Arts Movement, see Jonathan Fenderson, *Building the Black Arts Movement: Hoyt Fuller and the Cultural Politics of the 1960s* (Chicago: University of Illinois Press, 2019); Lisa Gail Collins and Margo Natalie Crawford's *New Thoughts on the Black Arts Movement* (New Brunswick: Rutgers University Press, 2006); James Smethurst, *The Black Arts Movement: Literary Nationalism in the 1960s and 1970s* (Chapel Hill: University of North Carolina Press, 2006); and Robert L. Douglas's *Resistance, Insurgence, and Identity: The Art of Mari Evans, Nelson Stevens, and the Black Arts Movement* (Trenton: Africa World Press, 2008). For synthetic works on African American theatre, see Mance Williams's *Black Theatre in the 1960s and 1970s: A Historical-Critical Analysis of the Movement* (Westport: Greenwood Press, 1985); Samuel Hay's *African American Theatre: An Historical and Critical Analysis* (New York: Cambridge University Press, 1994); Annemarie Bean's *A Sourcebook of African American Performance: Plays, People, Movements* (New York: Routledge Taylor and Francis Group, 1999); and James Hatch and Errol G. Hill's *A History of African American Theatre* (New York: Cambridge University Press, 2003).
23. James Smethurst, "The Black Arts Movement," in *Black Power 50*, eds. Sylviane A. Diouf and Komozi Woodard (New York: The New Press, 2016), 89.
24. Smethurst, "The Black Arts Movement," 50, 99. Jones, "Black West, Thoughts on Art in Los Angeles," 43.
25. Bernard Carragher, "Black Theater has Moved beyond Revolution," *New York Times* (April 29, 1979), 21.
26. Carragher, "Black Theater has Moved beyond Revolution," 21.
27. La Donna Forsgren, *Sistuhs in the Struggle: An Oral History of Black Arts Movement Theater and Performance* (Evanston: Northwestern University Press, 2020), 21. Mike Sell, "The Black Arts Movement: Performance, Neo-Orality, and the Destruction of the 'White Thing,' " in *African American Performance and Theatre History: A Critical Reader*, eds. Henry J. Elam Jr. and David Krasner (New York: Oxford University Press, 2001), 66.
28. Robin Kelley, *Freedom Dreams: The Black Radical Imagination* (Boston: Beacon Press, 2002), 6.
29. Gregory O'Malley, *Final Passages: The Intercolonial Slave Trade of British America, 1619–1807* (Chapel Hill: University of North Carolina Press, 2014), 6.
30. Cheryl Harris, "Whiteness as Property," in *Harvard Law Review* 106, no. 8 (1993), 1707. For other books on Black property and business ownership, see Dylan Penningroth, *The Claims of Kinfolk: African American Property and Community in the Nineteenth-Century South* (Chapel Hill: University of North Carolina, 2003) and Laura Warren Hill and Julia Rabig, eds. *The Business of Black Power*.
31. Penningroth, *The Claims of Kinfolk*, 132.

32. Penningroth, *The Claims of Kinfolk*, 104.
33. Karenga "Black Cultural Nationalism," 7.
34. Bernard L. Peterson, *The African American Theatre Directory, 1816–1960: A Comprehensive Guide to Early Black Theatre Organizations, Companies, Theatres, and Performing Groups* (Westport: Greenwood Publishing, 1997).
35. Patricia Collins, *Black Feminist Thought: Knowledge, Consciousness, and the Politics of Empowerment* (New York: Routledge, 2000), 2.
36. Alexis Pauline Gumbs, "Buying (Black) Power: The Story of *Essence* Magazine," in *The Business of Black Power: Community Development, Capitalism, and Corporate Responsibility in Postwar America*, eds. Laura Warren Hill and Julia Rabig (Rochester: University of Rochester Press, 2012), 104. Hill and Rabig compiled essays in their volume that each address the intermingled nature of cultural nationalism and the patriarchy as well as the stakes Black women had in the movement. For more on Black women in the Black Power Movement, see Christina Greene's *Our Separate Ways: Women and the Black Freedom Movement in Durham, North Carolina* (Chapel Hill: North Carolina University Press, 2005), Kimberly Springer's *Living for the Revolution: Black Feminist Organizations, 1968–1980* (Durham: Duke University Press, 2005), and Ashley D. Farmer's *Remaking Black Power*.
37. Gumbs, "Buying (Black) Power," 105–6.
38. The following texts assert BARTS as the start of the Black Theatre movement: Smethurst, "The Black Arts Movement," 91. Kellie Jones, "Black West, Thoughts on Art in Los Angeles," in *New Thoughts on the Black Arts Movement*, eds. Lisa Gail Collins and Margo Natalie Crawford (New Brunswick: Rutgers University Press, 2006), 43. Davarian L. Baldwin, " 'Culture is a Weapon in Our Struggle for Liberation:' The Black Panther Party and the Cultural Politics of Decolonization," in *In Search of the Black Panther Party: New Perspectives on a Revolutionary Movement*, eds. Jama Lazerow and Yohuru Williams (Durham: Duke University Press, 2006), 301.
39. Baraka, "The Revolutionary Theatre," 4.
40. Forsgren, *Sistuhs in the Struggle*, 20.
41. Doug McAdam, *Political Process and the Development of Black Insurgency, 1930–1970* (Chicago: University of Chicago Press, 1982), xii.
42. Jeanne Theoharis and Komozi Woodard, *Groundwork: Local Black Freedom Movements in America* (New York: New York University Press, 2005), 3.
43. Joseph, *Waiting 'Til the Midnight Hour*, 218–19.
44. Notable Black theatres founded in this period that did not survive to today include the Ebony Showcase Theatre (Los Angeles, 1950–1996), Free Southern Theater (Mississippi, 1963–1985), Performing Arts Society Los Angeles (1965–1975), New Lafayette Theatre (New York, 1967–1972), BLKARTSOUTH (New Orleans, 1968–1974), Kuntu Repertory Theatre (Pittsburgh, 1974–2013), and Penumbra Theatre (Minnesota, 1976–2012).
45. Notable Black theatres founded in this period that did not openly missionize cultural nationalism include the Ebony Showcase Theatre (Los Angeles, 1950), Detroit Repertory Theatre (Detroit, 1957), New Heritage Theatre

Group (New York, 1964), Negro Ensemble Company (New York, 1967), Amas Repertory Theatre (New York, 1968), Dashiki Theatre Project (New Orleans, 1968), New Federal Theatre (New York, 1970), DC Black Repertory Theatre (Washington DC, 1971), Black Ensemble Theatre (Chicago, 1976). Chicago has long been hailed as a thriving Black culture and arts scene. Despite Black cultural production and institution building in the city, Chicago's Black theatres were not directly tied to Black Power tenets. For a study of one of the most historically significant Chicago-based theatres, see Thomas Bauman's *The Pekin: The Rise and Fall of Chicago's First Black-Owned Theater* (Chicago: University of Illinois Press, 2014).

46. Margaret Wilkerson, "The Black Theatre Experience: PASLA (Performing Arts Society Los Angeles)," in *Theatre West: Image and Impact*, eds. Dunbar H. Ogden, Douglas McDermott, Robert K. Sarlós, Robert Károly Sarlós (Amsterdam: Rodopi Press, 1990), 76.

ONE

1. James Baldwin, *Notes of a Native Son* (1955; repr., Boston: Beacon Press, 2012) 140.
2. Errol Hill, "Forward," in *The African American Theatre Directory, 1816–1960: A Comprehensive Guide to Early Black Theatre Organizations, Companies, Theatres, and Performing Groups*, Bernard L. Peterson (Westport: Greenwood Press, 1997), ix.
3. Hall, "The Long Civil Rights Movement and the Political Uses of the Past," 1234.
4. W. E. B. Du Bois, *The Souls of Black Folk* (1907; repr., Scotts Valley: CreateSpace Independent Publishing, 2014), 3. The idea of African Americans possessing a double consciousness derives from Du Bois's *The Souls of Black Folk*, which he wrote in 1903. He used this term to describe the "twoness" that African Americans feel in their struggle to reconcile their identities between an African past and an American present.
5. Alice Childress, "A Candle in a Gale Wind," in Mari Evans, ed., *Black Women Writers* (New York: Anchor Books, 1984), 115.
6. For studies on nativism and histories on American xenophobia in this period, see Gary Gerstle's *American Crucible: Race and Nation in the Twentieth Century* (Princeton: Princeton University Press, 2001); John Higham, *Strangers in the Land: Patterns of American Nativism, 1860–1925* (New Brunswick: Rutgers University Press, 2002); and Peter Schrag, *Not Fit for Our Society: Immigration and Nativism in America* (Berkeley: University of California Press, 2010).
7. F. Garvin Davenport, Jr., "Thomas Dixon's Mythology of Southern History," *Journal of Southern History*, vol. 36, no. 3 (August 1970): 350.
8. Toll, *Blacking Up*, 5.
9. Collins, *Black Feminist Thought*, 76.
10. Peterson, *The African American Theatre Directory*, ix.
11. Doris E. Abramson, "The Great White Way: Critics and the First Black Playwrights on Broadway," in *Educational Theatre Journal* 28, no. 1 (1976): 45.
12. Peterson, *The African American Theatre Directory*.

13. Penningroth, *The Claims of Kinfolk*, 164.
14. W. E. B. Du Bois, "Krigwa Players," 134. W. E. B. Du Bois, 1868–1963. *Negro tabus in the American theatre, 1931*, Series 13: Plays, Reel 87: 1547, W. E. B. Du Bois Papers (MS 312) Special Collections and University Archives, University of Massachusetts Amherst Libraries, Amherst, Massachusetts, accessed April 15, 2018, http://credo.library.umass.edu/view/full/mums312-b233-i053. This mission statement appeared in all Krigwa playbills.
15. Du Bois, "Krigwa Players," 134.
16. W. E. B. Du Bois, "The Negro in Art: How Shall He Be Portrayed, A Questionnaire," *Crisis* (February–November 1926).
17. Georgia Douglas Johnson, "The Negro in Art: How Shall He Be Portrayed, A Questionnaire," *Crisis* (February–November 1926). Caroline Bond Day, "What Shall We play?," *Crisis* (September 1925), 221. Kathy A. Perkins, "Introduction," in *Selected Plays*, ed. Alice Childress (Evanston: Northwestern University Press, 2011), xv. Zora Neale Hurston, "Stories of Conflict: A Review of Wright's *Uncle Tom's Children*," *The Saturday Review of Literature* (April 1938), 32. Alain Locke, "Art or Propaganda," *Harlem*, vol. 1, no. 1 (November 1928), 12–13. Alain Locke, "Steps Toward the Negro Theatre," *Crisis* vol. 25, no. 2 (December 1922), 66, http://dl.lib.brown.edu/repository2/repoman.php?verb=render&id=1307029316296877&view=pageturner&pageno=18.
18. Izabella Penier, *Culture-Bearing Women: The Black Women Renaissance and Cultural Nationalism* (Berlin: De Gruyter Ltd., 2019), 6.
19. W. E. B. Du Bois, "The Conservation of Races," in *W. E. B. Du Bois Speaks: Speeches and Addresses, 1890–1919*, ed. Philip S. Foner (New York: Pathfinder Press, 1970), 78–79.
20. Robert A. Hill, *The Marcus Garvey and Universal Negro Improvement Association Papers*, vol. I (Berkeley: University of California Press, 1983), 65.
21. Hill, *The Marcus Garvey and Universal Negro Improvement Association Papers*, 63.
22. Keisha Blain, *Set the World on Fire: Black Nationalist Women and the Global Struggle for Freedom* (Philadelphia: University of Pennsylvania Press, 2018), 12.
23. Collins, *Black Feminist Thought*, 30.
24. Caroline Bond Day wrote an essay, "What Shall We Play," in *The Crisis* in September of 1925 regarding questions of the theatrical representation of race on American stages.
25. John M. Giggie, *After Redemption: Jim Crow and the Transformation of African American Religion in the Delta, 1875–1915* (New York: Oxford University Press, 2008), 24.
26. Daniel L. Fountain, *Slavery, Civil War, and Salvation: African American Slaves and Christianity, 1830–1870* (Baton Rouge: Louisiana State University Press, 2010), 70. Michael Gomez, *Exchanging Our Country Marks: The Transformation of African Identities in the Colonial and Antebellum South* (Chapel Hill: University of North Carolina Press, 1998), 245.
27. Lawrence W. Levine, *Highbrow/Lowbrow: The Emergence of Cultural Hierarchy in America* (Cambridge: Harvard University Press, 1998), 170.
28. Farmer, Remaking Black Power, 118.

29. Edward L. Ayers, *Southern Crossing: A History of the American South, 1877–1906* (New York: Oxford University Press: 1998), 31. Giggie, *After Redemption*, 24.
30. Randolph Edmonds, "The Negro Little Theatre Movement," *Negro History Bulletin* (January 1949), 82.
31. Du Bois, "Krigwa Players Little Negro Theatre: The Story of a Little Theatre Movement," *Crisis* (July 1926): 134.
32. Kevin K. Gaines, *Uplifting the Race: Black Leadership, Politics, and Culture in the Twentieth Century* (Chapel Hill: University of North Carolina Press, 2012), 181. Sharon Willis, *The Poitier Effect: Racial Melodrama and Fantasies of Reconciliation* (Minnesota: University of Minnesota Press, 2015), 5.
33. Evelyn Brooks Higginbotham, *Righteous Discontent: The Women's Movement in the Black Baptist Church, 1880–1920* (Cambridge: Harvard University Press, 1993), 187.
34. Spencer, *The Revolution Has Come*, 28–29.
35. Heather Andrea Williams, *Self-Taught: African American Education in Slavery and Freedom* (Chapel Hill: University of North Carolina Press, 2009), 7.
36. Charles V. Hamilton and Kwame Ture, *Black Power: Politics of Liberation in America* (New York: Knopf Doubleday Publishing, 2011), 157.
37. Paula Giddings, *Ida: A Sword Among Lions* (New York: Harper-Collins, 2008), 28. Kabria Baumgartner, *In Pursuit of Knowledge Black Women and Educational Activism in Antebellum America* (New York: New York University Press, 2019), 2.
38. Williams, *Self-Taught*, 67.
39. Adam Fairclough, *Teaching Equality: Black Schools in the Age of Jim Crow* (Athens: University of Georgia Press, 2001), 10.
40. William Edgar Easton, *Dessalines, A Dramatic Tale: A Single Chapter from Haiti's History* (1893; repr., Bibliolife Reproduction Series, 2010), vi. This play includes an oration from Frederick Douglass delivered at the dedication of the Haitian pavilion at the World's Fair in 1893.This four-act play was performed at the Freiberg's Opera House in Chicago instead of the fairgrounds of the exposition.
41. Easton, *Dessalines*, v.
42. Easton, *Dessalines*, v.
43. Koritha Mitchell, *Living with Lynching: African American Lynching Plays, Performance, and Citizenship, 1890–1930* (Champaign: University of Illinois Press, 2011), 10.
44. Grimké is the creator of the anti-lynching genre of theatre. She is followed by numerous other African American women in the 1920s and 1930s, including Georgia Douglas Johnson, who wrote plays to bring attention to the atrocities of lynching, as well as pressure Congress into passing anti-lynching legislation. For further reading, see Kathy A. Perkins and Judith L. Stephens's *Strange Fruit: Plays on Lynching by American Women* (Bloomington: Indiana University Press, 1998).
45. Robert Bernstein, "Never Born: Angelina Weld Grimke's *Rachel* as Ironic Response to Topsy," *Journal of American Drama and Theatre*, 19, no. 2 (Spring 2007): 68.
46. Peterson, *The African American Theatre Directory*, 58.
47. In her book, *Closer to Freedom: Enslaved Women and Everyday Resistance in the Plantation South* (Chapel Hill: University of North Carolina Press, 2004), Stephanie Camp discusses enslaved quarters as a significant site for resistance, in which slaves would display antislavery propaganda and hold secret parties.

Robin Kelley's book, *Race Rebels: Culture, Politics, and the Black Working Class* (Chapel Hill: University of North Carolina Press, 1990), demonstrates the lasting legacy of that tradition by examining the home as a site for resistance for the Black working class in the 1930s.
48. Perkins and Stephens, *Strange Fruit*, 9.
49. Penningroth, *The Claims of Kinfolk*, 137.
50. David Levering Lewis, *When Harlem Was in Vogue* (New York: Knopf, 1981), 196.
51. Wilkerson, "Black Theatre in California," 28–29.
52. W. E. B. Du Bois, "The Negro in Art: How Shall He be Portrayed?," *Crisis* (March 1926): 219–20. Alain Locke, "Art or Propaganda," *Harlem*, vol. 1, no. 1 (November 1928), 2.
53. Michael Kirby, *A Formalist Theatre* (Philadelphia: University of Pennsylvania Press, 2011), xi.
54. Ira Berlin, *The Making of African America: The Four Great Migrations* (New York: Viking Penguin, 2010), 5. Giggie, *After Redemption*, 24. Nicholas Lemann, *The Promised Land: The Great Black Migration and How it Changed America* (New York: Knopf Inc., 1991), 4. Isabel Wilkerson, *The Warmth of Other Suns: The Epic Story of America's Great Migration* (New York: Vintage Publishing, 2011), 535.
55. Peterson, *The African American Theatre Directory*.
56. Peterson, *The African American Theatre Directory*, 92.
57. Joseph McLaren, *Langston Hughes, Folk Dramatist in the Protest Tradition, 1921–1943* (Westport: Greenwood Publishing Group, 1997), 140.
58. Vincent Harding, Robin Kelley, and Earl Lewis, *We Changed the World: African Americans, 1945–1970* (New York: Oxford University Press, 1997), 175.
59. Lisa Krissoff Boehm, *Making a Way Out of No Way: African American Women and the Second Great Migration* (Mississippi: University Press of Mississippi, 2010), 10.
60. Komozi Woodard, *A Nation within a Nation: Amiri Baraka (LeRoi Jones) and Black Power Politics* (Chapel Hill: University of North Carolina Press, 2005), 34.
61. Elam and Krasner, *African American Performance and Theatre History*, 213.
62. Krissoff Boehm, *Making a Way Out of No Way*, 140.
63. Lynn Domina, *Understanding A Raisin in the Sun: A Student Casebook to Issues, Sources, and Historical Documents* (Westport: Greenwood Press, 1998), 18.
64. Ben Keppel, *The Work of Democracy: Ralph Bunche, Kenneth B. Clark, Lorraine Hansberry and the Cultural Politics of Race* (Cambridge: Harvard University Press, 1995), 190.
65. Keppel, *The Work of Democracy*, 24.
66. Joseph Agofure Idogho, "Lorraine Hansberry's A Raisin in the Sun: The African-Diasporas Identity Search and Racism/Desegregation Dialectics," in *Representing Africa in the Motherland and the Diaspora: Essays on Theatre, Dance, Music and Cinema*, ed. Kevin J. Wetmore Jr. (Cambridge: Cambridge Scholars Publishing, 2018) 20.
67. James V. Hatch and Ted Shine, eds. *Black Theatre, U.S.A.: Plays by African Americans* (New York: The Free Press, 1996), 105.
68. Amiri Baraka, "A Critical Reevaluation: *A Raisin in the Sun's* Enduring Passion," in *A Raisin in the Sun and The Sign in Sidney Brustein's Window*, ed. Robert Nemiroff (New York: Vintage Books, 1995), xiv.

69. Peniel E. Joseph, *Dark Days, Bright Nights: From Black Power to Barack Obama* (New York: Basic Civitas Books, 2009), 24–25. Fanon Che Wilkin, "Beyond Bandung: The Critical Nationalism of Lorraine Hansberry, 1950–1965," *Radical History Review*, issue 95 (Spring 2006): 192.
70. FBI, Subject: Lorraine Hansberry. File number: 100-393031, http://omeka.wustl.edu/omeka/exhibits/show/fbeyes/hansberry (accessed May 3, 2021).
71. Andrea Gill, "'Gilding the Ghetto' and Debates over Chicago's Gautreaux Program," in *The Business of Black Power: Community Development, Capitalism, and Corporate Responsibility in Postwar America*, eds. Laura Warren Hill and Julia Rabig (Rochester: University of Rochester Press, 2012), 190. These phrases were used by Stokely Carmichael, later known as Kwame Ture.
72. Waldo E. Martin, Jr., *No Coward Soldiers: Black Cultural Politics in Postwar America* (Cambridge: Harvard University Press, 2005), 32.
73. Martin, Jr., *No Coward Soldiers*, 32
74. John Henrik Clarke, *Malcolm X: The Man and His Times* (New York: Macmillan Publishers, 1969), 14.
75. OAAU's "Statement of Basic Aims and Objectives," cited in John Henrik Clarke, *Malcolm X: The Man and His Times* (Trenton: Africa World Press, 1969), 341.
76. Clarke, *Malcolm X*, 337. Molefi Kete Asante, *Malcolm X as Cultural Hero and Other Afrocentric Essays* (Trenton: Africa World Press, 1993), 38.
77. Farmer, *Remaking Black Power*, 94.
78. Farmer, *Remaking Black Power*, 98.
79. John Runcie, "The Black Culture Movement and the Black Community," *Journal of American Studies*, 1976 10(2), 187. Cruse, *The Crisis of the Negro Intellectual*, 14.
80. Hatch and Shine, eds. *Black Theatre, U.S.A*, 380.
81. Baraka, "The Revolutionary Theatre," 4.
82. Alice Childress, "For a Strong Negro People's Theatre," in *Masses and Mainstream* 4 (February 1951), 62.
83. Eric Lott, *Love and Theft: Blackface Minstrelsy and the American Working Class* (New York: Oxford University Press, 1993), 8.
84. Alice Childress, "For a Strong Negro People's Theatre," 63.
85. C. P. Epskamp and Kees Epskamp, *Theatre for Development: An Introduction to Context, Applications and Training* (London: Zed Books, 2006), 64. Holly Sidford, "Fusing Arts, Culture, and Social Change: High Impact Strategies for Philanthropy," from the National Committee for Responsive Philanthropy (2011), 4, http://heliconcollab.net/wp-content/uploads/2013/04/Fusing-Arts Culture and Social Change1.pdf (accessed June 19, 2019).
86. Kimberly Springer, "Black Feminists Respond to Black Masculinism," in Peniel E. Joseph's *Black Power Movement: Rethinking the Civil Rights-Black Power Era* (New York: Routledge Taylor and Francis Group, 2006), 106.
87. Forsgren, *Sistuhs in the Struggle*, 18.
88. Penier, *Culture-Bearing Women*, 43.
89. Penier, *Culture-Bearing Women*, 4.
90. Joseph, *Waiting 'Til the Midnight Hour*, 18. Nico Slate, "Introduction: The Borders of Black Power," in *Black Power beyond Borders: The Global Dimensions of the*

Black Power Movement, ed. Nico Slate (New York: Springer, 2012), 2. Nagueyalti Warren, "Pan-African Cultural Movements: From Baraka to Karenga," *Journal of Negro History*, vol. 75, no. 1–2 (Winter–Spring 1990), 16.

91. DeFrantz and Gonzalez, *Black Performance Theory*, 4.
92. DeFrantz and Gonzalez, *Black Performance Theory*, 4. Elam and Krasner, *African American Performance and Theatre History*, 65. Larry Neal, "The Black Arts Movement," *The Drama Review: TDR*, vol. 12, no. 4, Black Theatre (Summer 1968), 29. Cruse, *The Crisis of the Negro Intellectual*, 96.
93. Cruse, *The Crisis of the Negro Intellectual*, 534–35.
94. Farmer, *Remaking Black Power*, 129.
95. Williams, *Black Theatre in the 1960s and 1970s*, 66.
96. Judith E. Smith, "Finding a New Home in Harlem: Alice Childress and the Committee for the Negro in the Arts" American Studies Faculty Publication Series (2017), 21.
97. Hill and Rabig, *The Business of Black Power*, 2–3.
98. Michael O. West, "Conclusion: Whose Black Power? The Business of Black Power and Black Power's Business," in *The Business of Black Power: Community Development, Capitalism, and Corporate Responsibility in Postwar America*, eds. Laura Warren Hill and Julia Rabig (Rochester, University of Rochester, 2012), 292. Gill, "'Gilding the Ghetto' and Debates over Chicago's Gautreaux Program," 191.
99. David Zarefsky, *President Johnson's War On Poverty: Rhetoric and History* (Tuscaloosa: University of Alabama Press, 2005), 23.
100. Woodard, *A Nation within a Nation*, 160–61. Hill and Rabig, *The Business of Black Power*, 24–25. Christina Greene, "'Someday…the Colored and White will Stand Together': The War on Poverty, Black Power Politics, and Southern Women's Interracial Alliances," in *The War on Poverty: A New Grassroots History, 1964–1980*, eds. Annelise Orleck, Lisa Gayle Hazirjian (Athens: University of Georgia Press, 2011), 160.
101. Woodard, *A Nation within a Nation*, 219.
102. Williams, *Black Theatre in the 1960s and 1970s*, 80.
103. Hatch and Shine, *Black Theatre, U.S.A.*, 380.
104. Williams, *Black Theatre in the 1960s and 1970s*, 54.
105. Clayton Riley, "We will Not Be a New Form of White Art in Black Face," *New York Times* (June 14, 1970), section 2, 2.
106. William J. Maxwell, *F. B. Eyes: How J. Edgar Hoover's Ghostreaders Framed African American Literature* (Princeton: Princeton University Press, 2016), 3. The digital archives of collected FBI files on each of these artists can be found online at http://digital.wustl.edu/fbeyes/.
107. Alice Childress, "Black Writers' Views on Literary Lions and Values," Negro Digest 17 (January 1968), 86.
108. Williams, *Black Theatre in the 1960s and 1970s*, 78.
109. Hay, *African American Theatre*, 205.
110. *Black Theatre Alliance, Newsletter No. 1*, Sc Micro RS-235 r. 1: 1973–1977, Black Theatre Alliance Collection, Schomburg Collection, Schomburg Center

for Research in Black Culture, New York. A. Peter Bailey, "A Look at the Contemporary Black Theatre Movement," *Black American Literature Forum*, vol. 17, no. 1 (Spring 1983), 21.
111. Mance Williams, "The Color of Black Theatre: A Critical Analysis of The Black Theatre Movement of the 1960s and 1970s" (PhD diss., University of Missouri, Columbia, 1980), 188.
112. AUDELCO, "About AUDELCO," accessed May 2, 2019, http://www.audelco.org/about/.
113. Margaret Wilkerson, "Black Theater in California," *The Drama Review: TDR*, vol. 16, no. 4 (December 1972), 33–34.

TWO

1. Mona Vaughn Scott (current CEO of Black Repertory Group) in discussion with the author, April 2019.
2. Gloria Sewell Murphy, "Reports on Black Theatre U.S.A.: San Francisco-Oakland Bay," in *Black World/Negro Digest* (April 1976), 92.
3. Vaughn Scott, April 2019.
4. Robyn C. Spencer, *The Revolution Has Come: Black Power, Gender, and the Black Panther Party in Oakland* (Durham: Duke University Press, 2016), 33.
5. Robert O. Self, *American Babylon: Race and the Struggle for Postwar Oakland* (New Jersey: Princeton University Press), 23, 174.
6. Data collected from Bernard L. Peterson *The African American Theatre Directory, 1816–1960: A Comprehensive Guide to Early Black Theatre Organizations, Companies, Theatres, and Performing Groups* (Westport: Greenwood Publishing Group, 1997).
7. Delilah L. Beasley, *Negro Trail Blazers of California* (1919; repr., New York: James Stevenson Publisher, 2004), 208.
8. Donna Murch, *Living for the City: Migration, Education, and the Rise of the Black Panther Party in Oakland, California* (Chapel Hill: University of North Carolina Press, 2010), 15.
9. Gretchen Lemke-Santangelo, *Abiding Courage: African American Migrant Women and the East Bay Community* (Chapel Hill: University of North Carolina Press, 1996), 80.
10. Laura Warren Hill and Julia Rabig, *The Business of Black Power: Community Development, Capitalism, and Corporate Responsibility in Postwar America* (Rochester: University of Rochester, 2012), 23.
11. Shirley Ann Wilson Moore, *To Place Our Deeds: The African American Community in Richmond, California, 1910–1963* (Berkeley: University of California Press, 2001), 121–22.
12. Margo Natalie Crawford, "Must Revolution be a Family Affair?: Revisiting *The Black Woman*," in *Want to Start a Revolution?: Radical Women in the Black Freedom Struggle*, eds. Dayo F. Gore, Jeanne Theoharis, Komozi Woodard (New York: New York University Press, 2009), 187.
13. Morre, *To Place Our Deeds*, 93–94.

14. Morre, *To Place Our Deeds*, 88. "Warren asks Reports on Rent Raises," *Berkeley Gazette* (July 5, 1946), 1.
15. W. J. Rorabaugh, *Berkeley at War: The 1960s* (New York: Oxford University Press, 1989), 54–55.
16. Levine, *Highbrow/Lowbrow*, 145.
17. Margaret Wilkerson, "Black Theatre in California," *The Drama Review: TDR*, vol. 16, no. 4 (December 1972), 26. Though these theatres were heavily influential during this period, they are not the focus of interest for this analysis of Black Power theatre in California because they did not survive long or were more integrationist, as opposed to separatist.
18. Hay, *African American Theatre*, 191–92.
19. Wilkerson, "Black Theatre in California," 27.
20. Moore, *To Place Our Deeds*, 24–25.
21. Murch, *Living for the City*, 118.
22. Spencer, *The Revolution Has Come*, 25.
23. Murch, *Living for the City*, 31.
24. Spencer, *The Revolution Has Come*, 33.
25. Joseph, *Waiting 'Til the Midnight Hour*, 299. James Smethurst, *The Black Arts Movement: Literary Nationalism in the 1960s and 1970s* (Chapel Hill: University of North Carolina Press), 177.
26. Robyn C. Spencer, "Engendering the Black Freedom Struggle - Revolutionary Black Womanhood and the Black Panther Party in the Bay Area, California," in *Journal of Women's History*. 20, no. 1 (2008), 92.
27. Spencer, "Engendering the Black Freedom Struggle," 95–96. Suzanne Cope, *Power Hungry: Women of the Black Panther Party and Freedom Summer and Their Fight to Feed a Movement* (Chicago: Chicago Review Press, 2021), 170.
28. Samuel A. Hay, *Ed Bullins: A Literary Biography* (Detroit: Wayne State University Press, 1997), 97. Bullins was a well-known playwright, activist, and theatre founder in BAM. He was succeeded by Emory Douglas from 1967 until the group's demise.
29. Spencer, *The Revolution Has Come*, 2. Henry Elam, *Taking It to the Streets: The Social Protest Theater of Luis Valdez and Amiri Baraka* (Detroit: University of Michigan Press, 1997), 27.
30. Ed Bullins, "A Short Statement on Street Theatre," *The Drama Review: TDR*, vol. 12, no. 4 (Summer 1968), 93.
31. Hay, *Ed Bullins*, 82. Mike Sell, "The Black Arts Movement," 56.
32. Sell, "The Black Arts Movement," 77.
33. Dona Irvin, *The Unsung Heart of Black America: A Middle-Class Church at Midcentury* (Columbia: University of Missouri Press, 1992), 192.
34. Penningroth, *The Claims of Kinfolk*, 24.
35. Irvin, *The Unsung Heart of Black America*, 194. Dr. Mona Vaughn Scott, phone interview by Kerry Goldmann, April 18, 2019.
36. Data collected from Peterson's *The African American Theatre Directory*.
37. Nicholas Lemann's *The Promised Land: The Great Black Migration and How it Changed America* (New York: Knopf Inc., 1991), 269. Isabel Wilkerson, *The*

Warmth of Other Suns: The Epic Story of America's Great Migration (New York: Vintage Publishing, 2010), 531.
38. Mance Williams, *Black Theatre in the 1960s and 1970s: A Historical-Critical Analysis of the Movement* (Westport: Greenwood Press, 1985), 66.
39. Loren Schweninger, *Black Property Owners in the South, 1790–1915* (Chicago: University of Illinois Press, 1990), 80.
40. Lemke-Santangelo, *Abiding Courage*, 22.
41. Vaughn Scott, April 2019.
42. Lemke-Santangelo, *Abiding Courage*, 23.
43. Neil McMillen, *Dark Journey: Black Mississippians in the Age of Jim Crow* (Champaign: University of Illinois Press, 1990), 198.
44. McMillen, *Dark Journey*, 198.
45. Sean Vaughn Scott, "Our Story," Blackrepertorygroup.com, accessed June 27, 2018, http://www.blackrepertorygroup.com/our-story.html.
46. Phil James, "Black Repertory Group's Langston Hughes production 'Mulatto' Aligns with the Theater's Longstanding Mission," *Berkeleyside.com* (February 25, 2015), accessed April 2, 2019, https://www.berkeleyside.com/2015/02/25/Black-repertory-groups-langston-hughes-production-mulatto-aligns-with-the-theaters-longstanding-mission.
47. United Press, "Shipbuilding Wage Parley Opens in SF," *Berkeley Gazette* (February 18, 1946), 1–2.
48. Vaughn Scott, April 2019.
49. Vaughn Scott, April 2019.
50. Irvin, *The Unsung Heart of Black America*, 42.
51. Irvin, *The Unsung Heart of Black America*, 42.
52. Irvin, *The Unsung Heart of Black America*, 43.
53. Vaughn Scott, April 2019.
54. Lemke-Santangelo, *Abiding Courage*, 33.
55. Irvin, *The Unsung Heart of Black America*, 9.
56. "Shamrock Tea," *Oakland Tribune* (March 11, 1966), 29. Vaughn Scott, April 2019.
57. Vaughn Scott, April 2019.
58. Irvin, *The Unsung Heart of Black America*, 8. Murch, *Living for the City*, 52.
59. Spencer, *The Revolution Has Come*, 2.
60. Vaughn Scott, "Our Story."
61. Vaughn Scott, April 2019.
62. Vaughn Scott, April 2019.
63. Vaughn Scott, April 2019.
64. Vaughn Scott, "Our Story."
65. "Little Theaters," *Oakland Tribune* (November 30, 1968), 5-B.
66. Wilkerson, "Black Theatre in California," 30.
67. Wilkerson, "Black Theatre in California," 30.
68. Spencer, *The Revolution Has Come*, 22–23.
69. James, "Black Repertory Group's Langston Hughes production 'Mulatto' Aligns with the Theater's Longstanding Mission."
70. Irvin, *The Unsung Heart of Black America*, 194.

71. Irvin, *The Unsung Heart of Black America*, 194.
72. Sandra L. Richards, "Reports on Black Theatre U.S.A.: San Francisco-Bay Area," in *Black World/Negro Digest* (April 1974), 69.
73. Vaughn Scott, April 2019. Robert Hurwitt, "Nora Vaughn: Arts Heroes of Black History," *SFGate.com* (January 7, 2008), accessed June 25, 2019, https://www.sfgate.com/performance/article/NORA-VAUGHN-3231113.php.
74. Vaughn Scott, April 2019.
75. Vaughn Scott, April 2019.
76. Penningroth, *The Claims of Kinsfolk*, 191.
77. Shelia Washington, "Twenty Year Celebration for Black Repertory Group." Unprocessed. Black Repertory Group Theatre, Berkeley, California.
78. Miranda Ewell, "A Revitalized South Berkeley, an Awakened Interest in Black Culture, History, Literature," unknown newspaper. Unprocessed. Black Repertory Group Theatre, Berkeley, California.
79. Wilkerson, "Black Theatre in California," 29. " 'Purlie' Benefit," *Oakland Tribune* (March 17, 1972), 35.
80. Washington, "Twenty Year Celebration for Black Repertory Group."
81. Wilkerson, "Black Theatre in California," 33.
82. Wilkerson, "Black Theatre in California," 33.
83. Murphy, "Reports on Black Theatre U.S.A.," 91.
84. OAAU's "Statement of Basic Aims and Objectives," cited in John Henrik Clarke, *Malcolm X: The Man and His Times* (Toronto: Africa World Press, 1969), 341.
85. Murphy, "Reports on Black Theatre U.S.A.," 92.
86. Murphy, "Reports on Black Theatre U.S.A.," 92.
87. "Black Repertory to Present Three Plays," *Oakland Tribune* (March 3, 1973), 19.
88. Richards, "Reports on Black Theatre U.S.A.," 69.
89. Hurwitt, "Nora Vaughn: Arts Heroes of Black History."
90. Vaughn Scott, April 2019.
91. Wilkerson, "Black Theatre in California," 35.
92. Steve Isoardi, *The Dark Tree: Jazz and the Community Arts in Los Angeles* (Los Angeles: University of California Press, 2006), 83.
93. Isoardi, *The Dark Tree*, 83. Moore, *To Place Our Deeds*, 65.
94. Joseph, *Waiting 'Til the Midnight Hour*, 368.
95. Hurwitt, "Nora Vaughn: Arts Heroes of Black History."
96. Elizabeth Brown and George Barganier, *Race and Crime: Geographies of Injustice* (Berkeley: University of California Press, 2018), 186–87.
97. "Community Center: The Site," 3. Unprocessed. Black Repertory Group Theatre, Berkeley, California. Vaughn Scott, "Our Story."
98. Irvin, *The Unsung Heart of Black America*, 195.
99. Ewell, "A Revitalized South Berkeley."
100. Vaughn Scott, April 2019.
101. Ewell, "A Revitalized South Berkeley."
102. Nora Vaughn quoted in Nancy Scott, "Good News for Black Theatre," in *San Francisco Examiner* (November 11, 1987), 51.

103. Vaughn Scott, April 2019. "Black Rep Pans City for Poor Maintenance," unknown newspaper, 1. Unprocessed. Black Repertory Group Theatre, Berkeley, California.
104. "Black Rep Pans City for Poor Maintenance," 3.
105. Ewell, "A Revitalized South Berkeley."
106. "Community Center: The Site," 3.
107. Ewell, "A Revitalized South Berkeley."
108. Hurwitt, "Nora Vaughn: Arts Heroes of Black History."
109. Tracy Danison, "Arts/Stage: Community and Magic," *Berkeley Voice*. Unprocessed. Black Repertory Group Theatre, Berkeley, California.
110. Hurwitt, "Nora Vaughn: Arts Heroes of Black History."
111. Ewell, "A Revitalized South Berkeley."
112. Vaughn Scott, April 2019.
113. Wanda Ravernell, "Pride of the Community: Black Rep Gives Purpose to People Who Might Otherwise Have None," *Berkeley Gazette*. Unprocessed. Black Repertory Group Theatre, Berkeley, California.

THREE

1. Barbara Ann Teer, "A Stand for Ownership," unknown newspaper. Unprocessed. National Black Theatre, Harlem, New York.
2. Jessica B. Harris, "The Sun People of 125th Street: The National Black Theatre," *The Drama Review: TDR*, vol. 16, no. 4 (December 1972), 39.
3. Lundeana Marie Thomas, *Barbara Ann Teer and the National Black Theatre, Transformational Forces in Harlem* (New York: Garland Publishing Inc., 1997), 99. The street names were changed under local laws Number 10 and 11 and signed by Mayor Rudy Giuliani.
4. "The Quest," documentary produced by Abisola Patricia Ann Faison and The Griot Production Company, accessed June 13, 2023, https://www.youtube.com/watch?v=dQVhaZpjkCU.
5. Barbara Ann Teer quoted by Martha M. Jones, "Dr. Barbara Ann Teer's National Black Theatre," *Black Creation* vol. 3, no. 4 (Summer 1972), 19.
6. Hay, *African American Theatre*, 222.
7. Peterson, *African American Theatre Directory*, 6.
8. Barbara Ann Teer, "The Great White Way Is Not Our Way—Not Yet," *Negro Digest* (Apr. 1968): 29.
9. Lewis, *When Harlem Was in Vogue*, 11–12.
10. Adrienne Macki Braconi, *Harlem's Theaters: A Staging Ground for Community, Class, and Contradiction, 1923–1939* (Evanston, IL: Northwest University Press, 2015), 3.
11. Campbell Gibson and Kay Jung, *Historical Census Statistics On Population Totals By Race, 1790 to 1990, and By Hispanic Origin, 1970 to 1990, For Large Cities And Other Urban Places In The United States*, US Census Bureau, Population Division, Working Paper No. 76 (February 2005), 81, accessed June 21, 2019, https://www.census.gov/population/www/documentation/twps0076/twps0076.pdf.

12. Jonathan Shandell, *The American Negro Theatre and the Long Civil Rights Era* (Iowa: University of Iowa Press, 2018), 2.
13. Braconi, *Harlem's Theaters*, 198.
14. Shandell, *The American Negro Theatre and the Long Civil Rights Era*, 9.
15. Shandell, *The American Negro Theatre and the Long Civil Rights Era*, 30.
16. William Du Bois, "History of a Dream: Relating the Birth and Travails of the American Negro Theatre," *New York Times*, September 24, 1944, xi.
17. Brian Purnell, "'What We Need is Brick and Mortar': Race, Gender, and Early Leadership of the Beford-Stuyvesant Restoration Corporation," in *The Business of Black Power: Community Development, Capitalism, and Corporate Responsibility in Postwar America*, eds. Laura Warren Hill and Julia Rabig (Rochester: University of Rochester Press, 2012), 227. Peter Eisenstadt, "Rochdale Village and the Rise and Fall of Integrated Housing in New York," in *Civil Rights in New York City: From World War II to the Giuliani Era*, ed. Clarence Taylor (New York: Fordham University Press, 2011), 77. Michael W. Flamm, *In the Heat of the Summer: The New York Riots of 1964 and the War on Crime* (Philadelphia: University of Pennsylvania, 2017), 53.
18. Nikhil Pal Singh, *Black Is a Country: Race and the Unfinished Struggle for Democracy* (Cambridge: Harvard University Press, 2005), 74.
19. Cruse, *The Crisis of the Negro Intellectual*, 11.
20. Julie Burrell, *The Civil Rights Theatre Movement in New York, 1939–1966: Staging Freedom* (New York: Springer, 2019), 25.
21. Smethurst, *The Black Arts Movement*, 106.
22. Peter Bailey, "Annual Black Theatre Round-Up: New York City," *Black World/Negro Digest* (April 1972), 34.
23. Lisbeth Gant, "The New Lafayette Theatre. Anatomy of a Community Art Institution," *The Drama Review: TDR*, vol. 16, no. 4, Black Theatre Issue (December 1972), 47.
24. Barbara Ann Teer, "Needed: A New Image," in *The Black Power Revolt*, ed. Floyd B. Barbour (Boston: Collier Books, 1968), p. 222.
25. Du Bois, *The Souls of Black Folk*, 1–2.
26. "The Quest."
27. Biondi, *To Stand and Fight*, 249. Ula Taylor, "Elijah Muhammad's Nation of Islam: Separatism, Regendering, and a Secular Approach to Black Power after Malcolm X (1965–1975)," in *Freedom North: Black Freedom Struggles Outside the South, 1940–1980*, eds. Jeanne Theoharis and Komozi Woodard (London: Palgrave Macmillan, 2003), 183. Christopher M. Tinson, *Radical Intellect: Liberator Magazine and Black Activism in the 1960s* (Chapel Hill: University of North Carolina Press, 2017), 122.
28. August Meier and Elliott Rudwick, *CORE: A Study of the Civil Rights Movement, 1942–1968* (New York: Oxford University Press, 1973), 409.
29. Dhoruba Bin Wahad, Mumia Abu-Jamal, Assata Shakur, *Still Black, Still Strong: Survivors of the U.S. War against Black Revolutionaries* (Los Angeles: Semiotexte Press, 1993), 221.

30. Farmer, *Remaking Black Power*, 100–101.
31. Abisola Faison (NBT Director of Finance) in discussion with author, September 2023.
32. La Donna Lee Forsgren, *In Search of Our Warrior Mothers: Black Female Subjectivity in the Dramas of Martie Evans-Charles, Sonia Sanchez, and Barbara Ann Teer* (Evanston: Northwestern University Press, 2018), 227.
33. Curtis J. Austin, *Up Against the Wall: Violence in the Making and Unmaking of the Black Panther Party* (Fayetteville: University of Arkansas Press, 2006), 300.
34. Felicia Kornbluh, "Black Buying Power: Welfare Rights, Consumerism, and Northern Protest," in *Freedom North: Black Freedom Struggles Outside the South, 1940–1980*, eds. Jeanne Theoharis and Komozi Woodard (London: Palgrave Macmillan, 2003), 200.
35. Barbara Ann Teer quoted in Martha M. Jones, "Barbara Ann Teer's National Black Theatre," 18–19.
36. "The Quest."
37. Barbara Ann Teer, "The Culturnomics Prayer," pamphlet. Unprocessed. National Black Theatre, Harlem, New York.
38. Teer, "A Stand for Ownership."
39. Purnell, "What We Need is Brick and Mortar," 218–19. Kennedy created the community development corporation with the hope that it would form a political and private coalition that would empower leaders in the ghettos. However, politics and special interest groups constantly disrupted the merger between these groups.
40. Forsgren, *In Search of Our Warrior Mothers*, 191. Thomas, *Barbara Ann Teer and the National Black Theatre*, 39.
41. Sade Lythcott (current CEO of NBT) in discussion with author, September 2023.
42. Forsgren, *In Search of Our Warrior Mothers*, 192.
43. Faison, September 2023.
44. Faison, September 2023.
45. Barbara Ann Teer, "The Black Woman: She Does Exist," *The New York Times* (May 14, 1967), 15. Teer, "The Great White Way is Not Our Way—Not Yet," 22.
46. Faison, September 2023.
47. Collins, *Black Feminist Thought*, 68.
48. Faison, September 2023.
49. Charlie Russell, "Barbara Ann Teer: We are Liberators, Not Actors," *Essence* (March 1971), 49.
50. Forsgren, *In Search of Our Warrior Mothers*, 194.
51. Teer, "The Great White Way is Not Our Way—Not Yet," 25.
52. Thomas, *Babara Ann Teer and the National Black Theatre*, 41.
53. Lundeana Thomas, "Barbara Ann Teer: From Holistic Training to Liberating Rituals," *Black Theatre: Ritual Performance in the African Diaspora*, eds. Paul Carter Harrison, Victor Leo Walker II, and Gus Edwards (Philadelphia: Temple University Press, 2002), 368.
54. Forsgren, *In Search of Our Warrior Mothers*, 11.

55. Collins, *Black Feminist Thought*, 67.
56. Baraka, *The Autobiography of LeRoi Jones*, 299.
57. Lythcott, September 2023.
58. Larry Bivins, "Success without Compromise," *Newsday* (April 1988), 24.
59. Jim Williams, "The Need for a Harlem Theatre," in *Anthology of the American Negro in the Theatre: A Critical Approach*, ed. Lindsay Patterson (New York: Publishers Company, 1968), 169.
60. Thomas, *Barbara Ann Teer and the National Black Theatre*, 78.
61. Thomas, *Barbara Ann Teer and the National Black Theatre*, 78.
62. Faison, September 2023.
63. Faison, September 2023.
64. Faison, September 2023.
65. Faison, September 2023.
66. Faison, September 2023.
67. Thomas, *Barbara Ann Teer and the National Black Theatre*, 79.
68. Lythcott, September 2023.
69. Abiodun Jeyifous, "Black Critics on Black Theatre in America: An Introduction," *Drama Review: TDR*, vol. 18, no. 3, Criticism Issue (September 1974), 41.
70. Thomas, *Barbara Ann Teer and the National Black Theatre*, 75.
71. Teer, "The Great White Way is Not Our Way—Not Yet," 29.
72. Teer, "The Great White Way is Not Our Way—Not Yet," 29.
73. Teer quoted in Thomas, *Barbara Ann Teer and the National Black Theatre*, 78.
74. Teer, "The Great White Way is Not Our Way—Not Yet," 28.
75. Lythcott, September 2023.
76. Faison, September 2023.
77. Faison, September 2023.
78. Forsgren, *In Search of Our Warrior Mothers*, 228.
79. Forsgren, *In Search of Our Warrior Mothers*, 128.
80. Forsgren, *In Search of Our Warrior Mothers*, 128.
81. Lythcott, September 2023.
82. Faison, September 2023.
83. Barbara Ann Teer, "A Message From The Land of Vision: Breaking to New Ground Love," unpublished essay, written in May 2008, 3. Unprocessed. National Black Theatre, Harlem, New York.
84. Faison, September 2023.
85. Faison, September 2023.
86. Teer, "A Stand for Ownership."
87. Hornsford, "A Flair for Drama and a Head for Business," 12.
88. Lythcott, September 2023.
89. Faison, September 2023.
90. Faison, September 2023.
91. Lythcott, September 2023.
92. Harris, "The Sun People of 125th Street," 39.

93. La Donna Lee Forsgren, "Set Your Blackness Free": Barbara Ann Teer's Art and Activism during the Black Arts Movement," *Frontiers: A Journal of Women Studies*, vol. 36, no. 1 (2015), 139.
94. Forsgren, *In Search of Our Warrior Mothers*, 216.
95. Teer, "The Great White Way is Not Our Way—Not Yet," 27.
96. Harris, "The Sun People of 125th Street," 39.
97. NBT pamphlet, "NBT is a Celebration of Life AND A REBIRTH OF POWER," 1974. Unprocessed. National Black Theatre, Harlem, New York.
98. Anne Fliotsos and Wendy Vierow, *American Women Stage Directors of the Twentieth Century* (Champaign: University of Illinois Press, 2008), 412.
99. Forsgren, *In Search of our Warrior Mothers*, 226.
100. Forsgren, *In Search of our Warrior Mothers*, 201.
101. "Get to Know Sade Lythcott."
102. "NBT is a Celebration of Life AND A REBIRTH OF POWER."
103. Lythcott, September 2023.
104. Jones, "Barbara Ann Teer's National Black Theatre," 20.
105. "NBT is a Celebration of Life AND A REBIRTH OF POWER."
106. "Barbara Ann Teer and the National Black Theatre," in *Interreligious Foundation for Community Organization*, vol. iv, issue 1 (1972), 4.
107. Forsgren, *In Search of our Warrior Mothers*, 220.
108. Teer, "A Stand for Ownership."
109. Teer, "Culturnomics Prayer."
110. Valerie Harris, "Power Exchange 2: Barbara Ann Teer," *Heresies: A Feminist Publication on Art and Politics* (1979), 44.
111. Lythcott, September 2023.
112. Faison, September 2023.
113. Forsgren, *In Search of our Warrior Mothers*, 35.
114. Jones, "Dr. Barbara Ann Teer's National Black Theatre," 19.
115. Harris, "The Sun People of 125th Street," 42.
116. Jones, "Dr. Barbara Ann Teer's National Black Theatre," 19.
117. Teer, "Culturnomics Prayer."

FOUR

1. Eileen Morris quoted in interview with Olivia Flores Alvarez, "Best of Houston® 2013: Building Theater at Ensemble W/ Eileen Morris," *Houston Press*, October 10, 2013, accessed September 12, 2019, https://www.houstonpress.com/arts/best-of-houston-2013-building-theater-at-ensemble-w-eileen-morris-6366412.
2. George Hawkins quoted in Sharon Gray, "A History of the Ensemble Theatre and Its Productions: 1976–1999," (MA thesis, University of Houston, Houston, 1999), 65.
3. George Hawkins quoted by Everett Evans, *Houston Chronicle*, October 13, 1985, 4. Box 1677, Folder 10, Mayo and Holt Collection, Wittliff Collections, Texas State University, San Marcos, Texas.

4. Sandra Mayo and Evan Holt, "Interview with Eileen Morris," April 8, 2009, Box 1677, Folder 23, Mayo and Holt Collection, Wittliff Collections, Texas State University, San Marcos, Texas.
5. Michael Barnes, "Theater," *Handbook of Texas Online*, June 15, 2010, accessed March 4, 2019, https://tshaonline.org/handbook/online/articles/kkt01.
6. Mayo and Holt, *Stages of Struggle and Celebration*, 15.
7. Data collected from Peterson's *The African American Theatre Directory*.
8. Sandra Mayo and Elvin Holt, *Stages of Struggle and Celebration: A Production History of Black Theatre in Texas* (Austin: University of Texas Press, 2016), 10. The "Cakewalk" was a dance originally performed exclusively by enslaved black men on plantations. They would dance around a circle of numbers and eventually land on one hoping to win a prize from a number draw.
9. Sue Dauphin, *Houston by Stages: A History of Theatre in Houston* (Burnet, TX: Eakin Press, 1981), 395.
10. "Spectacular Feats of Daring Performed at the Camp Logan Show: Comedy Not Lacking in the Program of the 80th Infantry," *Houston Post*, December 8, 1917, 46. Buffalo Bill's Wild West Show was performed in blackface for the 80th infantry in Houston.
11. Dauphin, Houston by Stages, 398. Mayo and Holt, *Stages of Struggle and Celebration*, 217.
12. Tyina L. Steptoe, *Houston Bound: Culture and Color in a Jim Crow City* (Oakland: University of California Press, 2015), 60. William H. Frey, "The New Great Migration: Black Americans' Return to the South, 1965–2000," *The Brookings Institution* (May 2004), 5, accessed September 18, 2019, https://web.archive.org/web/20080428042235/http://www.brookings.edu/urban/pubs/20040524_Frey.pdf.
13. Frey, "The New Great Migration."
14. Brittny Mejia, "How Houston has become the most diverse place in America," *Los Angeles Times*, May 9, 2017.
15. Charles E. Jones, "Arm Yourself or Harm Yourself: People's Party II and the Black Panther Party in Houston, Texas," in *On the Ground: The Black Panther Party in Communities Across America*, Judson L. Jeffries, ed. (Jackson, MS: University Press of Mississippi: 2010), 7.
16. Martin Herman Kuhlman, "The Civil Rights Movement in Texas: Desegregation of Public Accommodations, 1950–1964," (PhD diss., Texas Tech University, Lubbock, 1994), 40.
17. Will Guzman, *Civil Rights in the Texas Borderlands: Dr. Lawrence A. Nixon and Black Activism* (Champaign: University of Illinois Press, 2015), 70. Casey Green, "Guardians Against Change: The Ku Klux Klan in Harris County, 1920–1925," *Houston Review* 10 (1988), 18, accessed September 13, 2019, http://www.houstonhistorymagazine.org/wp-content/uploads/2010/12/vol-8-no-1-KKK.pdf. Howard Beeth and Cary D. Wintz, *Black Dixie: Afro-Texan History and Culture in Houston* (College Station: Texas A&M University Press, 1992), 226.
18. Merline Pitre, *In Struggle Against Jim Crow: Lulu B. White and the NAACP, 1900–1957* (College Station: Texas A&M University Press, 2010), 56. Bruce

A. Glasrud and Merline Pitre, *Black Women in Texas History* (College Station: Texas A&M University Press, 2008), 214.
19. Kuhlman, "The Civil Rights Movement in Texas," 144, 207. Jones, "Arm Yourself or Harm Yourself," 8.
20. Alex Wukman, "Forgotten Houston July 1970: HPD vs. the Black Panthers," *Patch News*, June 9, 2016, accessed September 21, 2019, https://patch.com/texas/houston/forgotten-houston-july-1970-hpd-vs-black-panthers. Wukman illuminates the underrepresented history of Black Power in Houston and the assassination of one of their leaders, Carl Hampton, nearly fifty years following the events.
21. Jamie J. Wilson, *The Black Panther Party: A Guide to an American Subculture* (Santa Barbara: ABC-CLIO, 2018), 21.
22. Joshua Bloom and Waldo E. Jr. Martin, *Black Against Empire: The History and Politics of the Black Panther Party* (Berkeley: University of California Press, 2013), 315.
23. Jones, "Arm Yourself or Harm Yourself," 22.
24. Wukman, "Forgotten Houston July 1970."
25. Martin Waldron, "Black Militant Slain By Houston Police; Gun Fight Injures 4," *New York Times*, July 28, 1970, 1. Jones, "Arm Yourself or Harm Yourself," 26.
26. Smethurst, *The Black Arts Movement*, 321.
27. Doris Derby, Gilbert Moses, and John O'Neal, "A General Prospectus for the Establishment of a Free Southern Theater," 1964, Box 2, Folder 12, Zinn—Student Nonviolent Coordinating Committee Papers, Freedom Summer Collection, Wisconsin Historical Society, accessed September 21, 2019, http://content.wisconsinhistory.org/cdm/ref/collection/p15932coll2/id/28798.
28. Williams, *Black Theatre of the 1960s and 1970s*, 66.
29. Mayo and Holt, *Stages of Struggle and Celebration*, xiii.
30. Mayo and Holt, *Stages of Struggle and Celebration*, xiii.
31. Mayo and Holt, *Stages of Struggle and Celebration*, 218.
32. Dauphin, *Houston by Stages*, 402.
33. Dauphin, *Houston by Stages*, 402.
34. Bernard Carragher, "Black Theatre has Moved Beyond Revolution," *New York Times*, April 29, 1979, Section D, 1.
35. Carragher, "Black Theatre has Moved Beyond Revolution," 1.
36. Eileen Morris, in discussion with author, August 2023.
37. Wei-Huan Chen, "A Flood of Memories at the Ensemble Theatre," *Houston Chronicle*, October 26, 2018. Abner Fletcher, "Ensemble Theatre's 40th Anniversary," *Houston Public Media*, August 5, 2016, accessed October 15, 2019, https://www.houstonpublicmedia.org/articles/news/2016/08/05/163151/ensemble-theatres-40th-anniversary/.
38. Morris, August 2023.
39. Mayo and Holt, "Interview with Eileen Morris."
40. Morris, August 2023.
41. Mayo and Holt, "Interview with Eileen Morris."
42. Elvin Holt and Sandra M. Mayo, *Acting Up and Getting Down: Plays by African American Texans* (Austin, TX: University of Texas, 2014), 7.
43. William Albright, *Houston Post*, 4G.

44. Morris, August 2023.
45. "Blackshear to Speak to Negroes Tonight: Will Discuss What is Best for Emancipation Park," *Houston Post*, October 23, 1913, 9. "Emancipation Park: Park History," Houston Parks and Recreation Department, accessed November 2, 2019, https://www.houstontx.gov/parks/parksites/emancipationpark.html.
46. Kuhlman, "The Civil Rights Movement in Texas," 33.
47. Gray, "A History of the Ensemble Theatre and Its Productions," 38.
48. Faedra Chatard Carpenter, *Coloring Whiteness: Acts of Critique in Black Performance* (Ann Arbor: University of Michigan Press, 2014), 74.
49. Morris, August 2023.
50. Morris, August 2023.
51. Morris, August 2023.
52. Morris, August 2023.
53. Morris, August 2023.
54. Carpenter, *Coloring Whiteness*, 44. Steven Long, "Green Acres: Patriotism, picnics all part of legacy of Memorial Park," Houston Chronicle (September 1992).
55. Everett Evans, "Ensemble to Get in the Act for 13th Year – Theatre Keeps Its Focus on Black Culture," *Houston Chronicle*, October 15, 1989, 15. Box 1677, Folder 10, Mayo and Holt Collection, Wittliff Collections, Texas State University, San Marcos, Texas.
56. Evans, "Ensemble to Get in the Act for 13th Year," 15.
57. Gray, "A History of the Ensemble Theatre and Its Productions," 47–48.
58. Mayo and Holt, *Stages of Struggle and Celebration*, 221.
59. Morris, August 2023.
60. Chen, "A Flood of Memories at the Ensemble Theatre."
61. Gray, "A History of the Ensemble Theatre and Its Productions," 57.
62. C. Bernard Jackson, quoted in Bernard Carragher, "Black Theater has Moved beyond Revolution," *New York Times*, April 29, 1979, 21.
63. Morris, August 2023.
64. Morris, August 2023.
65. Mayo and Holt, *Stages of Struggle and Celebration*, 258–59.
66. Morris, August 2023.
67. Morris, August 2023.
68. Ensemble Theatre, "Our Story," Ensemble Theatre Website, accessed June 4, 2019, https://ensemblehouston.com/our-story.
69. Morris, August 2023.
70. George Hawkins quoted in Sharon Gray, "A History of the Ensemble Theatre and Its Productions 1976–1999," (MA thesis, University of Houston, Houston, 1999), 71.
71. Morris, August 2023.
72. Everett Evans, *Houston Chronicle*, May 9, 1984, 1. Box 1677, Folder 10, Mayo and Holt Collection, Wittliff Collections, Texas State University, San Marcos, Texas.
73. William Albright, *Houston Post*, February 2, 1984, 3E.
74. Morris, August 2023.

75. Morris, August 2023.
76. Morris, August 2023.
77. Morris, August 2023.
78. Morris, August 2023.
79. Morris, August 2023. Mayo and Holt, "Interview with Eileen Morris."
80. Everette Evans, *Houston Post*, n.d., n. page.
81. Mayo and Holt, *Stages of Struggle and Celebration*, 245.
82. Evans, "Ensemble to Get in the Act for 13th Year," 15.
83. "Our Story," The Ensemble Theatre Website.
84. Everett Evans, "*Hannah Davis* explores family's cultural clashes," *Houston Chronicle*, October 15, 1989, 15. Box 1677, Folder 10, Mayo and Holt Collection, Wittliff Collections, Texas State University, San Marcos, Texas.
85. Everett Evans, "Ensemble to Get in the Act for 13th Year," 15.
86. Carragher, "Black Theatre has Moved Beyond Revolution."
87. Mayo and Holt, "Interview with Eileen Morris."
88. Everett Evans, "Theater lives as Hawkins' legacy to city," *Houston Chronicle*, July 23, 1990, 1. Box 1677, Folder 23, Mayo and Holt Collection, Wittliff Collections, Texas State University, San Marcos, Texas.

FIVE

1. Childress, "But I Do My Thing," 9.
2. Alice Childress, "For a Strong Negro People's Theater," in *Masses and Mainstream* 4 (February 1951): 63.
3. Vaughn Scott, April 2019.
4. Dr. Nathan Hare to "To Whom it May Concern," Unprocessed. Black Repertory Group Theatre, Berkeley, California.
5. Vaughn Scott, April 2019.
6. Spencer, *The Revolution Has Come*, 12.
7. Keisha Blain, *Set the World on Fire: Black Nationalist Women and the Global Struggle for Freedom* (Philadelphia: University of Pennsylvania Press, 2018), 29.
8. Cathy Nessier, "Evaluation and Coordination Committee Chair of Junior League of San Francisco, letter to Nora Vaughn and Mona Vaughn Scott, November 15, 1989" Unprocessed. Black Repertory Group Theatre, Berkeley, California. Vaughn Scott, April 2019.
9. Mona Vaughn Scott, "Curriculum Vitae," emailed to author May 23, 2018, 20–21.
10. Vaughn Scott, "Curriculum Vitae," 21.
11. Vaughn Scott, "Curriculum Vitae," 21.
12. Frank O. Brown, M.D., "Recommendation for Mona Vaughn Scott," Unprocessed. Black Repertory Group Theatre, Berkeley, California.
13. Vaughn Scott, April 2019.
14. Peggy King, "Berkeley Students Tell it Like it is," *Oakland Tribune* (August 17, 1968), 7-B.
15. King, "Berkeley Students Tell it Like it is," 7-B.

16. David R. Johnson, "The History and Development of the Field of Drama Therapy in North America," in *Current Approaches to Drama Therapy* (Springfield, IL: Charles C. Thomas Publisher, 2009), 10.
17. B. M. Williams's "Minding our own biases: Using drama therapeutic tools to identify and challenge assumptions, biases and stereotypes," in *Drama Therapy Review*, 2(1) (2016), 12.
18. Hare, "To Whom it May Concern."
19. Vaughn Scott, "Curriculum Vitae," 7. Black Repertory Group, "Our Story."
20. Vaughn Scott, April 2019.
21. Shelia Washington, "Twenty Year Celebration for Black Repertory Group," unknown newspaper, 1. Unprocessed. Black Repertory Group Theatre, Berkeley, California.
22. Dr. Ruth B. Love, "Testimonials," Unprocessed. Black Repertory Group Theatre, Berkeley, California.
23. Mona Vaughn Scott "Letter to Senator Ted Kennedy," date unknown. Unprocessed. Black Repertory Group Theatre, Berkeley, California.
24. Vaughn Scott "Letter to Senator Ted Kennedy." Ravernell "Pride of the Community."
25. Vaughn Scott "Letter to Senator Ted Kennedy."
26. Vaughn Scott, "Curriculum Vitae," 10.
27. Andrzej Ceynowa, "Black Theaters and Theater Organizations in America, 1961–1982: A Research List," *Black American Literature Forum*, vol. 17, no. 2 (Summer 1983).
28. Victoria Horsford, "A Flair for Drama and a Head for Business: Barbara Ann Teer's National Black Theatre Turns 30," *KIP Business Report* (March 1998), 12. Unprocessed. National Black Theatre, Harlem, New York.
29. Lythcott, September 2023.
30. "Black Theatre Breaks Ground," *The Philadelphia Tribune* (May 16, 1989), p. C-1. Unprocessed. National Black Theatre, Harlem, New York.
31. George Goodman, "Black Theatre: Must it Appeal to Whites?," *New York Times*, Section 2 (January 10, 1982), 1. On the subject of the racial makeup of audiences, Goodman interviewed Douglas Turner Ward, owner of the Negro Ensemble Company; Woodie King Jr., owner of the New Federal Theatre, as well as playwrights Amiri Baraka and Ed Bullins.
32. Horsford, "A Flair for Drama and a Head for Business," 12.
33. Teer, "Culturnomics Prayer."
34. Sade Lythcott, interviewed by Kerry Goldmann, September 4, 2023.
35. Lythcott, September 2023.
36. Ana Escalante, "Sade Lythcott Is Building Her Own Legacy," in Glamour (February 11, 2022), accessed June 18, 2022, https://www.glamour.com/story/sade-lythcott-is-building-her-own-legacy.
37. "Pair Accused of Swindling National Black Theater," *Harlem World Magazine*. April 5, 2011, accessed July 21, 2019, https://www.harlemworldmagazine.com/pair-accused-of-swindling-national-Black-theater/.
38. Lythcott, September 2023.

39. Shirley Faison quoted in Linda Armstrong's "The Economic Crisis and the Black Theater," *New York Amsterdam News* (Mar 12-Mar 18, 2009), 35.
40. Armstrong, "The Economic Crisis and the Black Theater," 35.
41. "Stringer announces pact rescuing National Black Theater of Harlem," in *New York Beacon*, vol. 19, issue 24 (June 14, 2012), 2.
42. Ronald Bunn, "Coalition of Theatres of Color," *Routes-Mag*, May 2016, accessed June 14, 2019, http://routes-mag.com/coalition-of-theatres-of-color/.
43. National Black Theatre, "NBT Rentals," National Black Theatre Website, accessed July 23, 2019, https://www.nationalBlacktheatre.org/rentals.
44. Lythcott, "Get to Know Sade Lythcott."
45. Lythcott, "Get to Know Sade Lythcott."
46. Lythcott, "Get to Know Sade Lythcott."
47. Lythcott, September 2023.
48. Julia Jacobs, "National Black Theater Plans Next Act in a New Harlem High-Rise," *The New York Times* (June 4, 2021)
49. "Historic National Black Theatre to Break Ground on Mixed-Use Development in Harlem," *Real Estate Weekly* (June 23, 2022), https://rew-online.com/historic-national-black-theatre-to-break-ground-on-mixed-use-development-in-harlem%EF%BF%BC/.
50. Lythcott, September 2023.
51. Sade Lythcott, "State of Black Theatre: The Way Back Home," *Howlround Theatre Commons*, March 15, 2013, accessed July 25, 2019, https://howlround.com/way-back-home.
52. "Dr. Barbara Ann Teer's National Black Theatre Celebrates its 50th Anniversary," *Harlem World Magazine*, posted February 12, 2019, accessed March 29, 2019, https://www.harlemworldmagazine.com/dr-barbara-ann-teers-national-Black-theatre-celebrates-its-50th-anniversary/.
53. Faison, September 2023. Teer performed as a dancer in Sweden after graduating from college in the 1950s, and she maintained the personal relationships she developed.
54. Jacobs, "National Black Theater Plans Next Act in a New Harlem High-Rise."
55. Faison quoted in "The Economic Crisis in the Black Theatre," 35.
56. Faison quoted in "The Economic Crisis and the Black Theater," 19.
57. "Black Theatre Breaks Ground," C-1. Faison, September 2023.
58. National Black Theatre, "Our Story," National Black Theatre Website, accessed July 23, 2019, https://www.nationalblacktheatre.org/our-story.
59. Teer, "A Message From The Land of Vision," 4.
60. Thomas, *Barbara Ann Teer and the National Black Theatre*, xxi. National Black Theatre, "Who's Who," National Black Theatre Website, accessed July 23, 2019, https://www.nationalblacktheatre.org/whos-who-d. Faison quoted Armstrong's "The Economic Crisis and the Black Theater," 35.
61. "Harlem's National Black Theatre Receives Capital Grant Award Of $10 Million," in Harlem World (2022), accessed May 24, 2023), https://www.harlemworldmagazine.com/harlems-national-black-theatre-receives-capital-grant-award-of-10-million/.

62. Teer, "Culturnomics Prayer" pamphlet.
63. "Dr. Barbara Ann Teer's National Black Theatre Celebrates Its 50th Anniversary."
64. Morris, August 2023.
65. Everett Evans, "Theater lives as Hawkins' legacy to city," in *Houston Chronicle* (July 23, 1990), 1. (Mayo-Holt Collection, Box 1677, Folder 10)
66. Morris, August 2023.
67. "Eileen J. Morris," in *Howlround*, accessed June 21, 2022, https://howlround.com/commons/eileen-j-morris. Morris, August 2023.
68. Ensemble Theatre, "Our Story."
69. Morris, August 2023.
70. Morris, August 2023. Mayo and Holt, "Interview with Eileen Morris."
71. Ensemble Theatre, "Our Story." Mayo and Holt, *Stages of Struggle and Celebration*, 244.
72. Claudia Feldman, "Audrey Lawson, Church and Civic Leader, Dies at 83," *Houston Chronicle*, December 12, 2015.
73. Anthony D. Hill, *Historical Dictionary of African American Theater* (Lanham, MD: Rowman & Littlefield Publishers, 2018), 185.
74. Morris, August 2023.
75. Morris, August 2023.
76. Mayo and Holt, *Stages of Struggle and Celebration*, 262.
77. Morris, August 2023.
78. Evans, "Ensemble to Get in the Act for 13th Year," 15.
79. Mayo and Holt, "Interview with Eileen Morris."
80. Mayo and Holt, "Interview with Eileen Morris."
81. Mayo and Holt, "Interview with Eileen Morris."
82. Morris, August 2023.
83. Morris, August 2023.
84. Eileen Morris, "Indomitable Spirit: The Legacy, Vitality, and Sustainability of Black Theatre Today," in *Howlround*, March 16, 2013, accessed July 20, 2019, https://howlround.com/indomitable-spirit.
85. Morris, "Indomitable Spirit."
86. Morris, "Indomitable Spirit."
87. Morris, "Indomitable Spirit."
88. Everett Evans, "Writer Pulls Play from Ensemble Schedule," *Houston Chronicle*, March 28, 1999, Box 1677, Folder 10, Mayo and Holt Collection, Wittliff Collections, Texas State University, San Marcos, Texas.
89. "April 8 Jitney to Benefit African Grove Institute for the Arts," *Playbill*, April 7, 2000, accessed April 14, 2019, http://www.playbill.com/article/april-8-jitney-to-benefit-african-grove-institute-for-the-arts-com-88326.
90. Evans, "Writer Pulls Play from Ensemble Schedule."
91. Evans, "Writer Pulls Play from Ensemble Schedule."
92. "Newsmakers: Theatre Gala," *Jet*, October 9, 2006, Google Books, 34.
93. Mayo and Holt, "Interview with Eileen Morris."
94. Morris, "Indomitable Spirit."

95. Mayo and Holt, "Interview with Eileen Morris."
96. Gray, "A History of the Ensemble Theatre and Its Productions 1976–1999," 37. Hawkins learned the artistic and business side of theatre studying at Beale Street Repertory Theatre in Memphis, Tennessee, and the New Freedom Theatre in Philadelphia, Pennsylvania.
97. Chen, "A Flood of Memories at the Ensemble Theatre."
98. Ensemble Theatre, "Ensemble Venue Rentals," Ensemble Theatre Website, accessed September 18, 2019, https://ensemblehouston.com/visit/rentals.
99. Morris, August 2023.
100. "BWW News Desk, The Ensemble Theatre Artistic Director Eileen J. Morris Selected in Endeavor To Support Women In Theatre," *Broadway World*, February 24, 2018, accessed May 3, 2019, https://www.broadwayworld.com/houston/article/The-Ensemble-Theatre-Artistic-Director-Eileen-J-Morris-Selected-in-Endeavor-To-Support-Women-In-Theatre-20180224.

CONCLUSION

1. Neal, "The Black Arts Movement," 29.
2. Christopher L. Lebron, *The Making of Black Lives Matter: A Brief History of an Idea* (New York: Oxford University Press, 2017), xi.
3. Barbara Ransby, *Making All Black Lives Matter: Reimagining Freedom in the Twenty-First Century* (Oakland: University of California Press, 2017), 47.
4. There are several seminal texts to consult on the issue of mass incarceration and race. Michelle Alexander's *The New Jim Crow: Mass Incarceration in the Age of Colorblindness* sets the origin of racialized mass incarceration in Nixon War on Drugs in the 1970s. She argues that the waged War on Drugs had no correlating decrease in drug crime rates. Instead, the cyclical system created a new means of racial oppression after the demise of Jim Crow in the form of incarcerated isolation. Dan Berger's *Captive Nation: Black Prison Organizing in the Civil Rights Era* is in the same vein as Alexander in arguing the purpose of racial control. However, he diverges from her argument by setting the origin of Black mass incarceration earlier within the civil rights movement. Other scholars take racialized incarceration further back in American history. Khalil Muhammed's *Condemnation of Blackness: Race, Crime, and the Making of Modern America* uncovers the statistical roots of mass racialized incarceration back to the myth of Black criminality starting in the 1890s.
5. Gary Anderson, "Black Theatre Survey 2016–2017: A Report on the Health of Black Theatre in America." Blacktheatrematters.org, June 14, 2018, accessed June 11, 2024, https://blacktheatrematters.org/wp-content/uploads/2018/06/black-theatre-survey-2016–20173.pdf, 9, 12.
6. Anderson, "Black Theatre Survey 2016–2017," 17.
7. Lebron, *The Making of Black Lives Matter*, 39.
8. Margo Natalie Crawford, *Black Post-Blackness: The Black Arts Movement and the Twenty-First-Century Aesthetic* (Champaign: University of Illinois Press, 2017), 2.

9. Khalid Y. Long, "Staging Black Lives Matter," in *The Cambridge Companion to African American Theatre*, vol. 2, edited by Harvey Young (Cambridge University Press, 2023), 288.
10. Malorie Marshall, "National Black Theatre Hosts Plays and Events Honoring Trayvon Martin," *New York Amsterdam News*, February 8, 2014, accessed November 2, 2019, http://amsterdamnews.com/news/2014/feb/08/national-black-theatre-hosts-plays-and-events-hono/.
11. Edward J. Boyer, "Ebony Theater Tries to Keep Final Curtain from Coming Down," *LA Times*, February 1, 1993, accessed January 14, 2018, https://www.latimes.com/archives/la-xpm-1993-02-01-me-894-story.html.
12. "Diversity In The Arts: The Past, Present, and Future of African American and Latino Museums, Dance Companies, and Theater Companies," *A Study by the DeVos Institute of Arts Management at the University of Maryland* (September 2015), 9–10, accessed November 28, 2019, http://devosinstitute.umd.edu/What-We-Do/Services-For-Individuals/Research%20Initiatives/Diversity%20in%20the%20Arts. DeNeen Brown, "What is the State of Black Theater in D.C.?," *Washington Post*, January 6, 2012, accessed March 21, 2019, https://www.washingtonpost.com/lifestyle/style/what-is-the-state-of-black-theater-in-dc/2011/12/22/gIQArcQLfP_story.html.
13. Gray, "A History of the Ensemble Theatre and Its Productions," 65.
14. Lythcott, "State of Black Theatre: The Way Back Home."
15. Keli Goff, "Funding Crisis Threatens Black Theater," *The Root*, November 19, 2013, accessed February 18, 2019, https://www.theroot.com/funding-crisis-threatens-black-theater-1790898953. Kuntu Repertory Theatre, founded in 1974, was financially unsustainable by 2013, and Penumbra Theatre, founded in 1976, closed due to low funds the year prior.
16. "The Ensemble Theatre Participates in an International Celebration of African American Theatre," *Market Watch*, June 4, 2013, accessed December 4, 2019, https://www.marketwatch.com/press-release/the-ensemble-theatre-participates-in-an-international-celebration-of-african-american-theatre-2013-06-04.
17. Sidford, "Fusing Arts, Culture, and Social Change," 11.
18. Phyllis Joffe, "Black Theatre Funding," *NPR*, July 9, 1998, accessed November 13, 2019, https://www.npr.org/templates/story/story.php?storyId=1034259.
19. Sidford, "Fusing Arts, Culture, and Social Change," 26.
20. National Endowment for the Arts Grant Search, "Berkeley Repertory Theatre," accessed September 1, 2019, https://apps.nea.gov/grantsearch/.
21. National Endowment for the Arts Grant Search, "Alley Theatre," accessed September 1, 2019, https://apps.nea.gov/grantsearch/. National Endowment for the Arts Grant Search, "The Ensemble Theatre," accessed September 1, 2019, https://apps.nea.gov/grantsearch/.
22. Anderson, "Black Theatre Survey 2016–2017," 18.
23. Anderson, "Black Theatre Survey 2016–2017," 18.
24. Sidford, "Fusing Arts, Culture, and Social Change," 3.
25. Mona Vaughn Scott, in discussion with the author, July 2023. Lythcott, September 2023. Morris, August 2023.

26. "Dear White American Theater, Our Demands are in," We See You WAT (White American Theater), accessed July 2, 2021, https://www.weseeyouwat.com/.
27. For published articles addressing the "death" of the Black Theatre movement in the 1980s, see James V. Hatch, "Sittin' at the Banquet, Talkin' with Ourselves (An Open Letter to Theatre Scholars and Historians on the Status of Black Theatre Research and Publication)," *Black American Literature Forum*, vol. 16, no. 4, 1982; Winona L. Fletcher, "A Slender Thread of Hope: The Kennedy Center Black Theatre Project," *Black American Literature Forum*, vol. 17, no. 2, 1983; Addell Austin, "The Present State of Black Theatre," *The Drama Review: TDR* (1988), vol. 32, no. 3, 1988; and Donald M. Morales, "Do Black Theatre Institutions Translate into Great Drama?," *African American Review*, vol. 31, no. 4, 1997.
28. Christian Davenport, *How Social Movements Die: Repression and Demobilization of the Republic of New Africa* (New York: Cambridge University Press, 2015), 4.
29. Woodie King Jr., "Black Theatre: Present Condition," *The Drama Review: TDR*, vol. 12, no. 4, Black Theatre (Summer 1968), 116.
30. Vaughn Scott, April 2019.

BIBLIOGRAPHY

Primary Sources

MANUSCRIPT COLLECTIONS

Black Theatre Alliance Collection. Microfilm. Schomburg Collection, Schomburg Center for Research in Black Culture, New York.

Mayo and Holt Collection, Wittliff Collections, Texas State University, San Marcos, Texas.

Student Nonviolent Coordinating Committee Papers, Freedom Summer Collection, Wisconsin Historical Society. Accessed September 21, 2019. http://content.wisconsinhistory.org/cdm/ref/collection/p15932coll2/id/28798.

W. E. B. Du Bois Papers (MS 312) Special Collections and University Archives, University of Massachusetts Amherst Libraries, Amherst, Massachusetts. Accessed April 15, 2018. http://credo.library.umass.edu/view/full/mums312-b233-i053.

UNPROCESSED COLLECTIONS

"Black Rep Pans City for Poor Maintenance," unknown newspaper, 1. Unprocessed. Black Repertory Group, Berkeley, California.

Boggan, Jr., Vice Chancellor of Business and Administrative Services at UCB, to Nora Vaughn, June 12, 1990. Unprocessed. Black Repertory Group, Berkeley, California.

"Community Center: The Site," 3. Unprocessed. Black Repertory Group, Berkeley, California.

Hare, Nathan. Letter. "To Whom it May Concern," n.d. Unprocessed. Black Repertory Group, Berkeley, California.

Love, Ruth B. "Testimonials," Unprocessed. Black Repertory Group, Berkeley, California.

National Black Theatre Pamphlet, "NBT is a Celebration of Life AND A REBIRTH OF POWER," 1974. Unprocessed. National Black Theatre, Harlem, New York.

Nessier, Cathy, Evaluation and Coordination Committee Chair of Junior League of San Francisco, to Nora Vaughn and Mona Scott, November 15, 1989. Unprocessed. Black Repertory Group, Berkeley, California.

Teer, Barbara Ann. "A Message From The Land of Vision: Breaking to New Ground Love." Unpublished essay, written in May 2008, 3. Unprocessed. National Black Theatre, Harlem, New York.

Teer, Barbara Ann. "A Stand for Ownership," unknown newspaper. Unprocessed. National Black Theatre, Harlem, New York.
Teer, Barbara Ann. "The Culturnomics Prayer," pamphlet. Unprocessed. National Black Theatre, Harlem, New York.
Vaughn Scott, Mona. "Curriculum Vitae." Emailed to author, May 23, 2018.
Vaughn Scott, Mona. to Senator Ted Kennedy, date unknown. Unprocessed. Black Repertory Group, Berkeley, California.
Vaughn Scott, Mona. To #2idiotsproductions at the National Theatre of Ghana, April 30, 2019. Unprocessed. Black Repertory Group, Berkeley, California.
Washington, Shelia. "Twenty Year Celebration for Black Repertory Group," unknown newspaper, 1. Unprocessed. Black Repertory Group, Berkeley, California.

OTHER PRIMARY SOURCES

Bailey, A. Peter. "A Look at the Contemporary Black Theatre Movement." *Black American Literature Forum*, vol. 17, no. 1 (Spring 1983): 19–21.
Bailey, A. Peter. "Annual Black Theatre Round-Up: New York City," *Black World/Negro Digest* (April 1972): 31–36.
Baldwin, James. *Notes of a Native Son*. 1995. Reprint, Boston: Beacon Press, 2012.
Baraka, Amiri. "The Revolutionary Theatre." In *Liberator* (July 1965): 4–6.
Baraka, Amiri. "Black Revolutionary Poets Should Also Be Playwrights," *Black World/Negro Digest* (April 1972): 4–7.
"Barbara Ann Teer and the National Black Theatre," in *Interreligious Foundation for Community Organization*, vol. iv, issue 1 (1972): 1–6.
Bullins, Ed. "A Short Statement on Street Theatre." *The Drama Review: TDR*, vol. 12, no. 4 (Summer 1968): 93.
Childress, Alice. "A Candle in a Gale Wind." *Black Women Writers*. Ed. Mari Evans, 111–16. New York: Anchor Books, 1984.
Childress, Alice. "Black Writers' Views on Literary Lions and Values." In *Negro Digest* 17 (January 1968): 85–87.
Childress, Alice. "But I Do My Thing," in *The New York Times*, February 2, 1969.
Childress, Alice. "For a Strong Negro People's Theatre." In *Masses and Mainstream* 4 (February 1951): 61–64.
Childress, Alice. "Trouble in the Mind," in *Selected Plays by Alice Childress*, edited by Kathy Perkins. Evanston: Northwestern University Press, 2011.
Cruse, Harold. *The Crisis of the Negro Intellectual*. 1967. Reprint, New York: New York Review Books Classics, 2005.
Davenport, Jr., Garvin F. "Thomas Dixon's Mythology of Southern History," *Journal of Southern History*, vol. 36, no. 3 (August 1970): 350–67.
Day, Caroline Bond. "What Shall We play?," *Crisis* (September 1925): 221–23.
Du Bois, W. E. B. "The Conservation of Races." In *W. E. B. Du Bois Speaks: Speeches and Addresses, 1890–1919*, edited by Philip S. Foner, 83–95. New York: Pathfinder Press, 1970.
Du Bois, W. E. B. "Criteria of Negro art." *Crisis* (March 1926): 290–97.

Du Bois, W. E. B. "Krigwa Players Little Negro Theatre: The Story of a Little Theatre Movement." *Crisis* (July 1926): 134.

Du Bois, W. E. B. "The Negro in Art: How Shall He Be Portrayed?," *Crisis* (March 1926): 219–20.

Du Bois, W. E. B. *The Souls of Black Folk.* 1907. Reprint. Scotts Valley: CreateSpace Independent Publishing, 2014.

Easton, William Edgar. *Dessalines, A Dramatic Tale: A Single Chapter from Haiti's History.* 1893. Reprint, Bibliolife Reproduction Series, 2010.

Edmonds, Randolph. "The Negro Little Theatre Movement." *Negro History Bulletin* (January 1949): 82–86.

Ewell, Miranda. "A Revitalized South Berkeley, an Awakened Interest in Black Culture, History, Literature," unknown newspaper. Unprocessed. Black Repertory Group, Berkeley, California.

Faison, Shirley. Quoted in Linda Armstrong's "The Economic Crisis and the Black Theater," *New York Amsterdam News* (March 18, 2009), 35. Accessed July 23, 2019. http://assimediafinal.s3.amazonaws.com/site557/reseller84/company831/user28794/1460391469_UMEZ-Leveraging-the-Power-of-Cultural-Investments-20160226-WEB%20VERSION.pdf.

FBI. Subject: Lorraine Hansberry. File number: 100–393031. http://omeka.wustl.edu/omeka/exhibits/show/fbeyes/hansberry (accessed May 3, 2021).

Hurston, Zora Neale. "Stories of Conflict: A Review of Wright's *Uncle Tom's Children.*" *The Saturday Review of Literature* (April 1938): 32–33.

Horsford, Victoria. "A Flair for Drama and a Head for Business: Barbara Ann Teer's National Black Theatre Turns 30," *KIP Business Report* (March 1998).

James, Phil. "Black Repertory Group's Langston Hughes production 'Mulatto' Aligns with the Theater's Longstanding Mission." *Berkeleyside* (February 25, 2015). Accessed April 2, 2019. https://www.berkeleyside.com/2015/02/25/black-repertory-groups-langston-hughes-production-mulatto-aligns-with-the-theaters-longstanding-mission.

Jeyifous, Abiodun. "Black Critics on Black Theatre in America: An Introduction," *Drama Review: TDR*, vol. 18, no. 3, Criticism Issue (September 1974): 34–45.

Johnson, Georgia Douglas. "The Negro in Art: How Shall He Be Portrayed, A Questionnaire," *Crisis* (February-November 1926).

Karenga, Maulana. "Black Cultural Nationalism." *Black World/Negro Digest* 13(3) (1968), 5–9.

Karenga, Maulana. "Kawaida and Its Critics: A Sociohistorical Analysis," *Journal of Black Studies* (1977): 125–48.

King Jr., Woodie. "Black Theatre: Present Condition," *The Drama Review: TDR*, vol. 12, no. 4 (Summer 1968): 116–24.

Locke, Alain. "Art or Propaganda." *Harlem*, vol. 1, no. 1 (November 1928).

Locke, Alain. "Steps Toward the Negro Theatre," *Crisis* vol. 25, no. 2 (December 1922): 66–68. Accessed January 21, 2018. http://dl.lib.brown.edu/repository2/repoman.php?verb=render&id=1307029316296877view=pageturner&pageno=18.

Marvin X. "An Interview with Ed Bullins: Black Theatre," *Black World/Negro Digest* 18 (April 1969): 9–16.
Neal, Larry. "The Black Arts Movement." *The Drama Review* 12, 4 [T40], edited by Ed Bullins (1968): 29–39.
Richards, Sandra L. "Reports on Black Theatre: San Francisco-Bay Area." *Black World/Negro Digest* (April 1974): 66–71.
Russell, Charlie. "Barbara Ann Teer: We are Liberators, Not Actors," *Essence* (March 1971): 48–52.
Salaam, Kalamu Ya. "BLKARTSOUTH." *Black World/Negro Digest* (April 1972): 40–45.
Sewell, Gloria Murphy. "Reports on Black Theatre U.S.A.: San Francisco-Oakland Bay." *Black World/Negro Digest* (April 1976): 89–94.
Teer, Barbara Ann. Quoted by Martha M. Jones, "Dr. Barbara Ann Teer's National Black Theatre," *Black Creation* vol. 3, no. 4 (Summer, 1972): 18–20.
Teer, Barbara Ann. "The Great White Way is Not Our Way—Not Yet," *Black World/Negro Digest* (April 1968): 21–29.
Teer, Barbara Ann. "Needed: A New Image." In *The Black Power Revolt*, edited by Floyd B. Barbour, 219–38. Boston: Collier Books, 1968.
Williams, Jim. "The Need for a Harlem Theatre," in *Anthology of the American Negro in the Theatre: A Critical Approach*, edited by Lindsay Patterson, 169–75. New York: Publishers Company, 1968.

NEWSPAPERS

Berkeley Daily Gazette
Berkeley Voice
Houston Chronicle
Houston Post
Houston Press
Los Angeles Times
New York Times
Oakland Tribune
Philadelphia Tribune
San Francisco Examiner
San Francisco Gate
Washington Post

Secondary Sources

BOOKS

Abu-Jamal, Mumia. *We Want Freedom: A Life in the Black Panther Party*. Cambridge: South End Press, 2004.
Allen, Robert L. *Black Awakening in Capitalist America: An Analytic History*. Trenton: Africa World Press. 1990.

Asante, Molefi Kete. *Malcolm X as Cultural Hero and Other Afrocentric Essays*. Trenton: Africa World Press, 1993.

Austin, Curtis J. *Up Against the Wall: Violence in the Making and Unmaking of the Black Panther Party*. Fayetteville: University of Arkansas Press, 2006.

Ayers, Edward L. *Southern Crossing: A History of the American South, 1877–1906*. New York: Oxford University Press: 1998.

Baldwin, Davarian L. " 'Culture is a Weapon in Our Struggle for Liberation': The Black Panther Party and the Cultural Politics of Decolonization." In *In Search of the Black Panther Party: New Perspectives on a Revolutionary Movement*, edited by Jama Lazerow and Yohuru Williams, 289–305. Durham: Duke University Press, 2006.

Baraka, Amiri. *The Autobiography of LeRoi Jones*. Chicago: Lawrence Hill Books, 1997.

Baraka, Amiri. "A Critical Reevaluation: *A Raisin in the Sun's* Enduring Passion." In *A Raisin in the Sun and The Sign in Sidney Brustein's Window*, edited by Robert Nemiroff. New York: Vintage Books, 1995.

Baraka, Amiri. *Home: Social Essays*. Hopewell: Ecco Press, 1998.

Baumgartner, Kabria. *In Pursuit of Knowledge Black Women and Educational Activism in Antebellum America*. New York: New York University Press, 2019.

Beasley, Delilah L. *Negro Trail Blazers of California*. 1919. Reprint, Bibliolife Reproduction Series, 2004. https://archive.org/details/negrotrailblazer00beas/page/n8/mode/2up.

Beeth, Howard, and Cary D. Wintz. *Black Dixie: Afro-Texan History and Culture in Houston*. College Station: Texas A&M University Press, 1992.

Berlin, Ira. *The Making of African America: The Four Great Migrations*. New York: Viking Penguin, 2010.

Biondi, Martha. *To Stand and Fight: The Struggle for Civil Rights in Postwar New York City*. Boston: Harvard University Press, 2003.

Blain, Keisha. *Set the World on Fire: Black Nationalist Women and the Global Struggle for Freedom*. Philadelphia: University of Pennsylvania Press, 2018.

Bloom, Joshua, and Waldo E. Jr. Martin. *Black Against Empire: The History and Politics of the Black Panther Party*. Berkeley: University of California Press, 2013.

Braconi, Adrienne Macki. *Harlem's Theaters: A Staging Ground for Community, Class, and Contradiction, 1923–1939*. Evanston, IL: Northwest University Press, 2015.

Brown, Elizabeth, and George Barganier, *Race and Crime: Geographies of Injustice* Berkeley: University of California Press, 2018.

Brundage, W. Fitzhugh, ed. *Beyond Blackface: African Americans and the Creation of American Popular Culture, 1890–1930*. Chapel Hill: University of North Carolina Press, 2011.

Burrell, Julie. *The Civil Rights Theatre Movement in New York, 1939–1966: Staging Freedom*. New York: Springer, 2019.

Camp, Stephanie. *Closer to Freedom: Enslaved Women and Everyday Resistance in the Plantation South*. Chapel Hill: University of North Carolina Press, 2004.

Carpenter, Faedra Chatard. *Coloring Whiteness: Acts of Critique in Black Performance*. Ann Arbor: University of Michigan Press, 2014.

Carson, Clayborne. *In Struggle: SNCC and the Black Awakening of the 1960s.* Cambridge: Harvard University Press, 1981.
Clarke, John Henrik. *Malcolm X: The Man and His Times.* New York: Macmillan, 1969.
Cope, Suzanne. *Power Hungry: Women of the Black Panther Party and Freedom Summer and Their Fight to Feed a Movement.* Chicago: Chicago Review Press, 2021.
Collins, Patricia Hill. *Black Feminist Thought: Knowledge, Consciousness, and the Politics of Empowerment.* New York: Routledge Taylor and Francis Group, 2000.
Crawford, Margo Natalie. *Black Post-Blackness: The Black Arts Movement and the Twenty-First-Century Aesthetic.* Champaign: University of Illinois Press, 2017.
Cummings, Lindsay B. *Empathy as a Dialogue in Theatre and Performance.* New York: Springer Publishing, 2016.
Dauphin, Sue. *Houston by Stages: A History of Theatre in Houston.* Burnet, TX: Eakin Press, 1981.
Davenport, Christian. *How Social Movements Die: Repression and Demobilization of the Republic of New Africa.* New York: Cambridge University Press, 2015.
DeFrantz, Thomas F., and Anita Gonzalez, eds. *Black Performance Theory.* Durham: Duke University Press, 2014.
Domina, Lynn. *Understanding A Raisin in the Sun: A Student Casebook to Issues, Sources, and Historical Documents.* Westport: Greenwood Press, 1998.
Eisenstadt, Peter. "Rochdale Village and the Rise and Fall of Integrated Housing in New York." In *Civil Rights in New York City: From World War II to the Giuliani Era*, edited by Clarence Tyler, 77–94. New York: Fordham University Press, 2011.
Elam, Henry. *Taking It to the Streets: The Social Protest Theater of Luis Valdez and Amiri Baraka.* Detroit: University of Michigan Press, 1997.
Epskamp, C. P., and Kees Epskamp. *Theatre for Development: An Introduction to Context, Applications and Training.* London: Zed Books, 2006.
Fairclough, Adam. *Teaching Equality: Black Schools in the Age of Jim Crow.* Athens: University of Georgia Press, 2001.
Farmer, Ashley D. *Remaking Black Power: How Black Women Transformed an Era.* Chapel Hill: North Carolina Press, 2017.
Flamm, Michael W. *In the Heat of the Summer: The New York Riots of 1964 and the War on Crime.* Philadelphia: University of Pennsylvania, 2017.
Fliotsos, Anne, and Wendy Vierow. *American Women Stage Directors of the Twentieth Century.* Champaign: University of Illinois Press, 2008.
Forsgren, La Donna Lee. *In Search of Our Warrior Mothers: Black Female Subjectivity in the Dramas of Martie Evans-Charles, Sonia Sanchez, and Barbara Ann Teer.* Evanston: Northwestern University Press, 2018.
Forsgren, La Donna Lee. *Sistuhs in the Struggle: An Oral History of Black Arts Movement Theater and Performance.* Evanston: Northwestern University Press, 2020.
Fountain, Daniel L. *Slavery, Civil War, and Salvation: African American Slaves and Christianity, 1830–1870.* Baton Rouge: Louisiana State University Press, 2010.
Fuller, Hoyt W. "The New Black Literature: Protest or Affirmation." In *The Black Aesthetic*, edited by Addison Gayle, Jr., 346–68. Garden City: Doubleday Press, 1971.

Gaines, Kevin K. *Uplifting the Race: Black Leadership, Politics, and Culture in the Twentieth Century*. Chapel Hill: University of North Carolina Press, 2012.

Giddings, Paula. *Ida: A Sword Among Lions*. New York: Harper-Collins, 2008.

Giggie, John M. *After Redemption: Jim Crow and the Transformation of African American Religion in the Delta, 1875–1915*. New York: Oxford University Press, 2008.

Gill, Andrea. " 'Gilding the Ghetto' and Debates over Chicago's Gautreaux Program." In *The Business of Black Power: Community Development, Capitalism, and Corporate Responsibility in Postwar America*, edited by Laura Warren Hill and Julia Rabig, 184–273. Rochester: University of Rochester Press, 2012.

Glasrud, Bruce A., and Merline Pitre. *Black Women in Texas History*. College Station: Texas A&M University Press, 2008.

Gray-White, Deborah, Mia Bay, and Waldo E. Martin Jr. *Freedom on My Mind: A History of African Americans*. New York: Bedford St. Martin's Press, 2013.

Gomez, Michael. *Exchanging Our Country Marks: The Transformation of African Identities in the Colonial and Antebellum South*. Chapel Hill: University of North Carolina Press, 1998.

Greene, Christina. "'Someday . . . the Colored and White will Stand Together': The War on Poverty, Black Power Politics, and Southern Women's Interracial Alliances," in *The War on Poverty: A New Grassroots History, 1964–1980*, edited by Annelise Orleck, Lisa Gayle Hazirjian, 159–83. Athens: University of Georgia Press, 2011.

Gumbs, Alexis Pauline. "Buying (Black) Power: The Story of *Essence* Magazine." In *The Business of Black Power: Community Development, Capitalism, and Corporate Responsibility in Postwar America*, edited by Laura Warren Hill and Julia Rabig, 95–115. Rochester: University of Rochester Press, 2012.

Guzman, Will. *Civil Rights in the Texas Borderlands: Dr. Lawrence A. Nixon and Black Activism*. Champaign: University of Illinois Press, 2015.

Harding, Vincent, Robin Kelley, and Earl Lewis. *We Changed the World: African Americans, 1945–1970*. New York: Oxford University Press, 1997.

Hatch, James V., and Errol G. Hill. *A History of African American Theatre*. Cambridge University Press, 2003.

Hatch, James V., and Ted Shine, eds. *Black Theatre, U.S.A.: Plays by African Americans*, vol. 2. New York: The Free Press, 1996.

Hay, Samuel A. *African American Theatre: An Historical and Critical Analysis*. New York: Cambridge University Press, 1994.

Hay, Samuel A. *Ed Bullins: A Literary Biography*. Detroit: Wayne State University Press, 1997.

Higginbotham, Evelyn Brooks. *Righteous Discontent: The Women's Movement in the Black Baptist Church, 1880–1920*. Cambridge: Harvard University Press, 1993.

Hill, Anthony D. *Historical Dictionary of African American Theater*. Lanham, MD: Rowman & Littlefield Publishers, 2018.

Idogho, Joseph Agofure. "Lorraine Hansberry's A Raisin in the Sun: The African-Diasporas Identity Search and Racism/Desegregation Dialectics." In *Representing Africa in the Motherland and the Diaspora: Essays on Theatre, Dance, Music and*

Cinema, edited by Kevin J. Wetmore Jr., 18–30. Cambridge: Cambridge Scholars Publishing, 2018.

Irvin, Donna. *The Unsung Heart of Black America: A Middle-Class Church at Midcentury*. Columbia: University of Missouri Press, 1992.

Isoardi, Steve. *The Dark Tree: Jazz and the Community Arts in Los Angeles*. Los Angeles: University of California Press, 2006.

Jeffries, Judson L. *On the Ground: The Black Panther Party in Communities across America*. Jackson: University Press of Mississippi, 2010.

Johnson, David R., and Penny Lewis. *Critical Approaches to Drama Therapy*. Springfield: Charles C. Thomas Publisher, 2009.

Jones, Charles E. "Arm Yourself or Harm Yourself: People's Party II and the Black Panther Party in Houston, Texas." In *On the Ground: The Black Panther Party in Communities Across America*, edited by Judson L. Jeffries, 3–40. Jackson, MS: University Press of Mississippi: 2010.

Jones, Kellie. "Black West, Thoughts on Art in Los Angeles." In *New Thoughts on the Black Arts Movement*, edited by Lisa Gail Collins and Margo Natalie Crawford, 43–74. New Brunswick: Rutgers University Press, 2006.

Joseph, Peniel E. *Dark Days, Bright Nights: From Black Power to Barack Obama*. New York: Basic Civitas Books, 2009.

Joseph, Peniel E. "The Black Power Movement." In *Black Power 50*, edited by Sylviane A. Diouf and Komozi Woodard, 1–28. New York: The New Press, 2016.

Joseph, Peniel E. *Stokely: A Life*. New York: Civitas Books, 2016.

Joseph, Peniel E. *Waiting 'Til the Midnight Hour: A Narrative History of Black Power in America*. New York: Holt Paperbacks, 2007.

Kelley, Robin. *Freedom Dreams: The Black Radical Imagination*. Boston: Beacon Press, 2002.

Kelley, Robin. *Race Rebels: Culture, Politics, and the Black, Working Class*. New York: Free Press, 1996.

Keppel, Ben. *The Work of Democracy: Ralph Bunche, Kenneth B. Clark, Lorraine Hansberry, and the Cultural Politics of Race*. Cambridge: Harvard University Press, 1995.

King, Richard H. *Race, Culture, and the Intellectuals, 1940–1970*. Baltimore: Johns Hopkins University Press, 2004.

Kirby, Michael. *A Formalist Theatre*. Philadelphia: University of Pennsylvania Press, 2011.

Kornbluh, Felicia. "Black Buying Power: Welfare Rights, Consumerism, and Northern Protest." In *Freedom North: Black Freedom Struggles Outside the South, 1940–1980*, edited by Jeanne Theoharis and Komozi Woodard, 199–222. London: Palgrave Macmillan, 2003.

Lawson, Steven F., and Charles M. Payne, *Debating the Civil Rights Movement, 1945–1968*. Lanham: Rowman and Littlefield, 1998.

Lebron, Christopher L. *The Making of Black Lives Matter: A Brief History of an Idea*. New York: Oxford University Press, 2017.

Lemann, Nicholas. *The Promised Land: The Great Black Migration and How it Changed America*. New York: Knopf Inc., 1991.
Lemke-Santangelo, Gretchen. *Abiding Courage: African American Migrant Women and the East Bay Community*. Chapel Hill: University of North Carolina Press, 1996.
Levine, Lawrence W. *Highbrow/Lowbrow: The Emergence of Cultural Hierarchy in America*. Cambridge: Harvard University Press, 1998.
Lewis, David Levering. *When Harlem Was in Vogue*. New York: Knopf, 1981.
Long, Khalid Y. "Staging Black Lives Matter." In *The Cambridge Companion to African American Theatre*, vol. 2, edited by Harvey Young, 283–99 (Cambridge: Cambridge University Press, 2023).
Lott, Eric. *Love and Theft: Blackface Minstrelsy and the American Working Class*. New York: Oxford University Press, 1993.
Martin Jr., Waldo E. *No Coward Soldiers: Black Cultural Politics in Postwar America*. Cambridge: Harvard University Press, 2005.
Mahar, William J. *Behind the Burnt Cork Mask: Early Blackface Minstrelsy and Antebellum American Culture*. Urbana; University of Illinois Press, 1998.
Maxwell, William J. *F. B. Eyes: How J. Edgar Hoover's Ghostreaders Framed African American Literature*. Princeton: Princeton University Press, 2016.
Mayo, Sandra M., and Elvin Holt. *Stages of Struggle and Celebration: A Production History of Black Theatre in Texas*. Austin: University of Texas Press, 2016.
McAdam, Doug. *Political Process and the Development of Black Insurgency, 1930–1970*. Chicago: University of Chicago Press, 1982.
McLaren, Joseph. *Langston Hughes, Folk Dramatist in the Protest Tradition, 1921–1943*. Westport: Greenwood Publishing Group, 1997.
McMillen, Neil. *Dark Journey: Black Mississippians in the Age of Jim Crow*. Champaign: University of Illinois Press, 1990.
Meier, August, and Elliott Rudwick. *CORE: A Study of the Civil Rights Movement, 1942–1968*. New York: Oxford University Press, 1973.
Mitchell, Koritha. *Living with Lynching: African American Lynching Plays, Performance, and Citizenship, 1890–1930*. Champaign: University of Illinois Press, 2011.
Moore, Shirley Ann Wilson. *To Place Our Deeds: The African American Community in Richmond, California, 1910–1963*. Berkeley: University of California Press, 2001.
Murch, Donna. *Living for the City: Migration, Education, and the Rise of the Black Panther Party in Oakland, California*. Chapel Hill: University of North Carolina Press, 2010.
O'Malley, Gregory. *Final Passages: The Intercolonial Slave Trade of British America, 1619–1807*. Chapel Hill: University of North Carolina Press, 2014.
Penier, Izabella. *Culture-Bearing Women: The Black Women Renaissance and Cultural Nationalism*. Berlin: De Gruyter Ltd., 2019.
Penningroth, Dylan C. *The Claims of Kinfolk: African American Property and Community in the Nineteenth-Century South*. Chapel Hill: University of North Carolina Press, 2003.

Perkins, Kathy A., and Judith L. Stephens. *Strange Fruit: Plays on Lynching by American Women*. Bloomington: Indiana University Press, 1998.

Perkins, Kathy A. "Introduction." In *Selected Plays*, written by Alice Childress. Evanston: Northwestern University Press, 2011.

Peterson, Bernard L. *The African American Theatre Directory, 1816–1960: A Comprehensive Guide to Early Black Theatre Organizations, Companies, Theatres, and Performing Groups*. CT: Greenwood Publishing, 1997.

Phelan, Peggy. *Unmarked: The Politics of Performance*. New York: Routledge Taylor and Francis Group, 1993.

Pitre, Merline. *In Struggle Against Jim Crow: Lulu B. White and the NAACP, 1900–1957*. College Station: Texas A&M University Press, 2010.

Plummer, Brenda Gayle. "International Dimensions of the Black Power Movement." In *Black Power 50*. Ed. Sylviane A. Diouf and Komozi Woodard, 103–24. New York: The New Press, 2016.

Purnell, Brian. " 'What We Need is Brick and Mortar': Race, Gender, and Early Leadership of the Bedford-Stuyvesant Restoration Corporation." *The Business of Black Power: Community Development, Capitalism, and Corporate Responsibility in Postwar America*, edited by Laura Warren Hill and Julia Rabig, 217–44. Rochester: University of Rochester Press, 2012.

Ransby, Barbara. *Making All Black Lives Matter: Reimagining Freedom in the Twenty-First Century*. Oakland: University of California Press, 2017.

Self, Robert O. "The Black Panther Party and the Long Civil Rights Era." In *In Search of the Black Panther Party: New Perspectives on a Revolutionary Movement*, edited by Jama Lazerow and Yohuru Williams, 15–55. Durham: Duke University Press, 2006.

Sell, Mike. "The Black Arts Movement: Performance, Neo-Orality, and the Destruction of the " 'White Thing.' " In *African American Performance and Theatre History: A Critical Reader*, edited by Henry J. Elam Jr. and David Krasner, 56–80. New York: Oxford University Press, 2001.

Shabazz, Amilcar. *Advancing Democracy: African Americans and the Struggle for Access and Equity in Higher Education in Texas*. Chapel Hill: University of North Carolina Press, 2005.

Shandell, Jonathan. *The American Negro Theatre and the Long Civil Rights Era* (Iowa City: University of Iowa Press, 2018).

Shih, Bryan, and Yohuru Williams. *The Black Panthers: Portraits from an Unfinished Revolution*. New York: PublicAffairs Press, 2016

Singh, Nikhil Pal. *Black Is a Country: Race and the Unfinished Struggle for Democracy*. Cambridge: Harvard University Press, 2005.

Slate, Nico. "Introduction: The Borders of Black Power." In *Black Power beyond Borders: The Global Dimensions of the Black Power Movement*, edited by Nico Slate. New York: Springer, 2012.

Smethurst, James. *The Black Arts Movement: Literary Nationalism in the 1960s and 1970s*. Chapel Hill: University of North Carolina Press, 2006.

Smethurst, James. "The Black Arts Movement." In *Black Power 50*, edited by Sylviane A. Diouf and Komozi Woodard, 89–102. New York: The New Press, 2016.

Spencer, Robyn C. *The Revolution Has Come: Black Power, Gender, and the Black Panther Party in Oakland.* Durham: Duke University Press, 2016.
Springer, Kimberly. "Black Feminists Respond to Black Masculinism." In *Black Power Movement: Rethinking the Civil Rights-Black Power Era*, edited by Peniel E. Joseph, 105–18. New York: Routledge Taylor and Francis Group, 2006.
Springer, Kimberly. *Living for the Revolution: Black Feminist Organizations, 1968–1980.* Durham: Duke University Press, 2005.
Steptoe, Tyina L. *Houston Bound: Culture and Color in a Jim Crow City.* Oakland: University of California Press, 2015.
Taylor, Ula. "Elijah Muhammad's Nation of Islam: Separatism, Regendering, and a Secular Approach to Black Power after Malcolm X (1965–1975)." In *Freedom North: Black Freedom Struggles Outside the South, 1940–1980*, edited by Jeanne Theoharis and Komozi Woodard. London: Palgrave Macmillan, 2003.
Theoharis, Jeanne, and Komozi Woodard. *Groundwork: Local Black Freedom Movements in America.* New York: New York University Press, 2005.
Thomas, Lundeana Marie. "Barbara Ann Teer: From Holistic Training to Liberating Rituals." *Black Theatre: Ritual Performance in the African Diaspora*, edited by Paul Carter Harrison, Victor Leo Walker II, and Gus Edwards. Philadelphia: Temple University Press, 2002.
Thomas, Lundeana Marie. *Barbara Ann Teer and the National Black Theatre, Transformational Forces in Harlem.* New York: Garland Publishing Inc., 1997.
Tinson, Christopher M. *Radical Intellect: Liberator Magazine and Black Activism in the 1960s.* Chapel Hill: University of North Carolina Press, 2017.
Toll, Robert C. *Blacking Up: The Minstrel Show in Nineteenth-Century America.* New York: Oxford University Press, 1974.
Wahad, Dhoruba Bin, Mumia Abu-Jamal, and Assata Shakur. *Still Black, Still Strong: Survivors of the U.S. War Against Black Revolutionaries.* Los Angeles: Semiotexte Press, 1993.
Warren, Louis. *Buffalo Bill's America: William Cody and the Wild West Show.* New York: Vintage Books: 2006.
Warren Hill, Laura, and Julia Rabig, eds. *The Business of Black Power: Community Development, Capitalism, and Corporate Responsibility in Postwar America.* Rochester: University of Rochester Press, 2012.
Watts, Jerry Gafio. *Amiri Baraka: The Politics and Art of a Black Intellectual.* New York: New York University Press, 2001.
Wendt, Simon. "Armed Resistance and Radicalization of the Civil Rights Movement." In *The Black Power Movement: Rethinking the Civil Rights-Black Power Era.* Edited by Peniel E. Joseph, 145–66. New York: Routledge Taylor and Francis Group, 2006.
West, Michael O. "Conclusion: Whose Black Power? The Business of Black Power and Black Power's Business," in *The Business of Black Power: Community Development, Capitalism, and Corporate Responsibility in Postwar America*, edited by Laura Warren Hill and Julia Rabig, 274–303. Rochester, University of Rochester, 2012.

Wilkerson, Isabel. *The Warmth of Other Suns: The Epic Story of America's Great Migration*. New York: Vintage Publishing, 2011.

Wilkerson, Margaret. "The Black Theatre Experience: PASLA (Performing Arts Society Los Angeles)." In *Theatre West: Image and Impact*, edited by Dunbar H. Ogden, Douglas McDermott, Robert K. Sarlós, Robert Károly Sarlós, 69–83. Amsterdam: Rodopi Press, 1990.

Williams, Heather Andrea. *Self-Taught: African American Education in Slavery and Freedom*. Chapel Hill: University of North Carolina Press, 2009.

Williams, Jim. "The Need for a Harlem Theatre," in *Anthology of the American Negro in the Theatre: A Critical Approach*, edited by Lindsay Patterson, 169–75. New York: Publishers Company, 1968.

Williams, Mance. *Black Theatre in the 1960s and 1970s: A Historical-Critical Analysis of the Movement*. Westport: Greenwood Press, 1985.

Williams, Rhonda Y. *Concrete Demands: The Search for Black Power in the 20th Century*. New York: Routledge Taylor and Francis Group, 2014.

Wilson, Jamie J. *The Black Panther Party: A Guide to an American Subculture*. Santa Barbara: ABC-CLIO, 2018.

Woodard, Komozi. *A Nation within a Nation: Amiri Baraka (LeRoi Jones) and Black Power Politics*. Chapel Hill: University of North Carolina Press, 2005.

Zarefsky, David. *President Johnson's War On Poverty: Rhetoric and History*. Tuscaloosa: University of Alabama Press, 2005.

ARTICLES AND WEBSITES

"April 8 Jitney to Benefit African Grove Institute for the Arts." *Playbill*. April 7, 2000. Accessed April 14, 2019. http://www.playbill.com/article/april-8-jitney-to-benefit-african-grove-institute-for-the-arts-com-88326.

AUDELCO. "About AUDELCO." Accessed May 2, 2019, http://www.audelco.org/about/.

Abramson, Doris E. "The Great White Way: Critics and the First Black Playwrights on Broadway." *Educational Theatre Journal* 28, no. 1 (1976): 45–55.

Anderson, Sarah A. " 'The Place to Go': The 135th Street Branch Library and the Harlem Renaissance." *The Library Quarterly: Information, Community, Policy* 73, no. 4 (2003): 383–421.

Barnes, Michael. "Theater." *Handbook of Texas Online*. June 15, 2010. Accessed March 4, 2019, https://tshaonline.org/handbook/online/articles/kkt01.

Bernstein, Robert. "Never Born: Angelina Weld Grimke's *Rachel* as Ironic Response to Topsy." *Journal of American Drama and Theatre*, 19, no. 2 (Spring 2007): 61–75.

Brown, DeNeen. "What is the State of Black Theater in D.C.?," *Washington Post*, January 6, 2012. Accessed March 21, 2019. https://www.washingtonpost.com/lifestyle/style/what-is-the-state-of-black-theater-in-dc/2011/12/22/gIQArcQLfP_story.html.

Bunn, Ronald. "Coalition of Theatres of Color." *Routes-Mag*, May 2016. Accessed June 14, 2019, http://routes-mag.com/coalition-of-theatres-of-color/.

"BWW News Desk, The Ensemble Theatre Artistic Director Eileen J. Morris Selected in Endeavor To Support Women In Theatre." *Broadway World*. February 24, 2018. Accessed May 3, 2019. https://www.broadwayworld.com/houston/article/The-Ensemble-Theatre-Artistic-Director-Eileen-J-Morris-Selected-in-Endeavor-To-Support-Women-In-Theatre-20180224.

Ceynowa, Andrzej. "Black Theaters and Theater Organizations in America, 1961–1982: A Research List." *Black American Literature Forum*, vol. 17, no. 2 (Summer, 1983): 84–93.

Cha-Jua, Sundiata Keita and Clarence Lang. "The 'Long Movement' as Vampire: Temporal and Spatial Fallacies in Recent Black Freedom Studies." *The Journal of African American History* vol. 92, no. 2 (2007): 265–88.

"Dear White American Theater, Our Demands are in." *We See You WAT (White American Theater)*. Accessed July 2, 2021. https://www.weseeyouwat.com/.

"Diversity In The Arts: The Past, Present, and Future of African American and Latino Museums, Dance Companies, and Theater Companies." *A Study by the DeVos Institute of Arts Management at the University of Maryland* (September 2015): 9–10. Accessed November 28, 2019. http://devosinstitute.umd.edu/What-We-Do/Services-For-Individuals/Research%20Initiatives/Diversity%20in%20the%20Arts.

"Dr. Barbara Ann Teer's National Black Theatre Celebrates its 50th Anniversary," *Harlem World Magazine*, posted February 12, 2019. Accessed March 29, 2019. https://www.harlemworldmagazine.com/dr-barbara-ann-teers-national-black-theatre-celebrates-its-50th-anniversary/.

"Emancipation Park: Park History." Houston Parks and Recreation Department. Accessed November 2, 2019. https://www.houstontx.gov/parks/parksites/emancipationpark.html.

"The Ensemble Theatre Participates in an International Celebration of African American Theatre," *Market Watch*, June 4, 2013. Accessed December 4, 2019. https://www.marketwatch.com/press-release/the-ensemble-theatre-participates-in-an-international-celebration-of-african-american-theatre-2013-06-04.

Ensemble Theatre. "Ensemble Venue Rentals." Ensemble Theatre Website. Accessed September 18, 2019. https://ensemblehouston.com/visit/rentals.

Ensemble Theatre. "Our Story." Ensemble Theatre Website. Accessed June 4, 2019. https://ensemblehouston.com/our-story.

Escalante, Ana. "Sade Lythcott Is Building Her Own Legacy." *Glamour*, February 11, 2022. Accessed June 18, 2022. https://www.glamour.com/story/sade-lythcott-is-building-her-own-legacy.

Fletcher, Abner. "Ensemble Theatre's 40th Anniversary." *Houston Public Media*, August 5, 2016. Accessed October 15, 2019. https://www.houstonpublicmedia.org/articles/news/2016/08/05/163151/ensemble-theatres-40th-anniversary/.

Forsgren, La Donna Lee. " 'Set Your Blackness Free': Barbara Ann Teer's Art and Activism during the Black Arts Movement." *Frontiers: A Journal of Women Studies*, vol. 36, no. 1 (2015): 136–59.

Frey, William H. "The New Great Migration: Black Americans' Return to the South, 1965–2000." *The Brookings Institution* (May 2004), 5. Accessed September 18, 2019. https://web.archive.org/web/20080428042235/http://www.brookings.edu/urban/pubs/20040524_Frey.pdf.

Gant, Lisbeth. "The New Lafayette Theatre. Anatomy of a Community Art Institution." *The Drama Review: TDR*, vol. 16, no. 4, Black Theatre Issue (December 1972): 46–55.

Gibson, Campbell, and Kay Jung, *Historical Census Statistics On Population Totals By Race, 1790 to 1990, and By Hispanic Origin, 1970 to 1990, For Large Cities And Other Urban Places In The United States*, US Census Bureau, Population Division, Working Paper No. 76 (February 2005). Accessed June 21, 2019. https://www.census.gov/population/www/documentation/twps0076/twps0076.pdf.

Goff, Keli. "Funding Crisis Threatens Black Theater." *The Root*. November 19, 2013. Accessed February 18, 2019. https://www.theroot.com/funding-crisis-threatens-black-theater-1790898953.

Green, Casey. "Guardians Against Change: The Ku Klux Klan in Harris County, 1920–1925." *Houston Review* 10 (1988), 18. Accessed September 13, 2019. http://www.houstonhistorymagazine.org/wp-content/uploads/2010/12/vol-8-no-1-KKK.pdf.

Hall, Jacquelyn Dowd. "The Long Civil Rights Movement and the Political Uses of the Past." *The Journal of American History* 91, no. 4 (2005): 1233–63.

"Harlem's National Black Theatre Receives Capital Grant Award Of $10 Million." *Harlem World* (2022). Accessed May 24, 2023. https://www.harlemworldmagazine.com/harlems-national-black-theatre-receives-capital-grant-award-of-10-million/.

Harris, Cheryl. "Whiteness as Property." *Harvard Law Review* 106, no. 8 (1993): 1707–91.

Harris, Jessica B. "The Sun People of 125th Street: The National Black Theatre," *The Drama Review: TDR*, vol. 16, no. 4 (December 1972): 39–45.

Harris, Valerie. "Power Exchange 2: Barbara Ann Teer," *Heresies: A Feminist Publication on Art and Politics*, vol. 2, no. 4, issue 8 (1979): 42–44.

"Historic National Black Theatre to Break Ground on Mixed-Use Development in Harlem." *Real Estate Weekly* (June 23, 2022). Accessed July 28, 2022. https://rew-online.com/historic-national-black-theatre-to-break-ground-on-mixed-use-development-in-harlem%EF%BF%BC/.

Julia Jacobs, "National Black Theater Plans Next Act in a New Harlem High-Rise," *The New York Times* (June 4, 2021). Accessed December 2, 2022. https://www.nytimes.com/2021/06/04/theater/national-black-theater-dasha-zhukova.html.

Joffe, Phyllis. "Black Theatre Funding." *NPR*. July 9, 1998. Accessed November 13, 2019. https://www.npr.org/templates/story/story.php?storyId=1034259.

Lowney, John. "Black Power to Black Box Office." *African American Review* 34 (Spring 2000): pp. 39–59.

Lythcott, Sade. Interview by Jerry Grant, "Get to Know Sade Lythcott," on Google Open House, uploaded on October 12, 2018. Accessed June 2, 2019, https://www.youtube.com/watch?v=xbPB_t_8pGs.

Lythcott, Sade. "State of the Black Theatre: The Way Back Home," *Howlround Theatre Commons*. March 15, 2013. Accessed July 25, 2019. https://howlround.com/way-back-home.

Marshall, Malorie. "National Black Theatre Hosts Plays and Events Honoring Trayvon Martin." *New York Amsterdam News*. February 8, 2014. Accessed November 2, 2019. http://amsterdamnews.com/news/2014/feb/08/national-black-theatre-hosts-plays-and-events-hono/.

Miller, Henry. "Valorizing Ancestor Discourse: Harlem Renaissance Criticism and Theatre Theory." *Black Theatre Network Continuum Journal*, vol. 2, no. 2 (March 2016): 1–17.

Morris, Eileen. "Indomitable Spirit: The Legacy, Vitality, and Sustainability of Black Theatre Today." *Howlround*, March 16, 2013. Accessed July 20, 2019. https://howlround.com/indomitable-spirit.

National Black Theatre. "NBT Rentals." National Black Theatre Website. Accessed July 23, 2019. https://www.nationalblacktheatre.org/rentals.

National Black Theatre. "Our Story." National Black Theatre Website. Accessed July 23, 2019. https://www.nationalblacktheatre.org/our-story.

National Black Theatre. "Who's Who." National Black Theatre Website. Accessed July 23, 2019. https://www.nationalblacktheatre.org/whos-who-d.

National Endowment for the Arts Grant Search, "Alley Theatre." Accessed September 1, 2019, https://apps.nea.gov/grantsearch/.

National Endowment for the Arts Grant Search, "Berkeley Repertory Theatre." Accessed September 1, 2019, https://apps.nea.gov/grantsearch/.

National Endowment for the Arts Grant Search, "The Ensemble Theatre." Accessed September 1, 2019, https://apps.nea.gov/grantsearch/.

"Pair Accused of Swindling National Black Theater," *Harlem World Magazine*. April 5, 2011. Accessed July 21, 2019. https://www.harlemworldmagazine.com/pair-accused-of-swindling-national-black-theater/.

Runcie, John. "The Black Culture Movement and the Black Community." *Journal of American Studies*, 1976 10(2): 185–214.

Sidford, Holly. "Fusing Arts, Culture, and Social Change: High Impact Strategies for Philanthropy." The National Committee for Responsive Philanthropy (2011), 4. Accessed June 19, 2019. http://heliconcollab.net/wp-content/uploads/2013/04/Fusing-Arts_Culture_and_Social_Change1.pdf.

Smith, Judith E. "Finding a New Home in Harlem: Alice Childress and the Committee for the Negro in the Arts." American Studies Faculty Publication Series (2017): 1–22.

"Stringer announces pact rescuing National Black Theater of Harlem." *New York Beacon*, vol. 19, issue 24 (June 14, 2012).

Vaugh Scott, Sean. "Our Story." Black Repertory Group Website. Accessed June 27, 2018. http://www.blackrepertorygroup.com/our-story.html.

Warren, Nagueyalti. "Pan-African Cultural Movements: From Baraka to Karenga." *Journal of Negro History*, vol. 75, no. 1–2 (Winter–Spring 1990): 16–28.

Wilkerson, Margaret. "Black Theater in California." *The Drama Review: TDR*, vol. 16, no. 4 (December 1972): 25–38.

Wilkin, Fanon Che. "Beyond Bandung: The Critical Nationalism of Lorraine Hansberry, 1950–1965." *Radical History Review*, Issue 95 (Spring 2006): 191–210.

Wilson, W. J. "Revolutionary Nationalism versus Cultural Nationalism: Dimensions of Black Power Movement." *Sociological Focus* 1970 3(3): 43–51.

Wukman, Alex. "Forgotten Houston July 1970: HPD vs. the Black Panthers." *Patch News*, June 9, 2016. Accessed September 21, 2019. https://patch.com/texas/houston/forgotten-houston-july-1970-hpd-vs-black-panthers.

DOCUMENTARIES

"The Quest." Produced by Abisola Patricia Ann Faison and The Griot Production Company. Accessed June 13, 2023. https://www.youtube.com/watch?v=dQVhaZpjkCU.

DISSERTATIONS AND THESES

Brown, Scot D. "The US Organization: African-American Cultural Nationalism in the Era of Black Power, 1965 to the 1970s." PhD dissertation, Cornell University, Ithaca, 1999.

Gray, Sharon. "A History of the Ensemble Theatre and Its Productions 1976–1999." Master's thesis, University of Houston, Houston, 1999.

Kuhlman, Martin Herman. "The Civil Rights Movement in Texas: Desegregation of Public Accommodations, 1950–1964." PhD dissertation, Texas Tech University, Lubbock, 1994.

Williams, Mance. "The Color of Black Theatre: A Critical Analysis of The Black Theatre Movement of the 1960s and 1970s." PhD dissertation, University of Missouri, Columbia, 1980.

INDEX

African Grove Theatre, 55, 125; African Company and, 55
Afrocentrism, xvi, xxiii, 9, 14–5, 54, 60, 70, 71. *See also* Black-centrism; Eurocentrism
AIDS, 46, 106–8
Allen, Earl, 85–6
Alley Theatre, 91–2, 135, 137
American Negro Theatre, x, 56
Anderson, Gary, 132, 138
Antioch Church, 89
Audience Development Company (AUDELCO), 24, 45, 119, 128; Vivian Robinson and, 24

Baldwin, James, 15; *Amen Corner* and, 43
Baraka, Amiri, x, xiv, xx–xxi, 15, 17, 19, 22, 25, 33, 62, 65, 133, 134; "Revolutionary Theatre" and, xx–xxi, 17, 25, 26, 40, 52. *See also* Black Arts Repertory Theatre/School (BARTS)
Bay Area, 27, 28, 29, 30, 32, 33, 34, 36, 37, 40, 44, 51, 83, 111, 142; Alameda County and, 107, 109; San Francisco and, 33, 36, 107, 108. *See also* Berkeley; Oakland
Belle, Fannie, 95
Berkeley, xi, xx, xxi, xxii, xxiii, 34, 36, 41, 42, 44, 45, 46, 48, 51, 52, 60, 80, 103, 105, 106, 108, 110, 122, 125, 132, 137, 142; Black Power movement and, 28; race relations and, 29, 30, 45, 48, 132; property ownership and, 27–8, 29–30, 45–8, 50, 51. *See also* Bay Area; Black Repertory Group; Oakland; South Berkeley Playhouse; Vaughn, Nora
Berkeley Repertory Theatre, 48, 137
Black aesthetic, xvii, xxii, 5, 11, 18–9, 25–6, 61, 99, 133–4; Africa and, xxiii, 71, 74, 118; autonomy and, 35; white-washing and, xiv, xvi, 5, 29, 81–2
Black Arts Center Repertory Theatre, 85–6
Black Arts movement, x, xvii, xxv, 10, 13, 37, 43, 56, 80, 81, 133, 138, 140, 141, 143; cultural nationalism and, xvi, 19, 32, 55, 60, 63, 85, 134, 143; decline of, xxiv, 27, 46, 86, 101, 139; women and, xix, xx, xxi
Black Arts Repertory Theatre/School (BARTS), xiv, xx–xxi, 19, 33, 57, 62, 76–7, 84. *See also* Baraka, Amiri
Black-centrism, x, xi, xv, xix, 16, 17, 73, 86, 125. *See also* Afrocentrism; Eurocentrism
Black church: respectability politics and, 9, 39–40, 88–9; theatre support and, xix, 7–8, 13, 36–9, 48, 69. *See also* Antioch Church; Downs Methodist Church
Black community, xi, xxi, 8, 15, 16, 17, 19–20, 23, 27, 32, 46, 48, 57, 59, 60, 68, 79, 82, 84, 87, 99, 106, 108, 111, 137, 139–140, 142; the arts and, 3, 4, 11, 12, 14, 20, 21, 25, 34, 91; education and, 9–10, 23, 38, 70, 73, 107; social programs and, xix, xxii, 21, 36, 37, 43, 78, 106, 125, 126; theatre support from, 30, 34, 40, 42, 65, 99, 114, 123, 124, 126; uplift through theatre and,

192 INDEX

Black community *(continued)* ix, xiv, xxi–xxiii, 13, 20, 22, 25, 31, 35, 36, 41, 44, 51–2, 71–6, 78, 93, 94, 95, 106, 118, 120, 136, 143; women and, 7–9, 11, 14, 36. *See also* Black liberation; collective ownership; nationalism

Black Ensemble Theatre. *See* Ensemble Theatre

Black Feminism, xix–xx, 18, 61, 141, 142. *See also* Black women; Black womanhood

Black House Political and Cultural Center of San Francisco, 33

Black joy, xxiv, 91

Black liberation, xiii, 20, 39, 54, 71, 139, 141; economics and, 32, 43, 74, 118; education and, 58, 71–5, 96; nationalism and, xiv–xv, xii, 16, 19, 28, 32, 39, 72, 117–8; theatre and, xxiv, 25, 55, 86, 92, 116, 117, 129, 142, 143; women and, ix, xv, xx, 18, 58–9, 73, 131

Black Lives Matter, xxiv, 131–2, 133, 136, 139

Black Panther Party, xiii, 31, 33, 52, 57, 58, 59, 83; the arts and, 32–3, 57, 59; BPP New York chapter and, 58–60; Black Panther Party for Self-Defense and, xxii, 32; decline of, xiii, 27, 77–8, 103, 128; education and, 32, 43; People's Party II and, 83–4, 90, 122; the US government and, 32; women and, 32, 58, 59. *See also* Black liberation; nationalism; New York City; Oakland; police brutality

Black Power movement, x, xii, 9, 15, 28, 30–1, 32, 42, 55, 58, 63, 80, 83, 93, 104, 129, 132, 134, 141; decline of, xii, xiii, xxiv, 46, 76, 80, 86, 103, 106, 111, 139; economic self-determinism and, x, 20, 56, 140; nationalism and, xiv, xvi, xxv, 13, 16, 18, 28, 140; theatre and, xiv, xvii, xviii, xix, xx, xxi, xxiii, xxv, 25, 33, 36, 46, 66, 71, 86, 104, 112, 128, 142, 143;

women and, xi, xiv, xx, xxiii, 18, 24, 34, 52, 59, 142. *See also* Black Arts movement, Black liberation, Black Panther Party

Black Repertory Group, 25, 27–9, 33–52, 80, 96, 104, 133, 138; community programs and, xxii, 36, 106, 107, 109–10, 143; cultural nationalism and, 31, 44, 52, 54, 106, 108, 111, 120, 141; education and, 107–8, 109; funding and, 29, 37, 42, 43, 45, 75, 105–6, 134, 137; property ownership and, 27–8, 29, 37–9, 47–51, 97; mentioned, xi, xvi, xxiii, 66, 69, 80, 90, 101, 122, 125, 126, 128, 139. *See also* Berkeley; Vaughn, Birel; Vaughn, Nora

Black Theatre Alliance, 23, 115

Black Theatre Festival, 100, 111, 126, 128, 133, 137

Black theatre houses. *See* specific theatres

Black Theatre movement: alternative spaces and, 3, 7–8, 33, 35, 38–39, 63, 80, 87, 88, 116–7, 127; economic autonomy and, x, xvii, xviii, xix, 20, 24, 25, 31, 33, 52, 59, 74, 85, 91, 123, 134–5, 140; white audience and, xiv, xv, xvi, 5, 8, 11, 16, 20, 22, 45, 61, 62, 81, 85, 112, 125, 139; white funding and, x, xviii, 10, 17, 19, 21, 23, 29, 34, 43, 62, 123; white theatres and, xix, xxiv, 3, 17, 19, 20, 48, 55, 61, 66, 91, 97, 98, 135, 137–8, 139. *See also* Black Arts movement; Black-centrism; Black church; Black community; Black liberation; Black Power movement; Black women; education; nationalism

Black Theatre Network, 121, 140

Black women: as artists, 11, 13, 25, 51, 62, 91, 95, 127; Black liberation and, ix, x, xiii, xiv, xix, xx, xxv, 58–9, 73, 98, 142; cultural preservation and, 8, 11, 37–8, 52, 58, 60, 111, 140; education, 19, 58, 73, 109, 110, 127, 140;

INDEX

labor and, 30, 92, 93, 97; leadership and, xi, xviii, xix, xx, xxiv, 3–4, 6, 7, 9, 23, 24, 25, 28–9, 32, 35, 36–8, 41, 44, 52, 59, 60, 66, 69, 80, 83, 93, 97, 99, 101, 104, 106, 127, 140, 142, 143; misogyny and, xv, xx, 4, 5, 18, 30, 32, 62, 86, 106, 131; nation building and, xv, xvi, xxiii, 13–4, 15, 16, 17, 18, 19, 30, 32, 41, 52, 58, 59, 66, 128. *See also* Black feminism; Black Power movement; Black womanhood

Black womanhood, 62

Black World/Negro Digest, 43, 44

blackface, xv, 55

BOLD Theatre Women's Leadership Circle, 127

Br'er Rabbit, 87–8

Broadway, 14, 15, 23, 55, 56, 61, 65, 66, 70, 71, 79, 91, 92, 93, 117, 135; Off-Broadway, 63, 79; racism and, 55, 61. *See also* New York City

Brooks, Sylvia, 83

Brown, Michael, 131

Bullins, Ed, 32–3, 57, 64

California, 28, 30, 55, 82, 83, 84; Black Power movement and, 28; women and, 28–9. *See also* Bay Area; Berkeley; Oakland; Los Angeles

Carmichael, Stokely. *See* Ture, Kwame

Childress, Alice, ix–xi, xv, 4, 6, 17, 20, 22, 56, 103, 104, 133, 135; *Trouble in the Mind*, x; "For a Strong Negro People's Theatre," 17

Cleaver, Eldridge, 33, 59

Coalitions of Theaters of Color (CTC), 115

collective ownership, xviii, 11, 24, 37, 38, 42, 64, 66, 88, 140

colonization. *See* decolonization

Community Action Program (CAP), 21

Congress of Racial Equality (CORE), 58, 59

Connor, Joe, 84

cosmopolitanism, 18, 20

COVID-19, xxiv, 116, 138

crack-cocaine, 46

Cruse, Harold, 15, 19, 56–7, 133

Cullors, Patrisse, 131–2

Culturnomics. *See* Teer, Barbara Ann

cultural liberalism, 16

Dallas, 85

decolonization, x, xvii, 7, 31

Delany, Martin, xiii

Derby, Doris, xxiii, 84

Developmental Theatre, 17, 31, 79, 90

diaspora, xviii, 12, 42

Downs Methodist Church, 36–7, 38–9, 45, 48

drama therapy, xviii, 107, 108

Du Bois, W. E. B., 3, 5–6, 8–9, 10, 19, 25, 78, 82; and *second sight*, 58

Easton, William, 9–10

Economic Opportunity Act (EOA), 21, 23

education, 9; Black liberation and, xxii, 43, 58, 64, 71, 73, 75, 88, 133; theatre and, xiv, xxiii, 10, 13, 46, 54, 69, 71, 74, 107, 109, 110, 121, 126, 140. *See also* Black women and education

emancipation, xviii, 9, 12, 13, 81, 112, 132, 136, 140. *See also* enslavement

Emancipation Park, 88–9

Ensemble Theatre (Houston), xxiv, 25, 80–1, 83, 86, 88, 97, 120, 124–5, 128, 133, 136, 139, 143; collaboration and, 92, 101; community programs and, xxii, 95, 96, 121–2, 127; cultural nationalism and, 98, 100, 135, 141; education and, 96; funding and, 91, 93, 95, 96, 97, 100, 122–4, 126, 134, 137–8; property ownership and, 80, 87, 88, 89–90, 92, 98–9, 127; mentioned, xi, xvi, 85. *See also* Black Theatre movement; Hawkins, George; Houston; Morris, Eileen

enslavement, 8, 9, 11, 19, 81, 87. *See also* emancipation
Eurocentrism, xvi, 8, 53, 55, 70–1. *See also* Afrocentrism; Black-centrism
Evans, Everett, 96

Faison, Abisola, 63–4
Faison, Shirley, 68, 114
FBI, xiii–xiv, 15, 22, 45. *See also* Black liberation; police brutality
Federal Theatre Project, 56
Floyd, George, 138
Ford Foundation, 62, 70
Free Southern Theater, xxiii, 34, 84–5, 98

Garza, Alicia, 131–2
Garvey, Marcus, xiii, 6–7, 25
gentrification, 116, 135
Giovanni, Nikki, 73
globalization, 19, 119
Glover, Danny, 125
Grimké, Angelina Weld, 6, 10
Group Theatre, 34, 35, 38, 39. *See also* Black Repertory Group; Vaughn, Nora
Group Theatre Workshop, 62. *See also* Teer, Barbara Ann

Hamlin, Larry Leon, 133
Hampton, Carl, 83–4, 90
Hannah Davis, 100
Hansberry, Lorraine, 14–5; *A Raisin in the Sun* and, 43
Hare, Nathan, 105
Harlem, xxi, xxiii, 53–4, 59, 63, 66, 67, 72, 114, 115, 118; cultural nationalism and, 56–7, 58, 60, 70, 71, 75, 78, 120; property ownership and, 54, 55, 56, 57, 64, 69, 116, 142; race relations and, 56, 57, 58, 132. *See also* Harlem Renaissance; National Black Theatre; New York City; Teer, Barbara Ann
Harlem Renaissance, xvi, 7, 13, 40, 41, 51, 55, 138. *See also* Harlem

Hawkins, George, 79–81, 86–101, 120, 124, 126, 142; Black empowerment and, 96, 97, 121, 127; collaboration, 100, 101, 124; cultural nationalism and, 91, 98, 99, 100, 125, 135; financial issues and, 93–4, 95, 96–7, 101, 123; *Monday Night Follies*, 91; property ownership and, 80, 87, 89–90, 92, 96–7, 98, 99, 124; *Surprise, Surprise . . . A Love Story*, 91; *Who Killed Hazel Patton?*, 91; women and, xxiv, 80, 91, 95, 122, 127; mentioned, xi, 84, 104, 121, 125, 135. *See also* Ensemble Theatre; Houston; Morris, Eileen
Helen Gurley Brown Foundation, 128
Hooks, Robert, 62
Houston, xxi, 81, 82, 85, 86, 88, 91, 93, 96, 99, 103, 120, 122, 126, 127; property ownership and, 89, 142; race relations and, 80, 81–2, 83–4; Third Ward neighborhood and, 95, 100. *See also* Ensemble Theatre; Hawkins, George; Morris, Eileen; Texas
Houston Ensemble Theatre. *See* Ensemble Theatre
Hughes, Langston, 6, 51; Harlem Suitcase Theatre and, 87; *Mulatto*, 42; *Tambourines to Glory*, 42–3, 96

institution building, x, xx, xxiii, xxiv, 32, 34, 37, 39, 135, 143
institutional permanence, 68, 77, 104, 140
institutionalization, xv, xxv, 17, 52, 120, 143

Jackson-Randolph, Marsha, 80
Jim Crow, 9, 35, 42, 89, 132
Johnson, Georgia Douglas, 63
Johnson, James Weldon, 41

Karenga, Maulana, xiv, xv
Kennedy, Bobby, 105
Kennedy, Ted, 110
King Jr., Martin Luther, 63, 64
Ku Klux Klan, 31, 35, 131

Last Poets, The, 63, 66
Lawson, Audrey, 80, 99, 122, 123, 123
Ledet, Debora, 91, 95
LGBTQ community, 106-7, 127
Lillie, Vernell, 101
Longevity Award, 111, 126, 128
Los Angeles, 30, 41, 45, 134; Inner City Repertory Theatre of Los Angeles (ICRTLA), 92, 93; Watts, 30-1, 68; Watts Writers Workshop, 45. *See also* California
Lovelace, Mary, 34-5
lynching, 10, 35, 139
Lythcott, Michael, 112, 113-4, 115
Lythcott, Sade, 75, 112-4, 115-9, 120, 128, 132, 135, 138. *See also* National Black Theatre; Teer, Barbara Ann

Macbeth, Robert, 21, 57
Malaika, 16
Malcolm X, 16, 44, 58, 86
Marshall, Barbara, 85
Martin, Trayvon, 131, 134
Marvin X, 32, 33
mass incarceration, 46, 132
Merritt College, 32
minstrelsy, xv, 17, 29, 81-2, 88
Mississippi, 34, 35, 84, 85
Moreno, Jacob, 108
Morris, Eileen, xi, xxiv, 80-1, 87, 94-5, 96, 97-8, 120-7, 128, 132, 142. *See also* Ensemble Theatre; Hawkins, George
Moses, Gilbert, 84

National Black Theatre, 53-4, 63-70, 111-2, 113, 119, 128, 133, 134; community programs and, 72, 76-77, 96, 143; cultural nationalism and, 54, 57, 70-1, 74, 75, 78 118, 120, 141; education and, 73, 75; funding and, 77, 112, 114-5, 118, 119, 138; property ownership and, 54, 67, 68, 69-70, 77, 112, 115, 116-7, 118; mentioned, xi, 58, 59, 80, 85, 87, 90, 101, 123, 136, 139. *See also* Harlem; Lythcott, Sade; Teer, Barbara Ann

National Black Theatre Festival (now International), 111, 126, 128, 133, 137
National Endowment for the Arts, 77, 94, 120, 137-8
nationalism: Black, x, xiii, xiv, xv, xxv, 16, 25, 39, 43, 71, 72, 74, 99, 109, 125; cultural, xv, xvi, xxv, 6-7, 8, 13, 14, 15, 16, 19, 24, 25, 39-40, 57, 74, 75, 85, 108, 109, 125, 140; economic, 30, 108, 110; nation building, xxii, xxv, 7, 27, 28, 30, 33, 36, 45, 46, 52, 66, 100, 104, 110, 111, 117, 128, 141, 143; theatre and, xxi, xxii, xxiv, 17, 42, 44, 51-2, 70-1, 86, 88, 98, 99, 100, 105, 111, 120, 137, 140; women and, xxiii, 9, 15, 18. *See also* Black liberation; Black Panther Party; Hawkins, George; Teer, Barbara Ann; Vaughn, Nora
Neal, Larry, 142, 143
Negro Little Theatre Movement, 82
Neighborhood Youth Corps, 108
New Lafayette Theatre, 21, 57-8, 140
New York City, 55, 56, 66, 91, 118; Black Panther Party and, 58-9, 78; cultural nationalism and, 57; property ownership and, 55, 56, 69; race relations and, 25, 55, 59; theatre and, xxiii, 54-5, 57, 78, 81, 112, 115, 119. *See also* Broadway; Harlem
Newton, Huey P., 31-2, 33, 39
Nigeria, 70, 119

Oakland, 27, 28, 31-2, 36, 38, 46, 52, 105, 106, 108, 110; Black Panthers and, xiii, xxiii, 31, 32-3, 59; poverty and, xxiii, 29, 39, 41, 46, 51; race relations and, 29, 31, 39, 46; mentioned, 33, 37, 59, 60, 83. *See also* Bay Area; Berkeley; California
O'Neal, John, 84
Organization of Afro-American Unity (OAAU), 16

Pan-Africanism, 19, 74
People's Party II. *See* Black Panther Party

police brutality, 32, 46, 55, 56, 82, 83–4, 112, 131, 134, 138–9
poverty, 33, 39, 41, 44, 46, 51, 68, 74, 95–6; antipoverty programs, 21, 28–9, 60
Project1VOICE, 136, 140

radical imagination, xvii, 116
Reagan, Ronald, xvi, 23, 111–2
Rockefeller Foundation, xiv, 62
Russell, Charlie, 64–5

Seale, Bobby, 31–2, 33, 39
Second Great Migration, 13–4, 28, 36, 82, 100–101
Second World Black and African Festival of Arts and Culture, 70
segregation, 9, 30, 82, 83. *See also* Jim Crow
self-determinism, ix, x, 20, 22, 103, 140
Smith v. Allwright, 83
South Berkeley Playhouse, 41, 42–3, 45. *See also* Berkeley
St. Louis Black Repertory Theatre, 111
Student Nonviolent Coordinating Committee (SNCC), 16, 84
Sty of the Blind Pig, The (Dean), 43, 135

Taylor, Breonna, 138
Teer, Barbara Ann, xxiii, 53–4, 58–78, 112–3, 114, 115, 116, 117, 118, 119–20, 135, 142; Afrocentrism and, 54, 60, 63, 70–1; American Place Theatre and, 64–5; cultural nationalism and, 58, 59, 70–2, 74, 75, 78; Culturnomics and, 74, 77; "decrudding" and, 61, 64; education, 65–6, 73–4; the Negro Ensemble Company, 62–3; property ownership and, 60–1, 63, 64–5, 66–70, 75, 77, 118; mentioned, xi, 55, 57, 85, 86, 87, 96, 104. *See also* National Black Theatre; Lythcott, Sade
Teer, Frederica L., 54, 59, 67–8. *See also* National Black Theatre; Teer, Barbara Ann

Temple of Liberation for a Black Nation, 54, 69, 112. *See also* National Black Theatre; Teer, Barbara Ann
Texas, xxiv, 25, 81–2, 85. *See also* Houston
Tometi, Ayo, 131–2
Ture, Kwame, 16, 31, 105; mentioned, 25, 73

Universal Negro Improvement Association (UNIA), 6–7
Urban Theatre, 85

Vaughn, Birel, 34, 36, 37, 40, 46, 48
Vaughn, Nora, xxiii, 27, 33–6, 39–52, 104, 106; Black liberation and, 28, 34, 38, 39, 41–2, 46, 51, 52, 106, 108; cultural nationalism and, 27, 35–6, 39–40, 42, 43, 44, 45, 51–2, 99, 109, 142; property ownership and, 27–8, 35–6, 37, 38, 43, 44–5, 47–9, 51; mentioned, xi, 29, 31, 32, 54, 63, 65, 86, 87, 93, 99, 109, 110. *See also* Bay Area; Berkeley; Black Repertory Group; Oakland
Vaughn Scott, Mona, 45, 47, 104–6, 107–11, 128, 132, 141. *See also* Black Repertory Group; Vaughn, Nora

War on Crime campaign, 132
War on Drugs campaign, 132
War on Poverty initiative, 21
Watts Writers Workshop, 45
We See You WAT (White American Theater), 139
White, Lulu B., 83
white flight, 30
Wilson, August, 125, 135, 137
World War II, 18, 55; postwar era and, 13, 14, 28–9, 31, 36, 55–6

Zimmerman, George, 131, 137

ABOUT THE AUTHOR

KERRY L. GOLDMANN is senior lecturer of history at the University of North Texas, where she teaches courses on the histories of African Americans, Jewish Americans, and American culture. Her research centers on the intersecting histories of marginalized communities and art used for social change.

www.ingramcontent.com/pod-product-compliance
Lightning Source LLC
Chambersburg PA
CBHW032214230426
43672CB00011B/2549